P9-DXH-810

THIS LAND OF OURS

THE MACMILLAN COMPANY
NEW YORK · CHICAGO
DALLAS · ATLANTA · SAN FRANCISCO
LONDON · MANILA

IN CANADA
BRETT-MACMILLAN LTD.
GALT, ONTARIO

THIS
LAND OF OURS

Community and Conservation Projects
for Citizens

by
ALICE HARVEY HUBBARD

New York
THE MACMILLAN COMPANY
1960

First Printing

The Macmillan Company, New York
Brett-Macmillan Ltd., Galt, Ontario

Printed in the United States of America

Library of Congress catalog card number: 60-6163

To Edward

ACKNOWLEDGMENTS

Because of its nature, this book necessitated the cooperation of hundreds of people, and I am grateful to all of them, for they gave generous and willing assistance on every hand. I am especially indebted to Adrian C. Fox of the Soil Conservation Service, C. W. Mattison of the United States Forest Service, and Richard Pough of the Natural Area Council for reading the manuscript and making comments and suggestions based upon their broad knowledge and experience in this field. I am also indebted to Jack Culbreath of the Fish and Wildlife Service, Joseph Doherty of the United States Rural Development Program, Jack Durham of the Public Health Service, Walter B. Langbein of the Geological Survey of the United States Department of the Interior, Dr. Ruth Patrick of the Academy of Natural Sciences, Ernest Grigg of the Community Development Program of the United Nations, and P. V. Acharya, Liaison Officer of the Food and Agriculture Organization of the United Nations, for reading the parts of the manuscript relating to their specialties. And I am greatly indebted to Gordon Webb of the United States Department of Agriculture for help in checking facts and figures pertaining to our natural resources.

The source of most of the projects included in this book is either a personal interview or files and unpublished materials placed at my disposal by the persons responsible for carrying out the projects, and again I thank them for sharing their experiences with others through this book. For permission to use published material in discussing the

vii

topics indicated, I make grateful acknowledgment to: *The Rotarian* for "The Rotarian Painting Bee" and "Rotarian Leadership in Tennessee," adapted from an article by George Laycock; *The American City* magazine for "How De Soto Planned Its Future Growth" and "Pocket-Sized Playgrounds in New Haven;" *The Christian Science Monitor* and Jessie Ash Arndt for "Boulder City's Hospital" and other projects; The Curtis Publishing Company for "The Brandywine Creek Story" from an article by Arnold Nicholson in the *Country Gentleman*, for "Teamwork in Tupelo" from an article by Hodding Carter in *The Saturday Evening Post*, and for "A Conservation Crusade Along a Mail Route," copyright 1956, The Curtis Publishing Company, reprinted by special permission of *Ladies' Home Journal*.

My thanks to the League of Ohio Sportsmen for permission to include "I Am a Stream," John C. Gibbs of the Conservation Foundation for "Industrial Wastes in the Kalamazoo," The Garden Club of America for "Maplewood's Fallen Leaves an Asset," the Center for Information on America for "The Threat to Walden" from *Vital Issues* (Vol. VII, No. 3), the Brooklyn Botanic Garden for "A Fragrance Garden for the Blind," Action for "Block Projects in Chicago," the National Federation of Women's Institutes for permission to quote from an article by Lady Brunner in "Home and Country," *Life* magazine for permission to quote from "The World We Live In" series (November 8, 1954, issue), the *San Francisco Examiner* for permission to quote from "The Big Push" by Will Stevens, Mrs. Mildred White Wells for permission to include Community Achievement Contest projects of the General Federation of Women's Clubs, and Mrs. F. B. De Mel of Ceylon, Asian representative of the Associated Country Women of the World, for permission to use material from "Twenty-five Years," a history of the *Lanka Mahila Samiti*.

My thanks also, for their generous help, to Mrs. Blanche P. Wilks of the National Council of State Garden Clubs, Inc., Mrs. Roland C. Bergh of the Garden Club of America, Richard W. Tupper of the American Automobile Association, John Baker of the National Audubon Society, Bernhard A. Roth of the Soil Conservation Service, and Newton B. Drury of the Department of Natural Resources of California.

These acknowledgments would not be complete without an expression of appreciation to Mrs. Austin Phillips who first aroused my interest in conservation, Mrs. Frank G. Boudreau who has been so unfailingly helpful, Mrs. Richard I. Land whose faith was a tower of strength when I needed it most, my husband and friends whose "clipping service" was of immeasurable help, and for the inspiring encouragement of Mrs. Frederic R. Kellogg, Honorary Life President of the National Council of State Garden Clubs, Inc.

FOREWORD

All over the United States people are awakening to the fact that the open countryside, so long a part of our way of life, is vanishing almost before our eyes and that the old idea of inexhaustible resources is a myth which must be discarded.

This realization is usually brought home to us by some incident, such as the disappearance of a wooded area that was always a part of the community; the increasing distance we must travel for outdoor recreation, articles relating to the destruction of some favorite haunt, and water shortages. When the realization does come, the reaction of thoughtful people invariably is: "What can we do about it?"

This book, believed to be the first of its kind in the conservation field, offers down-to-earth suggestions as to what we can do by showing what others have done and how they did it. Essentially it is a book of "grass roots" community and conservation projects, successfully carried out by public-spirited individuals and groups throughout the country. More than 180 projects are detailed. They range in scope from a petunia contest in a small California town to the Community Development Program of the United Nations and the International Union for Conservation of Nature and Natural Resources.

Although designed primarily for garden clubs, youth groups, women's clubs, men's service clubs, organized communities, and other civic-minded groups, this book is not solely for them. It is for all people everywhere who are interested in building better communities, as well as for those who simply want a better understanding of the conservation problems facing our country today.

The thought of writing such a book came to me when I realized the urgent need for public support of conservation and the tremendous potentialities that exist for such support in our numerous organized groups. It occurred to me that if enough of these groups would participate through local projects and educational programs a movement could perhaps be started—a crusade for conservation and community betterment. As I sought projects to illustrate the points I wanted to make, I found that such a movement was already under way. Information about programs and projects poured in from all sections of the country in such a flood that I realized it was not only under way, but steadily growing stronger. As the book took shape, it seemed to me that the people of the United States, through these demonstrations of democracy in action, were drawing a portrait of themselves and their country that was more characteristic than any I could make, so I stood aside and let them draw it. The projects are typical of the manner in which our people have been tackling community problems since pioneering days.

The compilation is necessarily illustrative and not exhaustive. Indeed, one of my most difficult problems has been to choose from hundreds of fine projects the ones I should use. Many others, just as fine, will forever haunt me because I had to leave them out. I make no claim that the projects are completely up-to-date because no record can keep pace with such a dynamic movement.

The general plan of the book was suggested by Richard Pough, president of the Natural Area Council. The inspiration for making it a "how to do it" book came from a bit of philosophy of one of our great conservationists, Theodore Roosevelt:

"Do what you can, where you are, with what you've got."

ALICE HARVEY HUBBARD

CONTENTS

CHAPTER I

GUARDING OUR HERITAGE
OF NATURAL BEAUTY

Ours is not only a beautiful and bountiful land, but a land of striking contrast and almost infinite variety. From the rocky coast of Maine to Florida and the lazy lagoons and bayous of Louisiana; from the sweeping grasslands of the Great Plains to the rain-drenched forests of the Pacific Northwest, nature speaks "a various language." Each state has its treasure of river, lake, mountain, or desert; of butte, canyon, and mesa; mysterious swampland, sun-tanned fields of grain; hot spring and geyser, or sweep of ocean shore.

So varied is our landscape that, in Idaho, we even have a place like an area of the moon. It is a tortured section of earth, a great rift in its crust. Here, once, volcanic eruptions spat lava into the air to form cones 800 feet high, and oozing streams of liquid rock hardened slowly into craters, vents, tunnels, and a host of weird formations. The spot is not completely sterile, as the moon is believed to be, but the scant vegetation that sprouts seldom reaches maturity, and even the birds shun it.

Contrast this, or the Badlands of the Dakotas, with the Everglades of Florida. This vast area of saw grass and water prairie with its swampland smell teems with subtropical fauna and flora. The egret, roseate spoonbill, great blue heron, the wild turkey, and the bald eagle are only a few of the spectacular birds that haunt the swamp. It is the home too of the alligator, crocodile, loggerhead turtle, and the fan-

1

tastic manatee, said to be the prototype of mermaids reported in
Florida waters. Among the many mysterious plants in this vast
wilderness are the strangler fig, mangrove, and the gumbo limbo
with its thick, twisted limbs.

We have many other masterpieces in our outdoor museum. There
is Bryce Canyon, a sandstone fairyland of towers, bastions, and
pinnacles in sunset colors; Crater Lake high in the Cascades, with
fathomless crystal clear water that is blue beyond belief; Carlsbad Cav-
erns, an endless labyrinth of corridors, chambers, and arched palaces;
the Painted Desert, and Okefenokee Swamp. We have Old Faithful
and the Artist's Palette of Yellowstone; the noble sequoias of California, trees native to no other country; the Petrified Forest with
its agate logs and fossilized plants; Hawaii's Fern Jungle, a green
paradise where ferns grow forty feet tall; and the grim, unconquerable
region of Superstition Mountain, once sacred to the Indians. This is
the place where the saguaro grows, a giant cactus that can store a ton
of water in a single rain.

There is the rugged grandeur of the Rockies, home of the bighorn
sheep and a haven of wildflowers. In the northernmost part of this
mountain chain are some sixty glaciers, the Indians' Land of Shining
Mountains. New Mexico has its White Sands, a desert where the
sand on a sunswept day rivals the snow in brilliance. And North
Carolina counts among her treasures the "Smokies," veiled in their
deep blue haze, where giant trees shelter mountain laurel and rhododendron which grows in wild, pristine abundance. Yosemite's beauty
must be seen to be believed; it lies not far from the terrible Death
Valley. Nor can we forget the Grand Canyon—a drama of eternity.

Protecting the Masterpieces: Our National Parks

The rarest and most majestic of our masterpieces have been set aside
as national parks by Congress or as national monuments by presi-
dential designation. We are indebted to the men who fought to protect them from commercial exploitation "because their special and
unique qualities make them the concern of all the people."

Yellowstone, the first national park in the world, was established
in 1872. This is a 2,213,000-acre tract, believed to have more
geysers than all the rest of the world together, the most famous having

no peers in size, power, or variety. The whole area is volcanic, with over 3,000 hot springs and geysers. Wildlife is scrupulously protected here and more than 200 species of birds and many animals live in the park. Today the National Park Service, established in 1916, is administering some 177 places of scenic, historic, and scientific interest, totaling approximately 23 million acres.

Public Watchfulness Essential

It would be folly, however, to take the security of these treasures for granted, even though they have been set aside as the property of the people. Because our liberty was dearly bought, we guard it zealously, but we have always been careless of our natural resources—perhaps because nature was so lavish in her gifts. We cannot continue to rely on a few interested individuals and organizations to fight for the integrity of our public lands. There is too much pressure to exploit them from too many sources. Administrations change and interpretations of what is important to all the people can change too. In heated controversy, arguments as to the "best interests" of the public can be so confusing that the public becomes confused too. It is imperative that we be ever on guard.

Opposition to the proposed building of a dam in Dinosaur National Monument not long ago was a convincing indication that the American people want these heritages held inviolate. This area, one of "great scientific interest," was set aside in 1915. It contains the petrified bones of prehistoric animals that roamed North America a hundred million years ago. The public might never have realized the significance of the proposed dam before it was too late had it not been for alert conservation groups. The dam would have not only impaired the beauty and scientific value of Dinosaur Monument but endangered the integrity of all such areas by establishing a precedent for their invasion. People realized, many for the first time, that national parks and monuments are *not* secure, and they expressed their opposition in a flood of indignant letters to their congressmen and senators. It is noteworthy that it was not a minority group that opposed the building of this power dam in a national preserve, but alerted and outraged citizens all over the country.

However, an occasional flurry of interest, interspersed with long periods of apathy, will never insure our national parks against violation. Pressure groups may be checked temporarily, but they are seldom defeated by spasms of interest on the part of the public. They wait until the tumult dies, then bring the tabled issue back, knowing that it is harder to *rekindle* interest than to arouse it in the first place. Ours must be a consistent interest and watchfulness. Elected officials must be made to feel the weight of public opinion, made to know exactly what the people want. And in this conservation groups can make a strong contribution. Such groups have no axe to grind, being non-profit, non-political organizations. When they champion an issue, people know it is in the best interest of the community or country. Thus they have the confidence of the public and greater influence than the size of their membership would indicate. They can play an important role in safeguarding our national parks and monuments, our national forests, the public domain, state and even private forests, and in other phases of conservation too. By their nature they are in a position to achieve certain things that no other organizations are as well qualified to do. This is particularly true in the field of education.

We all know that we cannot take the security of public lands for granted. We know that, as citizens, it is our responsibility to protect them. But for a long time we have been leaving it to the other fellow. In a democracy, the government, in the last analysis, will do only what public opinion wants it to do. As long as we are careless of our property, all public-owned lands will be in danger of exploitation. We must be urgently aware of our duty to demand from our representatives that the integrity of our natural masterpieces and other public lands be maintained. This requires a program of public education, sustained over a period of time, which civic and conservation-minded groups are in a unique position to advance.

Adequate Appropriations for Maintenance

A part of that educational program should be insistence that public lands be administered properly. We are often said to be the most generous people in the world, and in some ways we may be. In others we are niggardly. Although millions use our parks and forests every year, the budgets for their administration have never been adequate to operate, maintain, and protect them properly. Surely there is no need in a country as rich as ours for the administrators of the people's property to be continually harassed trying to make ends meet. It is our responsibility as owners of these treasures to make *sure* Congress appropriates enough money to maintain them properly, and that the money is used for that purpose.

Rescuing Smaller Areas from Destruction

Magnificent as they are, the national parks and monuments include only a small portion of the beauty of our country. Every community has little gems of nature that contribute to the tapestry of our land. They need champions too, if they are to be saved from the saw and bulldozer. Here again, organized groups have a unique opportunity for constructive action. Such groups can help either by lending support to conservation agencies anxious to save these areas, or by carrying out projects of their own. In fact, one person is often the spearhead in such a project, enlisting the support of organized groups. There are hundreds of instances where people have saved areas of rare beauty or scientific value and made them the property of the community, in the same spirit that the great masterpieces were made the property of the nation. We include a few examples to show how such projects may be carried out.

Mettler's Woods in New Jersey

At the time this country was settled, the eastern portion was mantled with what forestry experts consider the mightiest deciduous forest in the world. Of these primeval woods only 1,600 square miles, less than half of one per cent, remain in an unspoiled state. One area is a sixty-five acre tract in New Jersey, fifty miles from New York City. It escaped exploitation because, until recently, it had been in the possession of one family since 1701. *Life* magazine, which described this woodland in its "The World We Live In" series, says: "The trees and plant life it harbors represent an unbroken succession dating back to the end of the ice ages when deciduous trees reconquered the land in the wake of the last glacier." It further states that "no less than four full centuries are required for the creation of a climax forest (at its peak of development) of this kind."

Generation after generation of the Mettler family, owners of this virgin forest, refused tempting offers to log it, and as consistently protected it from fire. Just as nature intended, litter, leaves and fallen trees were left undisturbed on the forest floor to decompose and replenish the soil. For years, nearby Rutgers University used the woods as a living laboratory.

In the fall of 1950, a storm did so much damage that the owner called in a lumber company to salvage the fallen trees. The offer made by the company, which had long wanted the tract, was such that the owner felt he could not refuse it. However, he was reluctant to sell the forest for logging purposes and to deprive the university of its laboratory. A group of conservationists in New Brunswick, New Jersey, organized "The Citizens' Scientific and Historical Committee for the Preservation of Mettler's Woods," with the purpose of buying the area and putting it under the trusteeship of Rutgers University. Wholly in sympathy with the purpose of the group, Mr. Mettler offered to take considerably less than the lumber company offered and to wait until the money could be raised.

Leading conservationists of the area supported the project. Richard Pough, at that time president of Nature Conservancy, later president of the Natural Area Council, urged: "To understand the present we must know the heritage of the past. This is as true of natural communities as it is of human societies. Throughout the nation we have set aside primeval areas—to name a few, the redwoods of California, pine forests in Minnesota, and cove forests in the Great Smokies— but in this part of the country, none. It is imperative that we save this one."

"When in war a 700 year-old cathedral is threatened by unsubtle guns, all men sharply perceive the blasphemy and bitterly deplore it," the Rutgers staff pointed out. "Is not the present threat to this leafy cathedral, whose cornerstone was laid at least seven times 700 years ago by the Master Architect Himself, of at least equal concern?"

Through the contributions of individuals and organized groups, not only was the money raised to save the area, but an adjoining forest was purchased too. Interestingly, the United Brotherhood of Carpenters and Joiners of America was one of the most generous contributors. It gave $75,000 toward the purchase as a memorial to William L. Hutcheson, in the interest of the source of the carpenters' craft.

Connecticut's Mianus Gorge

Across the Hudson River, near Greenwich, Connecticut, is another fragment of virgin forest. This scenic valley, with a tumbling brook called the Mianus River, has soaring cliffs from which the gorge can best be seen, cascades and waterfalls, springs, deer yards, old silica mines, pink and white quartz beds, trout and pickerel pools, swamps and fields. Magnificent stands of ancient hemlocks tower a hundred feet above the gorge and other native trees—oaks, beeches, and dogwoods—grow in abundance. On the highland behind the gorge one even finds apple trees, seedlings from orchards abandoned a century ago. Some still bloom and bear edible fruit, helping to support the wildlife that makes its home in and around the gorge. The area is a natural habitat for birds, some of which are rare in this part of the country. There is a wealth of flowers too, with many found here that never grow in areas disturbed by man.

Inspired by the success of the Mettler's Woods project, Mr. and Mrs. Anthony Anable of Stamford, Connecticut, set out to save Mianus Gorge in somewhat the same way. The first objective was to purchase eighty acres, then add to it as more money was raised. In December, 1953, "The Mianus River Gorge Conservation Committee" was formed, headed by conservation-minded people in both Connecticut and New York. The Nature Conservancy of Washington, D.C., became interested and made this project a part of its program, with the Anables as secretary and treasurer of the campaign. (Nature Conservancy is a private, non-profit organization of national scope whose purpose is to "set up and administer wilderness islands" throughout the country and to insure their remaining intact in perpetuity for educational, scientific, and cultural purposes.)

The first objective was reached and more than 100 additional acres were added. The committee is now working to acquire approximately 200 surrounding acres. Contributions have been received from four large foundations, sixty garden clubs, several Audubon chapters, Daughters of the American Revolution chapters, and many other groups and individuals. Some gifts came from as far afield as Arizona and California, Holland and Australia.

"The centuries-old hemlocks in the gorge," Richard Pough told the garden clubs which supported the project, "guard a wealth of scientific data. Secrets of climate, the evolution of plants and wildlife, mysteries of soil and water, are hidden in this unexploited wilderness."

The area is to be kept in its primitive state, with only the sketchiest foot trails providing access.

Pearson's Falls in North Carolina

Pearson's Falls is one of those places familiar to every community, a wooded glen just outside of town that everybody loves and takes for granted. It is six miles north of Tryon, North Carolina—250 acres of wild beauty along the Pacolet River. On the west and south are hills so steep that they are nearly inaccessible, covered with a climax forest consisting mostly of deciduous trees. Toward the southern tip of the glen, Colt Creek pours over a precipice, forming falls and rapids which rush over high, jutting rocks to the Pacolet. Throughout the area the flora is so abundant and varied that botanists have been attracted to it for years.

One spring day a few years ago, a group of garden club members went to the glen to see what wildflowers were in bloom. To their amazement they saw a sawmill set up and learned that this beloved spot was to be lumbered. There was not time to arouse the community, so this small group of women borrowed money and bought the glen themselves as a club project. The members raised the money through contributions, plant sales, flower shows, and card parties.

A year or so after they had finished paying for it, Oliver M. Freeman, retired botanist of the Washington Arboretum, moved to Tryon. He was immediately drawn to the glen, recognized the importance of its flora, and began a study of it, offering to make a mounted collection of specimens if the club would erect a suitable building to house it. This became the club's next project and a herbarium was established.

"More than 5,000 specimens have been collected and identified," Mr. Freeman reports, "with more than 1,200 of them mounted." While no herbarium is ever complete, he points out, this one is a good representation of the flora in the area and will be valuable to present and future botanists. "The current activity is the checking of each family for completeness and the mounting of at least one specimen of each species," he says. "This work has led to the finding of 405 new or noteworthy plants in the region."

Lady-Slippers in the Black Hills

Because our land *is* one of such variety and contrast, every effort to save the flora and fauna of each section helps preserve the character of the country as a whole, giving significance to any project, however small.

At one time yellow lady-slippers grew abundantly in the rugged Black Hills, land of Calamity Jane and Wild Bill Hickok. Today they have all but disappeared, one of those things nobody notices until "they're just not there anymore." That is why J. M. Atkinson of Rapid City felt that he had struck gold when he came upon a host of them in bloom in a secluded valley. Like a prospector staking a claim, he marked the location and made several return trips to check the seed for harvesting time. He gathered them when they were just ripe enough, then searched through many little draws and valleys until he found a location similar to the habitat of the parent plants. He planted the seed carefully. Two years passed before he was able to return. He had almost forgotten which of the shady, damp little draws he had used in his experiment, but suddenly the terrain took on meaning and he found them blooming as bountifully as if nature had put them there. Perhaps one day the Black Hills will again be covered with golden lady-slippers in the spring.

The Salt Marsh of Conanicut

We turn now from the Black Hills to the sand pits, barrier beaches, lagoons, and salt marshes of Narragansett Bay. Conanicut Island is about nine miles long and a mile or two wide, its southern tip lying in the entrance to the bay. Title to the island, then known as Quinunicutt, passed from the Narragansett Indians to a small band of Rhode Island colonists in 1637, a year after Roger Williams planted the first settlement at Providence. For some reason the people who settled Conanicut became increasingly anxious about "ye marsh and grasse" through the years that followed. In 1657 a group of landowners held a meeting and appointed seven of their number "to make a full and firm purchase of the island" to insure its safety for themselves and their heirs. And for over 300 years the salt marsh remained inviolate.

But as they watched seemingly limitless expanses of the country's farmland, woodland, and shore being transformed into housing de-

velopments and commercial or industrial areas, the people of Conanicut again became anxious about the safety of "ye marsh and grasse."
America's vanishing landscape was not something these people of the
country's most densely populated state could regard lightly. At one
time there were numerous salt marshes in the area: now theirs was
one of only a few left unspoiled.

The Conanicut salt marsh is a typical example of how nature cares
for her own. Although the tides sweep over parts of these treeless wetlands daily, the soil remains, for it is pinned in place by coarse grasses
and rushes, often knee-high. The marsh peat in the lower area,
washed by every tide, is held in place with cord grass, preventing the
tide from eating into the salt meadow beyond. The meadow, reached
only by the highest tide, is covered with other grasses, intermingled
with small stands of samphire and sea lavender. At the upper limit
of tidal influence, the tall, dense panic grass takes over, as if walling
off the sea. Fringing the marsh are cattails, alder, dogwood, and pink-
flowered marsh mallows. Just as the dry, treeless plains of the West
provide a home for the prairie dog and other creatures that need little
water, the salt marsh provides a habitat for birds and marine life. The
black duck, green heron, sharp-tailed sparrow, and the red-winged
blackbird breed there, and it is the daily feeding ground of many
other birds. But perhaps its greatest usefulness to birdlife is as a
sanctuary and resting place during migrations. Dropping from the
sky for an hour, a night, or a few days, come many migrants, among
them the little blue heron, yellow-crowned night heron, the snowy and
the American egret, least tern, clapper, Virginia rail, and the snow
goose.

The marsh was dear to all the islanders, but for each it had its
special meaning. Little boys fished and crabbed there, people interested in birds went there to watch and study them, students of marine
life collected specimens, botany students from nearby universities
used it for field trips, school children came for nature study, and
people of all ages enjoyed its tranquility.

As the original settlers had done, a group of Conanicut people—
members of the Jamestown Garden Club—held a meeting to determine how they could make their marsh secure for themselves and
future generations. Again as their ancestors had done, they decided

to make "a full and firm purchase." Club funds were to be used as an initial payment, and a committee was appointed to raise the rest of the money.

The club developed its project in a businesslike way. Conservation and soil experts in the area were consulted and a survey was made of the botanical, ornithological, and marine life. The purpose was to determine the value of the marsh from a conservation point of view and its suitability as a project. With the unanimous approval and vigorous support of these specialists, the club took its next step, a visit to the town authorities. Did *they* approve? Would they accept the gift of the marsh to the town? Would they cooperate in maintaining it as a wildlife sanctuary after it became town property? Would they support the project? "We will," the town fathers replied, "with the greatest of pleasure and appreciation. We like the marsh too." The next trip was to the editor of the local newspaper. Would *he* help? "I most certainly will," he told the committee. "I used to go crabbing there when I was a boy, and my little fellow does the same thing now."

Everywhere they turned, club members received the same enthusiastic support. A local banker, interested in birds, offered legal service. School children wrote essays on the flora and fauna in "our marsh." Contributions poured in, ranging from five cents to generous checks. Although the club had thought the project might take years, the townspeople responded so generously that the drive was completed within a few months.

The marsh has been protected by the club in several ways. When the deed was presented to the town council, it was requested that a citizens' committee on salt marsh affairs be appointed, consisting of a chairman and individuals qualified to represent the marsh. The deed itself stipulates that the marsh is given to the town "on condition that the grantees and their successors shall use the premises for recreation purposes as a wildlife preserve and upon use of the premises for any other purpose, title to the premises shall forthwith revert to the grantors or their successors." The deed further stipulates that should the town fail in its duty or the Jamestown Garden Club cease to exist, the whole area would come under the guardianship of a national or state conservation agency.

New York's Bergen Swamp

The wanton destruction of buffalo made William Cody (Buffalo Bill) a hero in his day, but if someone destroyed any of the buffalo left today the whole country would be aroused. Yet we are destroying nature's gems on a staggering scale, sometimes without realizing *what* we are destroying. Most communities look upon swamps as eyesores and fill them in as a matter of course. However, the swamp is important in many ways. One function is to help maintain the water table. As our communities spread, the open areas where rainfall can be absorbed into the ground become fewer. When we destroy the swamp we destroy one of nature's storage tanks. Furthermore, a swamp is a little world of its own, another living laboratory for scientific study. If there must be a utilitarian purpose for everything we save, there is always the possibility that, among its abundant plant life, scientists may find another of those strange elements that can greatly benefit mankind.

Bergen Swamp is about twenty-five miles from Rochester, New York. Always there have been people who loved and appreciated it. But through the years nothing had been done to make it secure, even though the matter had often been discussed by naturalists, botanists, and members of nearby educational institutions. To Mrs. Walter B. Slifer, of Rochester, the swamp was an expression of one of nature's most beguiling moods and she visited it for that reason alone. It had often occurred to her that it should be safeguarded, but the general attitude toward swamps was such that she felt little could be done without a tangible reason.

One day a friend sent her a copy of an article written by Professor William P. Alexander of the Buffalo Museum of Sciences entitled "Swamp Drainage Is Seen As a Scientific Calamity." This was what she needed. Armed with the article, she called together a group of people she felt would be interested and asked for suggestions. Among them were a botanist, a zoologist, a lawyer, and a forester, also garden club leaders and nature lovers. If the swamp was to be preserved, the group realized, community support was necessary. This meant changing the prevailing attitude toward the swamp, educating people to appreciate its beauty and scientific value. The "Bergen Swamp Preservation Society, Inc." developed from this meeting. Many pamphlets have been written by the society in its successful campaign to save the swamp, but probably it was a beautifully illustrated booklet called "Swamp Treasure," that did most to awaken people throughout the state to the value of the swamp.

The Society has succeeded in purchasing several hundred acres and will buy more as funds are raised until its goal of 2,000 acres is reached. The Federated Garden Clubs of New York State, Inc., and the Garden Club of America have both contributed heavily to the project.

A comprehensive plant survey of Bergen Swamp has been made by Dr. Walter C. Muenscher of Cornell University. In an area less than a mile square, 2,392 species were found, including the pitcher plant and round-leafed sundew which trap and digest insects. The small white lady-slipper, large yellow, the stemless, and the showy lady-slipper were discovered growing together in one little area—a rare occurrence. Other plant residents included the fringed polygala, grass-of-Parnassus, pink azalea, and the little known lizard's tail which has heart-shaped leaves and slender spikes of feathery white blossoms. Among the birds are a number of warblers not usually found in this area—black-throated green, black and white, magnolia, Canada, hooded, and mourning warblers. Bergen Swamp is also the haunt of the barred owl, great horned owl, screech owl, and whippoorwill.

Avoiding Overdevelopment

Larchmont's Country Atmosphere

Although Larchmont, New York, is forty-five minutes from Broadway, people who live there like to think of it as country. It is part of a tract of land on Long Island Sound purchased from the Siwanoy Indians in 1661 by John Richbell, an English trader, for "two coats, and ten shillings in wampum, 22 coates, one hundred fathom of wampum, 12 shirts, ten paire of stockings, twenty hands of powder, twelve barrs of lead, two firelocks, ffifteene hoes, ffifteene hatches, three kettles." It gets its name from the larch tree, and although there are few larches there today, the place is known for its beautiful trees.

In spite of its proximity to New York City, Larchmont remained a small village with many wooded areas long after most communities in the suburban areas had become small cities. Not until after World War II did it begin to feel the impact of housing developments.

Larchmont did not object to being built up, but the residents watched with increasing concern the practices of many of the builders. They would buy up most of the available land in a community, strip it of topsoil and trees, and then sell the topsoil back to the buyers. This would leave them with a home barren of beauty in a spot that had formerly had a sylvan charm that would take a lifetime to duplicate. With the wooded areas disappearing fast, the general feeling was that something must be done quickly or the character of the community would be changed completely.

The Garden Club of Larchmont decided to take the leadership in preserving the town's country atmosphere. Its first objective was to have a number of vacant lots throughout the community set aside as play areas. They were not to be the usual type, with hard packed earth, but were to have well kept grass and a background of shrubs and trees. Contractors would be urged to save the largest and most beautiful trees in areas where they were building, and to landscape new homes in keeping with the character of the community. A third objective was to persuade county authorities to set aside a long strip of county-owned land that winds through a section of Larchmont— not as a park, but in its natural state. The area has a brook, an old mill site, a variety of trees, and attracts hundreds of birds. It was the only large wooded area left, where once there had been so many.

Through the cooperation of local authorities, the first two parts of the plan were accomplished without much difficulty, but there was a problem with the county-owned land because real estate men wanted it for a housing development. They argued that it was not bringing any financial return either to the community or to the county, and that if houses were built on it the tax rolls would be materially increased. Lawyers to whom the garden club members turned for help showed that this was not necessarily true. They pointed out that real estate values go down when a community becomes over-crowded. Open areas such as this, they said, are essential as a buffer against over-crowding and to help maintain property values by keeping the community attractive. If Larchmont lost its country atmosphere, many living there would seek what they wanted elsewhere, and people buying new homes, who had been attracted to Larchmont by its wooded charm, would not be pleased either.

The local newspaper editor and civic groups supported the club wholeheartedly. County officials finally concluded that the people of Larchmont were right and set the land aside as a woodland area.

Housing Developments on Oahu

Since World War II, the loss of natural and created beauty through housing developments, shopping centers, highways, gas stations, and industrial sites, has become of increasing concern to communities all over the nation. Sadly enough, the more attractive the area, the greater is the threat to the trees and open spaces that make it so. The housing problem facing Oahu, third largest of the Hawaiian Islands and the location of Waikiki Beach, is a good illustration of this point.

From the time it was organized in 1912, the primary objective of the Outdoor Circle, a public-spirited group of women with headquarters at Honolulu, has been to preserve and enhance the natural beauty of the islands. Following a plan drawn for Honolulu in 1906 by Charles Mulford Robinson, civic adviser to Rochester, New York, the group is responsible for innumerable beautification and community improvement projects, among them the planting of thousands of shrubs and trees. So many thousands of plantings were made on the hillsides, along the roads, around public buildings, and in other places, that the Circle maintained its own nursery for twenty years, until the Parks Board took it over.

"Only if you have read the old missionary diaries which speak of the dry dust plains and the barren slopes of Punchbowl and Diamond Head, do you realize that Honolulu was once far from a verdant, semitropical, lovely land," Mrs. Alice Spalding Bowen reports in her history of the Circle. "Most visitors who delight in flowering trees stretching for miles along the streets of residential districts are unaware that most of these trees were planted under the auspices of the Outdoor Circle."

With millions of tourists drawn to the islands by their beauty, it is inevitable that many would remain or return to settle there. Hawaii, particularly Oahu, must now provide for a staggering increase in population. "Fifty thousand acres of natural growth must be cleared for new land development within the next few years," a Circle committee reports to members, adding that 7,500 acres in roadways will be paved; 650 miles of new roads built; sixty-three new subdivisions, many with shopping centers, have been planned; twenty-two new commercial and industrial centers will have acres of paving. These things spell progress, members of the Circle and thoughtful Hawaiians realize, but they also realize that if the beauty of the islands is destroyed, their economic foundation, the tourist business, will be destroyed with it. "Sun-baked thoroughfares, barren housing areas, and hot glaring shopping centers do not appeal to visitors," the Circle remarks. "Neither do they appeal to our own people."

Planning ahead, the Outdoor Circle has launched a plant replacement program for Oahu and other islands. Extensive tree planting is an important part of the program and covers residential, commercial, industrial, and street improvement districts, with a special "Subdivision Tree Committee." The effects of mass planting in Europe are being studied, along with tree planting programs on the mainland, with authorities in the field giving technical advice as to the plants most suitable. Again the thought is to work out a plan whereby the new developments will fit into the existing landscape rather than mar it.

Preserving the Natural Elements of the Past

The Threat to Walden

European nations are wiser than we in recognizing the importance of preserving some of the past, with Rome the classic example of past and present living side by side in harmony. Because we are still a young nation, our heritage of man-made creations cannot compare with that of older countries; but this cannot be said of our rich heritage of natural beauty. If we would preserve these gems of nature, we must recognize before it is too late the many ways in which they are threatened.

Henry David Thoreau is regarded as one of America's significant spokesmen. For two years this poet-naturalist, who made study of the outdoors his occupation, lived in a shanty on the shore of Walden Pond, near Concord, Massachusetts, on land owned by Ralph Waldo Emerson. His book, *Walden: or Life in the Woods*, an account of his thoughts and observations there, made Walden Pond world famous. The Center for Information on America, in Washington, Connecticut, recently gave the following report on what is happening to Walden:

"The four families which once owned the surrounding land, wishing to 'preserve the Walden of Emerson and Thoreau, its shores and woodlands,' deeded the tract to Massachusetts. As such, it is visited yearly not only by Americans but by people from many lands, drawn by the world-wide reputation and influence of these two writers and thinkers.

"But Walden, besides thus becoming a shrine of quiet beauty and inspiration, also possesses another attraction. It has clear, cool water and a pleasant beach. The Middlesex County Commissioners, in charge of the reservation, and aware of a considerable demand, presently established at the south end of the pond a general swimming and bathing area. Then other things began to happen. Across the road that skirts the area's east side, and beyond state property, trailer camps and hot-dog stands mushroomed up. Today it requires a considerable stretch of imagination to picture in the busy scene the former tranquility of Walden. For many American visitors, as well as for foreign pilgrims, like the ambassador from India who came to pay his respects to a man whose writings helped Mahatma Gandhi lead his people to independence, this change looks like a catastrophe and irreparable loss.

"The conflicting uses to which Walden has been put were brought to public attention recently when the county commissioners began further enlarging the bathing area. Protests from all over were backed up even by an editorial in the *Times* of London. On October 1, 1957, Judge E. R. Dewing, of the Massachusetts Superior Court, on the petition of a 'Save Walden' committee, issued a temporary injunction stopping the bulldozers which already had ripped up an acre or so of trees and shoved part of a hillside into the pond.

" 'This does not sound as if it were following out the purpose of the establishment of this reservation,' remarked the judge—and his words point up the whole problem that faces us everywhere in the management of our great outdoors.' "

Lubbock's Prairie Dog Town

Mackenzie Park in Lubbock has a community called "Prairie Dog Town," population 300 prairie dogs, which is the talk of Texas. Captivated by the merry antics of these fascinating little animals, more than a million tourists visit the town every year. ·

While prairie dogs are common from Montana to northern Mexico, this colony is of interest conservation-wise because it *has* been preserved and is all that is left of a giant prairie dog town inhabited by some 400 million of these animals at the turn of the century. The prairie dog, like other small animals of its type, is one of nature's farmers. In digging its tunnels, it plows the soil, helping to make it rich and absorbent. Some of the colonies were from twenty to thirty miles long. One continuous colony in Texas is reported to have been 250 miles long and nearly 150 wide, covering 25,000 square miles— a *real* plowing job.

But, while the prairie dog is essential in nature's plan, it became a "pesky nusiance" in Lubbock, which just had too many. Consequently, ranchers and farmers asked the government to help exterminate them, with townspeople concurring. Within a few years they were "pushed off the prairie in the name of progress."

The present Prairie Dog Town was established in 1936, when Mackenzie Park was being developed. Four of the dogs were scurrying to and fro over the land, getting in the way of the park superintendent. "I just don't know what to do with these little rascals," he remarked dolefully, adding that he guessed he'd have to poison them. A tall Texan, Kennedy N. Clapp, was standing nearby. "Why poison them?" he asked quietly. "Why not preserve them?"

Mr. Clapp was given seven acres of the park to use for his town, provided he could confine the animals to that area. This turned out to be a project in itself. "They would always get out of any enclosure I made," he recalls, "and would sometimes start new holes in the middle of nearby golf courses." This did not endear his prairie dogs to golfers, so Clapp sought advice. The National Zoo suggested using chicken wire. "It took me three years," he says, "and a lot of trials and errors to get what I wanted. I finally sank chicken wire eighteen inches into the ground and extended it eighteen inches above ground with six inches of tin at the top. A cement-block fence has since been erected around the plot."

Because of his understanding of these animals, Mr. Clapp is called the "Mayor of Prairie Dog Town." When asked why he has worked so hard to save a creature most Texans have little love for, he replied: "Because I'm interested in conservation from all angles and down the middle."

Mr. Clapp says "dog" is a misnomer. "They are rodents, really," he explains, "members of the squirrel family, marmots, near relatives of the woodchuck. Full-grown, the greyish to reddish animals are from twelve to fifteen inches in length, weigh from two to three pounds, and have a short black-tipped tail that wags as if attached to a spring. Their homes are L-shaped burrows, usually twelve to twenty feet long and six to fifteen feet horizontally. The entrance is banked with earth to keep out water and the size of the mound depends upon its location and rainfall. Mound and hole resemble a miniature volcano.

"From three to six feet below the entrance is a small room to which the animal retires when first frightened into his hole. There he may be heard barking and scolding. If he hears the intruder approaching too near, down he slips to the bottom. Here there is a place where he may halt, turn around, and go back up for a peep, or come out if the 'all clear' is sounded by other residents. They have their own 'civil defense' system, and no vegetation within 100 feet of their burrow is allowed to be more than six inches high. As an intruder approaches, signals are relayed throughout the town. The dogs 'freeze' until the danger has passed.

"Construction of a home is always watched with delight by tourists. If the earth is damp, the dogs make mud balls and remove them to the surface. If the earth is dry, it is carried out in armfuls. Noses and heads are used to tamp the earth firmly around the entrance hole and inside the crater. When there is general repairing of mounds, one may anticipate rain. Those here seem contented with their lot, and even seem to enjoy putting on a show for visitors. I hope this small colony may be preserved."

The Indian Mounds of Mississippi

Every school child knows the story of Pompeii, but most of them would be stumped if asked to describe evidences of former cultures in their own country, such as the cliff dwellings in Mesa Verde and the Indian mounds. These ruins may not be as important historically as Pompeii and cannot be classified as natural beauty, but they are part of our heritage.

Mesa Verde in Colorado, said to have the largest and best preserved cliff dwellings in the world, was established as a national park in 1906. The Mound City Group of twenty-three prehistoric mounds in

Ohio was designated a national monument in 1923. Many other evidences of ancient Indian culture in Arizona, New Mexico, Georgia, Colorado, and elsewhere have been protected in the same way. Doubtless the spectacular 1,350 foot-long Serpent Mound in southern Ohio will be preserved, as well as the Elephant Mound in Wisconsin, both totemic representations. Nevertheless, an effort by a small group to save its own evidences of such a culture is significant because it is another indication that people do appreciate our heritage and want to save it.

Twenty years ago there were many mounds from the Canadian border to the Gulf of Mexico, with the greatest concentration in Ohio and Mississippi. They are disappearing rapidly. These mounds are believed to have been used for burial purposes, as foundations for temples and other buildings, or as fortresses, and are in some way connected with tribal totems and religious ceremonies. Some are 2,000 years old, others apparently of historical times. Stone, copper, mica, obsidian, and meteoric iron have been found in them, giving evidence of widespread trade. The people knew weaving and pottery making, and their stone carvings of animals, human figures, and especially of pipes are considered excellent.

There is a forty-acre area of mounds in the Mississippi Delta, north of Greenville, which is the finest group in the state. Members of the local garden club, fearing that they would be destroyed, took the preservation of the entire area as a club project. They painstakingly raised the money to buy the land, then put it in the name of the city of Greenville. Next they planted a backdrop of native plants, using material known to the Indians. They hope to develop the park as a national attraction.

The Redwoods of California

If a survey were made to determine the best-loved masterpieces of nature in this country, the sequoias in California would be high on the list. These noble trees, native to North America alone, have stirred the imagination of men beyond all others. In a way it is strange that our country, still young, should have the largest tree in the world, the tallest known standing tree, and what is believed to be the oldest living thing on earth—and that all of them should be in one section of the country. On the other hand, perhaps it is not strange at all.

The Old World has its cathedrals of unsurpassed beauty, built by men. These groves are our temples, created by God.

The California sequoias are of two species: *Sequoia sempervirens,* the coast redwood, and *Sequoia gigantea,* the Sierra redwood, often called the "big tree." The coast redwood is limited to a narrow belt 450 miles long and about forty wide along the Pacific coast. This belt runs from the southwestern corner of Oregon southward to the Santa Lucia Mountains in San Luis Obispo County. The coast redwood grows at a maximum elevation of 2,000 feet. These lofty lords of the tree world soar upward like majestic columns. Their fluted, chocolate brown trunks are often bare of branches for a hundred feet above a forest floor carpeted with ferns and flowers. The trees grow close together, shutting out direct sunlight, but in the morning and evening, long shafts of light stream down through their interlacing branches as from a stained-glass window. "Founder's Tree," tallest of all trees, is a coast redwood 364 feet high. Many trees along the Avenue of the Giants are over 2,000 years old. The coast redwood reaches its best development in Humboldt and Del Norte counties, on flats and river bottoms sheltered from the coastal winds, where it forms dense, pure stands of tremendous volume and impressiveness. The wood of this tree is of high commercial value.

The Sierra redwoods (these are designations adopted by the California Park System) grow along the western slopes of the Sierra Nevada mountain range in central California, at elevations of 4,500 to 8,000 feet. They are limited to a 250-mile strip where they are found in isolated groves. There are about seventy-two groves, ranging in size from ten to 4,000 acres. Most of the trees are in Tulare and southern Fresno counties. The Sierra redwood does not grow as tall as the coast redwood, which averages from 250 to 275 feet, with some much taller. However, it is a much more massive tree with an average diameter of fifteen to twenty feet, and sometimes more than twenty-five. The cinnamon red bark is usually from twelve to twenty-four inches thick near the base, although a thickness of more than three feet has been measured. The roots supporting this vast bulk do not penetrate to a depth much more than six feet, but reach out laterally from 200 to 300 feet, with the roots of a single tree sometimes covering three acres. The Sierra redwood grows in company with other conifers of great height, although none are as tall as itself. The General Sher-

man tree, largest living tree in the world, is a Sierra redwood 273 feet
high and nearly 115 feet in circumference. It is said that its first large
limb, about 130 feet from the ground, is about seven feet thick. This
tree is in Sequoia National Park. The oldest living tree, aside from
the recently discovered age of the bristlecone pine which also grows
only in this country, is thought to be one of the Sierra redwoods, some
of which are estimated to be more than 3,000 years old. The wood
of this species is inferior commercially to the coast redwood, one
reason, perhaps, why it has been better protected.

The sequoia is named for a famous Indian chief of the Cherokee
tribe, Sequoyah, who created the Indian alphabet. Many poets and
writers have attempted to describe this tree, but the words of Edwin
Markham are in some ways the most fitting—"forms of immortality
standing here among the transitory shapes of time."

Unlike other trees, the redwoods defy decay, disease, and fire. Since
the glacial ages, when they were almost exterminated by ice sheets,
their only enemy seems to have been man. There is little doubt that
the sequoias in California would have been destroyed during the
reckless tree-cutting period in the United States had it not been that
they were just too overpowering to tackle in great numbers. What a
loss it would have been, for all that most of us ask of these superb
monarchs of the forest is that they simply stand there to be admired.

Over 90 per cent of the Sierra redwoods have been set aside in
national parks and forests or are in the custody of the state of California, including most virgin stands. When negotiations are completed
some 97 per cent will be in public ownership, a dramatic illustration
of the attitude of the people of the United States toward natural
wonders today.

The situation of *Sequoia sempervirens* is somewhat different and
much more complex. The coast redwood lumber industry is among
the most important in the state and most of these trees are privately
owned. While the bulk of the Sierra redwoods are safeguarded, federal holdings include only a small portion of the coast redwoods.
However, California has set aside nearly 70,000 acres in state parks
and hopes to increase the acreage to 100,000 or more. Those now in
state possession represent perhaps 6 or 7 per cent of the remaining
virgin stand, which once covered about 1,500,000 acres. Due to
their commercial value, the cost of acquiring either species is very

high. One grove of coast redwoods in Humboldt County cost nearly $5,000,000, while the two groves of Sierra redwoods in the California park system were purchased at a cost of almost $3,500,000. The California holdings were acquired on a matching system; that is, the state put up half the money and the Save-the-Redwoods League raised the rest. The Avenue of the Giants is one of the most recent purchases, acquired at a cost of $1,200,000. Over a million acres of coast redwoods are in private ownership.

How these giants survived the saw is in some ways even more inspiring than their survival through the ages. A brief account can only hint at the drama. It began in the days before our national park and forest system was established, when about the only friends they had were a few conservationists like John Muir. Such men were dismissed as impractical idealists and dreamers by exploiters—as some still are today. The battle to save as many as possible of the trees is by no means finished and, like the old movie serials, there have been many episodes, with the trees saved, grove by grove, often "just a little ahead of the saw." The Sierra redwoods fared better than the coast redwoods. In 1890, Sequoia, Yosemite, and General Grant National Parks were established, all containing groves of "big trees." Saying this, however, is like saying we won our freedom in 1781. The mere statement of fact gives no idea of the long struggle to achieve it. Even after these areas were rescued, there was still controversy over them. In 1892 a bill was introduced into Congress to cut away nearly half of Yosemite. Its passage would have meant the loss of some of the most beautiful scenery in the park. Furthermore a precedent would have been set for other invasions of national park and forest areas. "We are not building this country of ours for a day," Muir pleaded. "It is to last through the ages."

Up to 1917, however, no coast redwoods were publicly owned. All were in the hands of lumbermen, with the cream being rapidly destroyed. Appalled at the devastation of what many now consider the finest forests in the world, three conservationists—Dr. John C. Merriam, Madison Grant, and Henry Fairfield Osborn—organized the Save-the-Redwoods League. Through the years this group has raised millions of dollars to buy up the trees. Contributions have included large donations, such as the millions the Rockefellers have given, and the dollars of countless people in all walks of life. The project of the

garden club of Lodi, California, is a typical example of how the
money was raised.

In 1948 the League was conducting a drive to purchase the South
Calaveras Grove, owned by a lumber company and about to be logged.
This magnificent stand of Sierra redwoods is in northern Tuolumne
County, southwest of a tract that had already been set aside as a state
park. But while the grove in the park contained only 158 of these
trees, the Valley of Big Tree Creek has nearly a thousand, intermingled
with large and beautiful sugar pines, as well as firs, cedars, dogwoods,
and other trees. As their conservation project, the hundred members
of the Lodi Garden Club voted to help raise money to save this grove.

"We began our campaign with a Tag Day," says Mrs. H. B.
Rencher, then president. "Our mayor cooperated and signed a proclamation, declaring March 13, 1948, Tag Day during Conservation
Week. We made tags of redwood tips tied with brown ribbon and
pinned one on each person donating money. Our containers were ice
cream cartons wrapped with redwood bark to resemble trunks of redwood trees. We collected $239.45.

"Our interest was shared by many organizations. The local Kiwanis
Club and the Farmers and Merchants Bank both had 'thank you'
cards printed for us, and when money was sent in, either to the club
or the bank, we acknowledged the donation with a card. All garden
clubs in our district assisted in raising money for our fund. We worked
six years raising money. When the big drive of the Save-the-Redwoods
League ended in 1954 with Mr. Rockefeller's gift of $1,000,000, we
turned in $2,510, the largest check from a single garden club. Ours
was a very small part of the purchase price, $2,800,000, but we were
proud of what we did."

They are everywhere, these precious heritages, and everywhere little
detachments of citizens are fighting to save them. It may be sand
dunes in Indiana, acres of trilliums in Pennsylvania, a cypress swamp
in Maryland, or a sunken holly forest on Long Island. Or it may be
the pitiful remnant of the whooping cranes. There is no flourish of
trumpets for those who fight this type of battle and no flags wave
when they pass by. But in their own way they are like so many soldiers,
defending this land of ours.

CHAPTER II

OUR ROADSIDES

Advantageous as it may be to us as motorists, the multi-billion dollar road building program now under way will make drastic changes in our landscape. Will we be pleased? Or will we realize too late that far more natural beauty has been destroyed than we counted on? Will we find this network of interstate highways so commercialized and littered that we do not enjoy using it and visitors from other countries receive an unfavorable impression?

It is inevitable that much countryside charm will be lost in constructing the highways, but fortunately our country is large enough not to lose its character completely by the changes. This project has in fact almost limitless potentialities for enhancing the beauty of the country. Whether it does or not, and to what extent, depends upon us, the people who use the highways and pay for them. As in all matters concerning our land, we are the ultimate authority on what happens, provided we make our voices heard.

The new superhighways will be engineering miracles of magnificent sweep, but they should have an appropriate setting. We have permitted too many thoroughfares to become littered, billboarded alleys and if we crisscross the country with mile upon mile of such ugliness, future generations are not going to thank us. Even if the highways make our parks, forests, and monuments more accessible, what will it profit us if the beauty of the country as a whole is destroyed.

Some of our parkways and highways are breathtakingly beautiful, through careful landscaping or the preservation of natural scenery.

They are well kept, free of billboards, and without litter. This is the type of highway we have a right to expect and upon which we should insist. Wherever possible, the natural charm of the countryside should be preserved, and where it must be sacrificed, it should be replaced with created beauty in harmony with the surroundings.

Highway plantings also have practical uses—safe driving and a reduction of maintenance costs by the prevention of roadside erosion. Neither factor is within the scope of this book but such considerations alone would make carefully planted highways a necessity. Tests by the New Jersey Turnpike Authority have proved that plantings of shrubs and trees in the strips between divided highways practically eliminate headlight glare, the cause of many accidents.

These considerations aside, let us think about roadside beauty that may be lost—or achieved. One engineer has summed the matter up in these words: "The taxpayers can have whatever they are willing to pay for. Time is one of the biggest factors in construction costs, and in figuring bids an engineer counts heavily on what a bulldozer can do. It is usually easier, quicker, and cheaper for us to clear everything out of the way and let the landscaper take over after we're finished, rather than work around existing shrubbery and trees. We're like everybody else, we have to make a living and the fellow that puts in the lowest bid is the one most likely to get the job. Still, we like nature too. What we've all got to do as taxpayers is make up our minds what we want. We'll have to pay more for road construction if we want the countryside saved, or else have fewer highways. It would probably be worth it to most people, if they saw the thing straight. As for myself, I'd like to see us hang on to as much of the America we've always known as we can. You've got to figure too that landscaping costs money, so maybe we ought to think a little more about saving the countryside. But it's not up to us, just because we build the roads. It is something everybody should start thinking about before it's too late."

There perhaps is the crux of the matter: What do we want? If we want as much of the countryside saved as possible, we shall have to insist upon it with our votes, our voices, and our actions. If we want the rest landscaped to conform, we shall have to see to that too—and promptly. Otherwise, the beauty of the roadsides will be lost by default. By the same token, they will be hemmed in with billboards.

Where the existing landscape cannot be kept, it still need not be destroyed completely. Shrubs, plants and small trees can be salvaged to beautify homes, public buildings, and even whole communities. Many people have created wildflower gardens on their own property by beating the bulldozer to the plants. In other instances the highway flowers have been removed to sanctuaries and parks. Shrubbery and small trees have often been saved in the same way. Several projects will be described to show how effective salvaging may be done in any community.

But it is not just the new roads and highways that need our attention. There are thousands of miles of existing roadsides that should be cleaned up and beautified. In most instances this is something that can be handled on a local basis through the leadership of civic groups. We have more leisure to travel than at any time in the history of our country, spend more time on the road than any other people, and drive the most beautiful cars. However, we are being forced to drive farther and farther every year to find the refreshing greenery we should be enjoying all along the way, because we have permitted our roadsides to be stripped of their natural beauty. And all too often the roadside becomes a garbage can for passing cars. We pride ourselves on personal cleanliness, but where our roadsides are concerned we are among the dirtiest of people.

Controlling Billboard Advertising

America's Present Problem

Judging from the comments of people in various parts of the country, many are under the impression that the congressional legislation passed in the spring of 1958 will either eliminate billboards entirely from the new interstate highways or control them strictly. Unhappily, neither is the case: the "battle of the billboards" is far from won.

The Federal Government is shouldering 90 per cent of the cost of the highways, individual states paying the rest. The bill which was finally passed was a watered-down version of the original. It simply offers the states a bonus for banning such advertising and no state need agree. An additional ½ per cent of the cost will be borne by the Federal Government in states that agree to control billboard advertising. Thus the hundreds of thousands of public-spirited citizens

who deluged their congressmen with postcards, letters, and telegrams,
stating that they did not want billboards on their new highways have
won only the first round of what may be a long, hard fight.

The billboard lobby is rich and powerful. It fought tooth and nail
against this bill and unquestionably will continue to fight through the
state legislatures. If we are to defeat it and make *sure* our new highways are free of billboards, we must write our state representatives as
we did our congressmen, and get friends, acquaintances, and members
of organized groups to do the same, in an even stronger campaign.

Although numerous groups worked hard to secure a law controlling
billboard advertising, many congressmen credit "that enormous force,
the women of America," especially garden club members, with the
passage of the congressional bill.

Hawaii's Billboard Boycott

People who have visited Hawaii speak glowingly of its charm and
beauty, but would the rest of the world be so enthusiastic about these
island gems if they were infested with billboards? Suppose there were
huge tobacco and whisky signs on Diamond Head, an immense pickle
sign obstructing the view of Manoa Valley, a soap sign in letters ten
feet high perched atop Punchbowl, the Pali cluttered with them and
the highways hemmed in.

Such signs were there once and many more. When the Outdoor
Circle of Honolulu started its campaign against billboards in 1913,
forty-three local and many mainland firms were using this form of
advertising on tiny Oahu, to say nothing of the other islands. The
situation was especially bad in and around Honolulu. There had been
individual attempts to correct matters but no organized effort.

The Circle opened its campaign on May 10, 1913, backed staunchly
by Lorrin A. Thurston, local newspaper editor. Placing his paper at
the disposal of Circle members, he put out a special antibillboard
edition which today is a collector's item. Pictures of the more offensive
billboards were featured, showing how they marred the landscape and
shut out scenic beauty. There were interviews with residents and
visitors, who expressed their disapproval; essays by school children;
and an editorial by Mr. Thurston that was "packed with real dyna-
mite."

The Circle kept the issue constantly before the public through a stamp campaign. Members had rubber stamps made with letters half an inch high, bearing the single word "antibillboard." Using red ink, they stamped checks, receipts, bills, letterheads, personal correspondence, everything that would carry their message. After the campaign had continued long enough for advertisers to realize the Circle was in dead earnest, a committee called upon local merchants and asked their cooperation. The committee called to the attention of the merchants the fact that this "orgy of billboards" was not only antagonizing their island customers, but harming the tourist business by ruining the beauty that attracted visitors to Hawaii. Meanwhile, Mr. Thurston's newspaper kept up a running report on the progress of the drive. Over a period of time, most local merchants discontinued billboard advertising.

Feeling a responsibility toward the advertising company selling billboard space on the islands, the Circle decided to buy and scrap it. A visit to the Territorial Tax Office revealed that the company was making tax returns on an investment of $2,500. Circle members voted to raise this amount, plus what would probably be asked for good will. But when Mrs. Cherilla Lowrey, then president, approached the company, she was told that the price was $18,000, an impossible sum for a small group of women to raise.

Refusing to be defeated, the Honolulu group asked sister groups on the islands to join in a letter-writing campaign, with the letters going directly to the manufacturers of the products advertised on the billboards. These firms were asked to cooperate in helping to rid Hawaii of billboards, and it was explained that Circle members would be prejudiced in favor of products advertised in other ways. "One morning the advertisement of a popular and well-known brand of baking powder appeared on one of the largest billboards," says Mrs. A. N. Campbell, who headed the committee, "but instead of realizing increased sales, the manufacturer received an avalanche of letters stating that as long as the advertisement remained, the writers would use another brand and recommend it to their friends." She adds: "After all, advertisers want the good will of the public and when the public takes the trouble to tell them that their methods are wrong they should be grateful." This one was and lost no time in cabling from the mainland that the advertisement was being eliminated.

By 1917, there were only six billboard users on the islands. The old rickety billboards had disappeared and those that remained were large and impressive. No local merchants were using such advertising, but there were still some manufacturers from the mainland who refused to cooperate. For ten more years the Circle battled. Members won the support of the Tourist Bureau, the Board of Supervisors of the city and county of Honolulu, and the Chamber of Commerce. They also continued their efforts to buy the company contracting for billboard space.

By 1927, only two billboard users were left. With the support of business houses gone and the increased antagonism of the community, the Outdoor Circle was finally able to buy the company for $4,000. Before scrapping it, the club obtained a signed agreement from leading individuals and firms, promising to continue their support of the billboard ban.

The Circle did not stop there. "The year 1927 was a legislative year," Mrs. Campbell relates. "We had a bill drawn, forbidding the erection of billboards on the Island of Oahu except in a very limited area in the heart of the city at well-nigh prohibitive rates. On April 27, 1927, the bill was introduced in the Senate, passed by both houses, and signed by the governor.

Campaigns Against Roadside Littering

A Helping Hand from Industry

Having their products strewn along the roadside is another manner in which manufacturers receive adverse publicity. Recognizing this, industry in many instances has taken the lead in efforts to break the littering habit of our people. A notable example is "Keep America Beautiful, Inc."

To pinpoint the origin of the drive to clean up our roadsides would be neither possible nor fair. The need for action was there. Throughout the country individual citizens and groups were simultaneously seeking legislation to prevent the countryside from becoming a dump for pop bottles, beer cans, empty cartons, banana peels, and other refuse—not to mention burning cigarettes tossed near dry wooded areas. It was a spontaneous revolt, springing up all over the country. Keep America Beautiful, however, is typical of these movements. It is a national public service organization for the prevention of litter, non-profit and non-partisan, with headquarters in New York. It encourages volunteer groups to work closely with government officials and is supported by business firms, national trade associations, various departments of the Federal Government, and more than fifty of the nation's leading civic, service, and professional organizations. More than 70 million persons belong to it. Among the cooperating groups are women's clubs, garden clubs, religious groups, youth organizations, educators, professional groups, conservationists, sportsmen, and rural groups.

Like many projects of national or international scope, the corporation started with the activities of a small group. In 1939, Mrs. Cyril G. Fox of Media, Pennsylvania, organized the Pennsylvania Roadside Council in an effort to improve the condition of roadsides in and around her community. The Council did so well that in 1944 Mrs. Fox was asked to organize a special committee in Philadelphia to work on its litter problem. "As the Cleaner Streets Committee and working closely with the city's director of public works, we waged an intensive campaign with the slogan, 'Don't be a Litterbug,' " she explains. "Illustrating our slogan was a drawing of a revolting looking bug emerging from a battered rubbish can surrounded by trash. Since we started our campaign, Philadelphia has repeatedly received annual awards from the National Cleanup, Paintup, Fixup Bureau as the cleanest city of its size in America."

In 1951, Mrs. Fox, a garden club member, was made Roadside Chairman of the National Council of State Garden Clubs, Inc., a group of approximately 13,000 clubs (several in foreign countries), with a total membership of nearly half a million women. Capitalizing on her Philadelphia experience, she set up a system whereby cleanup drives were organized by garden clubs in other states. It soon became apparent that to put the campaign over on a national scale, the clubs would need an eye-catching emblem and effective publicity material. "I consulted the advertising executive that was handling my husband's account," Mrs. Fox recalls. "He turned our problem over to a group of artists in Philadelphia, asking them to see what they could do. One of them, Ben Brunner, created the aggressive little meanie that is now used by all our clubs."

The president of the National Council at that time, Mrs. William Walters, supported the campaign enthusiastically and arranged for the publicity material to be sold at cost. There were brochures, stickers for car bumpers, "meanie" seals for stationery, enameled signs for parks and as roadside markers, litterbug pins for children, and posters for schools, office buildings, stores, and factories.

"The first big break we got after the release of our publicity," says Mrs. Fox, "came through the public relations manager of the Owens-Illinois Glass Company, who saw the possibilities of our campaign. He ordered a supply of the seals, then wrote a form letter outlining the need to check the throwing of bottles and cans along the roadsides. The letter, along with our little bug, was sent to industrial organizations all over the country, such as brewers, bottlers, and can manufacturers. I was invited to meet with the heads of some of these industries in New York to discuss plans for a national program, which they would subsidize, to fight the litter problem. My committee and I suggested an educational program along the lines we were using and "Keep America Beautiful" came into being in 1953. I was asked to serve as chairman of the steering committee of the advisory council. The board of the National Council of State Garden Clubs, Inc., voted its approval, joined the organization, and I accepted the privilege of serving."

The second big break came in June 1954, when the *Reader's Digest* included an article about litterbugs by William S. Dutton. Everyone who saw the magazine was confronted with the question: "Are You a Litterbug?" printed on the cover. Deploring the "appalling mess of trash along our highways," Mr. Dutton asked, "Who are the guilty?" Quoting the report of Howard Chase, who had directed a nationwide survey the previous winter, he replied: "All of us except the bedridden, the jailed, and the newly born." Since the *Digest* is published in a dozen or more languages, as well as in Braille, the debut of the "litterbug" was on an international scale.

The Staggering Cost of Littering

The conservation field needs more men like William C. Stolk, president of the American Can Company, who is largely responsible for the creation of Keep America Beautiful. According to KAB, as much as 100,000 tons of litter are dumped on the nation's highways in one holiday week-end, while countless additional tons are scattered over city streets, parks, recreation areas, and beaches. The cost of cleaning up the primary highways alone is $50,000,000 a year and, if the cost of cleaning city streets, parks, and resorts is added, the figure becomes staggering. One report sets the annual cost at from $15 to $50 *per mile* —money which certainly could find a better use.

However, cost is only part of the story. Litter is a safety hazard and a health menace. It causes erosion in highway drainage, provides breeding places for flies and mosquitos, and diverts manpower from constructive work. It is a nuisance to farmers, a cause of many highway accidents, and responsible for millions of dollars worth of fire damage every year. There is also a loss that cannot be measured in dollars and cents, the distressing appearance of littered highways.

Most states today either have, or are considering, laws prohibiting the throwing of refuse along the highways, with fines as high as $250 provided. In Missouri, a Cass County judge has devised a punishment that really fits the crime. He sentences offenders to clean up about a mile of right-of-way under the watchful eye of a state policeman.

Noteworthy Results in Maryland

One of the principal problems of KAB is providing appropriate containers for litter disposal in strategic places. This is not too difficult in a community. And if enough containers are provided at such places as roadside parks and picnic areas there is no excuse for trash being thrown on the ground. The real problem is the automobile. It is all too easy to toss an empty carton from a speeding car, and unless there is a place in the car to put it, the tossing habit is going to be difficult to break in spite of punitive measures. With this in mind, KAB designed a litterbag. It bears the "meanie" insignia of the National Council of State Garden Clubs, Inc., is sturdily constructed, and has a paper strap to hold it in place on the car door. Distribution of the bag has been handled in various ways. One of the most successful methods was devised by Maryland.

In one year the state had removed 8,000 truckloads of trash from its highways at a cost of $21 a truckload. "These are unserviceable, unprofitable, unproductive dollars," the governor declared; "this is money that could have gone into making roads safer and more comfortable to ride." The state anti-littering law provides fines up to $250 and jail sentences up to ninety days for throwing trash on public highways. State police were instructed to take special care that thoughtless violators were cautioned and willful violators punished. The governor also appointed a special Highway Receptacle and Litter-bag Committee as a subdivision of Keep Maryland Beautiful. It is composed of representatives from two veterans' organizations, two automobile clubs, the garden clubs, Izaak Walton League, Maryland Homemakers, Automobile Trade Association, Motor Truck Association, and the Maryland Travel Club.

Service stations were asked to cooperate by using standardized receptables. These were 120-pound grease barrels, cleaned and painted in the colors of the stations. Each barrel was identified by two decalcomanias—one at the top reading "Travel Trash" and the other, at the bottom, reading "Keep Maryland Beautiful." The KMB insignia was used in service station windows. Trash receptacles were also placed along the highways, at vacation spots, and other places where trash tended to collect. Other containers were placed in transit buses with placards using the "Don't be a Litterbug—Keep Maryland Beautiful" slogan. Business firms catering to motorists, tourists, and vacationists were asked to have the bags stamped with their name as a trade item or advertising medium. Large organizations, too, were asked to cooperate. A semi-permanent bag, with a disposable container, was devised, which was found to be most effective.

Maryland's plan is to make the litterbag fashionable, standard equipment for motorists, and the state's campaign, started in 1955, is still being conducted along that line. Television watchers are reminded of the drive by repetitions of the slogan and school children are taught to use litterbags. Sometimes the bags are used as favors at parties. The Disabled American Veterans popularized this idea by using it at a dinner. Usually the litterbag is introduced to the community on a "Litterbag Day," with a special publicity drive. Each county has a well organized cleanup, anti-litter, Keep Maryland Beautiful program, and generally some single group or organization has charge of litterbag distribution.

Wilshire's Special Prize

The nation-wide campaign against litter has won the enthusiastic support of children, who sometimes put grown-ups to shame by their eager participation in clean-up drives. In California a couple of years ago the Wilshire Garden Club and the County of Los Angeles Parks and Recreation Department co-sponsored a contest to beautify the community. The contest was for children under eighteen and included the cleaning of vacant lots, front and backyard plantings, and the designing of hanging baskets and window boxes. Mrs. Vera May Lewis, senior recreation director of the department, had charge, working with the garden club which was providing the awards.

Near the Carver School in Willowbrook, one of the poorer areas, was a two-and-a-half acre dump, heaped with revolting trash. Eleven little Negro boys who live in the area got to thinking about the contest. They had no idea what the prizes were, but hoped that if they worked *awfully* hard they could win what they wanted more than anything in the world. For two months—a long, long time in the life of little boys—they worked, carrying the debris away, armful by armful. Then they leveled the hard-packed ground very, very carefully, and made bases in the proper places. Yes, they got the prize they had hoped for—eleven baseball suits.

Action in England

The United States is not alone in its litter problem. The English counterpart of our drive is a "Keep Britain Tidy" group, under the chairmanship of Lady Brunner, a member of the National Federation of Women's Institutes. It operates under the Ministry of Housing and Local Government and is supported by Queen Elizabeth and other members of the royal family, the prime minister, and more than thirty volunteer organizations. Propaganda materials similar to ours, also slides and films, are furnished to youth groups. On April 21, the queen's birthday, the Girl Guides are asked to do something for the queen by signing a pledge not to litter for a specified time. The reason for limiting the time, according to Lady Brunner, is that "the young find it hard to take a long-term view and a promise valid for a little while is better than a far-reaching one broken."

Adult volunteers serve as wardens at England's beauty spots, organize "Tidy Village Competitions" in the counties, and conduct anti-litter drives at agricultural fairs, horticultural shows, and camps. The winning village retains for a year a movable sign, presented by the Councils for the Preservation of Rural England and Wales. The campaign also includes long distance coaches and the British Railways. As in this country, the matter of disposal is a problem, and

Keep Britain Tidy has been experimenting with various types of litterbags. The press and the British Broadcasting Company have consistently supported this program.

Novel Ideas in the Litterbug Drive

Nowhere is our genius for inventiveness better evidenced than when we are confronted with a challenge, and the anti-littering campaign seems to foster imaginative ideas. In Chicago, trash receptacles were wired to say "Thank you" when people put trash in them. New Haven, Connecticut, dressed Mickey Mouse as a street cleaner to help in its drive. The garden club of Paris, New York, organizes an annual spring cleaning day, on which the entire community turns out to clean up the village green. Garden club members in Escondido, California, distributed leaflets to stores for use as package enclosures and left stickers for drivers at filling stations. Then they organized a scavenger hunt. Fifty children formed groups and gathered debris from along the five highways leading into the city and loaded it into trucks provided by the Kiwanis Club. When the job was finished they were treated to refreshments and a swim in the city pool. In Kamiah, Idaho, the Valley Garden Club sponsors drives in three towns—Kamiah, Stites, and Kooskia—and has sponsored litterbug clubs in all grade schools. Each grade has a club and competes with the others. The garden clubs of Virginia make effective use of a camera. "Before" and "after" color slides of cleaned and beautified roadsides are shown at schools, group meetings, and public gatherings.

In Corinth, New York, the garden club starts its annual cleanup campaign with a proclamation by the mayor. So successful has this club been in working with the schools that three Corinth high school girls won first prizes in the 1955 anti-litter slogan contest of the National Council of State Garden Clubs, Inc. In Oregon, a mountainous display of trash, the collection of a single day, was piled beside a state highway with an appropriate sign. Motorists were shocked at this dramatic revelation of their littering habits. Tennessee police officers handed slips to offenders, saying, "This is not a ticket, but *you* are a litterbug!" Frank Lovejoy, in his television program called "Meet McGraw," helps the cause by being careful to avoid throwing cigarettes and other litter on the streets. When he has the opportunity, he sets the example by using a litterbag in his car.

New York City has used ingenious methods in its drive, conducted under the slogan, "A Cleaner New York Is Up to You." Programs involving fines and lectures had failed, so at the suggestion of Young & Rubicam, an advertising agency which had volunteered its services, the Citizens Committee tried humor. Posters, radio and television jingles, and other publicity is all in a light vein, with Miss Clean City telling reporters she is "bitter with men who litter," preferring "picker-uppers." A giant litter basket, described as "the world's largest" (sixteen feet high), was set up in Times Square for two months as a reminder to use the regular ones. Later it was moved to Battery Park and on to other locations. Proctor & Gamble furnished 108,000 bars of soap, which were used in Rockefeller Plaza to spell out in eight-foot letters "A Cleaner New York Is Up to You." But perhaps the cleverest idea was the talking trashcan. Trashcans in areas of heavy traffic were wired so that when passersby tossed paper into the street, the voice of a Sanitary Department employee, parked nearby, would say in an injured tone: "Aw, please mister pick up that paper and put it where it belongs. Why ignore me? I'm a nice guy." When the startled offender complied, the can said, "Thank you!" Here too children have been valuable allies. They march in parades, write essays about keeping the streets clean, clear up rubble-strewn vacant lots and make them into little parks and flower gardens, and write and stage anti-litter plays to which parents are invited.

Sportsmen too have joined in the drive. *Outdoor Boating* magazine, in a recent issue, tells of a "cleanup day" project carried out by the Phoenix Sportsmen's Association, of Phoenix, Arizona. These men were so annoyed by littering that they decided to act. Their first project was to clean up Tonto Creek, "one of the most beautiful trout streams in the Southwest." This project was so successful that they moved on to another maltreated spot, Canyon Lake, "one of the more picturesque bodies of water in the state." The project received such acclaim that other groups soon borrowed the idea, and the Arizona Game Protection Association adopted it as a state-wide project. The Phoenix Sportsmen's Association suggests five steps to groups wishing to undertake similar projects: (1) appoint a committee, (2) select a project, (3) survey the project to see what materials are needed, (4) organize a campaign and set a date, (5) *do the job!*

Garden Club and County Cooperation

Cleanup campaigns are most successful when planned on a long-range cooperative basis. The manner in which the drive in Monterey, California, was handled illustrates this. The garden club in Pacific Grove had been conducting an anti-litter campaign for some time when Mrs. C. C. Brockman, the president, wrote a letter to the local newspaper describing the club's work as part of a national drive of garden clubs to clean up roadsides.

The letter was published and A. B. Jacobsen, then chairman of the Monterey County Board of Supervisors, asked her for more information. Later a conference was held with representatives present from nearby Fort Ord, the city councils, oil companies, the district attorney, supervisors, state highway officials, sheriffs, schools, and other groups. Mrs. Brockman represented the garden clubs in the area. A tape recording was made of the meeting and of those that followed so that the discussions could be studied by the Board of Supervisors. A coordinated plan of action was then worked out for the county.

"At first," Mrs. Brockman says, "some of the committee thought we should have a sticker of our own, but when Mr. Jacobsen asked my opinion I pointed out that the National Council material was already in use all over the country. I said I thought it would be better to use that, because it was already familiar to many tourists, than to take a different line."

Mrs. Brockman won her point and Mr. Jacobsen was authorized to use the publicity material of the National Council of State Garden Clubs, Inc. The board of supervisors voted an appropriation of $1,500 to launch the campaign, ordering 100,000 litterbags and 500,000 windshield stickers to be distributed through service stations. The oil companies donated 900 additional drums for use as trash containers. These were painted an attractive green and placed at service stations and along beaches and highways. An anti-litter drive was started in schools throughout the county, and Mrs. Brockman set out on a speaking tour to enlist the support of service clubs and other civic groups. The newspapers cooperated by keeping up a steady fire of editorials and articles, with plenty of "before" and "after" pictures. Laws prohibiting the throwing of trash along the highways were strictly enforced, with arrests made and fines imposed where necessary. The united effort resulted in an extremely successful campaign.

"Once you start a program of this nature," Mrs. Brockman advises, "you've got to keep it going, or it doesn't mean anything. You should have a long-range plan, and be prepared from the beginning to carry on the campaign consistently. We're teaching our children that outdoor good manners are just as important as good manners at the table, or anywhere else."

How Cities Have Worked Together

Cleanup campaigns have a way of engendering other improvements. Once the roadsides are cleared of debris, there is usually an urge to beautify them. Then one notices that the community could stand a good house cleaning and some improvements too. Frequently all that is needed to start things rolling is a "majority of one." So it was with three California beach towns.

The membership of the South Bay Garden Club is composed of women from Hermosa, Manhattan, and Redondo Beaches. Rivalry between the towns has always been spirited, but it was not until Mrs. R. O. Young joined the club that an intensive clean-up-and-beautify drive was launched. She had lived in a number of other places and that may be why she noticed unsightly debris that long-time residents had learned to overlook and saw possibilities for improvements that had not occurred to others.

The group cleaned up the roadsides in an anti-litter campaign in conjunction with the National Council of State Garden Clubs, Inc. So noticeable was the improvement that a goodly portion of the population pitched in one afternoon and planted fourteen tons of mesembryanthemum along the four miles of railroad that connect the towns. This cooperative effort led to a general cleaning up of the beaches, streets, and the grounds of public buildings, business houses, and homes. After that it seemed quite logical to embark upon a beautification program, with the three towns competing for a trophy.

Traffic islands near the shore were planted in one town. In another the owner of an amusement park was persuaded to clean up and im-

prove it, and business men were surprised to find themselves tearing
off gingerbread fronts and modernizing their shops. The third town
worked on landscaping, and an oil company decided that its property
would look better with trees and planted several hundred.

A major problem was an anti-aircraft base located in the center
of a residential area. The grounds needed landscaping and the building needed paint inside and out. But a woman who had lost her only
son in World War II solved the problem by "adopting" the whole
base. She helped the boys with planter boxes and landscaping and
persuaded the commanding officer to have the buildings painted in
colors that harmonized with the surrounding homes. Another club
member, who is past seventy, made a hundred pairs of curtains for
the windows. These touches of home appealed to the boys and they
were soon competing among themselves to improve the appearance
of the base. Club members made flower arrangements for the mess
hall and day room and contributed flowers and shrubs for planting.

The program is continuing, with business men, youth groups,
service clubs, church organizations, school and city officials, women's
clubs, and other civic groups participating. Mrs. Young says the club
created community interest in its projects mainly through personal
contacts, but that local newspapers, radio and television stations,
deserve much of the credit for sustaining it.

Saving Roadside Trees from Destruction

Oskaloosa's Reaction to the Bulldozer

As we have said before and will stress throughout this book, when
the people of the United States let their wishes be known to their
elected representatives they get what they want. An incident that
occurred in Oskaloosa, Iowa, in 1949, provides an example. Oskaloosa
is a quiet town of ten to twelve thousand people. It is hot there at
corn-growing time, but Iowans accept heat philosophically, because
without it they would not have such tall corn. Of course corn grows
in other states, but Iowa *is* corn, and corn is Iowa. If you have ever
watched those emerald seas emerge from the mists at dawn, or seen
them ripple in a sunset breeze, you can understand the strong feeling
these people have for the earth and its fruit. Our story, however, is
about trees. Iowans like trees almost as much as they like corn. They

want open corn fields where the sun beats down, but around their homes and along their streets they want tall, full-grown trees. It seems you cannot talk about Iowa without mentioning corn, and you cannot speak of corn without mentioning summer heat. And when you mention heat, you speak of shade trees. That is Iowa, the setting of our story.

Oskaloosa is a town where trees line the streets, forming cathedral-like arches high overhead. The trees are mainly elms, maples, and other hardwoods that take a long time to grow. The State Highway Commission decided to widen one of the residential streets to make a four-lane highway, which meant that 137 beautiful shade trees would be destroyed. The townspeople disliked the idea. To them the trees were more important than a four-lane highway. A petition of protest with hundreds of signatures was presented to the highway commission, but, to their dismay, the people learned that this meant nothing. Only legal action could save the trees, and that would require time and money. Undaunted, the little group set out to raise the money for a court battle. Subscriptions poured in, but before enough money had been raised, the bulldozers arrived. Attorneys advised an injunction, but said that unless a miracle occurred, the trees would be down before it could be obtained. The women of the town then decided to create their own miracle. They formed a human chain around each bulldozer and refused to budge. Working in relays, they blocked the machines until the injunction came through and the men could take over the responsibility. Then the townspeople went to battle. Yes, they won. The beautiful old trees are still shading the street.

Resistance in Winnipeg

The Oskaloosa incident is perhaps not important in itself; the interesting thing is that there have been so many such incidents. One wonders if people are not beginning to decide that they will take so much, and no more, in the name of "progress." In Winnipeg, Canada, an old elm that everyone loved was left in the middle of Wolseley Avenue when it was paved, with traffic flowing around it. City and elm grew, and civil authorities decided that the tree would have to go. Again, the people felt differently about it. When the workmen came to cut it down, a group of women had formed a chain around the elm and would not move. The mayor finally ordered the workmen away, to the accompaniment of cheers. The women said the old elm, which slowed traffic, was a safety factor—not a hazard.

Transplanting Turnpike Trees

When a turnpike was being built through Berlin, Ohio, the route was plotted through the largest and most beautiful stand of dogwoods and fruited shrubs in the area. Many people were concerned about them and how they could be saved. The garden club finally wrote to the governor, asking if some provision could be made either to protect the dogwoods or to transplant them. The governor advised that he had referred the club's query to the Ohio Turnpike Commission, but when construction was started in 1954 no arrangement had been made.

The group decided to transplant as many of the dogwoods and shrubs as possible themselves, placing them in the community as a civic improvement project. A local nurseryman, George Pickett, addressed the group and explained the proper transplanting methods, illustrating his talk with slides and diagrams. Then he toured the village with club representatives and made suggestions about plantings. Among the sites chosen were the grounds of schools, churches, and public buildings, and the town pump. To save as many plants as possible, club members agreed to transfer any material not used in the village plantings to the grounds of their own homes. The Future Farmers of America, who had been invited to Mr. Pickett's talk, agreed to help with the transplanting.

The next regular meeting of the club was designated "transplanting day," and the membership turned out *en masse*, together with the Future Farmers and other interested citizens. As it happened, two days were required for the job but the whole stand of dogwoods and most of the shrubs were saved.

Loss of Bird Habitats

Among the other tragedies of a vanishing countryside is the destruction of song bird habitats. A newspaper columnist recently spoke of the number of readers who had written her deploring that "there are no more birds." And there have been numerous comments from other sources. We cannot expect to have the abundance of birds we have always had, if we continue our destruction of their shelter and breeding places. Ornithologists have long been concerned about this. Now that the practice of blanket spraying along roadsides has become widespread, the matter is even more serious.

In an effort to counteract this habitat loss, many civic groups are putting bird houses and feeding stations along the roadsides. The garden club in Narberth, Pennsylvania, maintains nesting boxes in the Penn Valley for bluebirds, a long-range project. The boxes are cleaned, repaired, and maintained regularly with the help of the Penn Valley Boy Scouts. In connection with its project the club prepared an educational booklet called "Solving Your Bird Problems," which it sells to help maintain a banding station at Washington Crossing Park.

Roadside Beautification

"Blue Star" Highways of the Garden Clubs

A striking illustration of what can be accomplished in roadside beautification is the "Blue Star Drive" of the National Council of State Garden Clubs, Inc. This project which grew from the beautifying of six miles of highway by the New Jersey garden clubs in 1944, today includes over 25,000 miles of highways all over the country and more are being added every year. It is one of the most extensive projects ever undertaken by garden clubs, and the first attempted on a nation-wide scale. Its success paved the way for the anti-litter drive and other national projects.

The Blue Star Memorial Highways take the name from the blue star in the service flag. They are a living memorial to "all those who have served or will serve in the nation's armed forces." A standard marker with a blue star identifies them. The purpose of the project is manifold. It was organized to serve as a demonstration of roadside beautification, to show member clubs what could be accomplished through united strength, as a protest against billboards, to educate the public to higher standards of roadside development, and to determine how the National Council could best work with civil authorities for major achievement.

At the close of World War II, the National Council, like other public-spirited groups, was seeking a suitable means of honoring service men and women. It was generally agreed that, as garden clubs, it would be better to help beautify and preserve the country the men had fought for than to build stone monuments. The New Jersey clubs had just finished beautifying a section of one of the state's busiest highways as a war memorial, working with the New Jersey highway commissioner, Spencer Miller, Jr., when Mr. Miller, as guest speaker at the annual meeting of the National Council in 1945, suggested that this program be projected on a nation-wide basis. Council representatives replied that it was just the project they were seeking and began immediately to investigate its possibilities.

The New Jersey clubs had chosen their project because so many of our highways have become billboard alleys, and they hoped to counteract the trend. As highway commissioner, Mr. Miller helped them, both in choosing the section to be landscaped and in carrying out the project. The club raised the money for shrubs and trees, raising $25,000 the first year, and the highway department undertook planting and maintenance. Among the original plantings were 10,000 dogwoods, used in attractive groupings with other trees and shrubs. This part of the highway was memorialized by the state legislature in 1945. Later the section was extended. Enabling legislation was passed, permitting the State Highway Department to purchase the rights of way on either side of the highway, with control of the roadsides. This legislation paved the way for the beautiful Garden State Parkway of today. The original section became the first Blue Star Drive and former Governor Driscoll set up a Blue Star Council, including two garden club representatives, to develop more such highways in the state.

Using the New Jersey project as its model, the National Council made a study of the inter-regional highways of the United States. A Blue Star Highway System was outlined, consisting of one east-west and seven north-south highways. Highway commissioners were informed of the plan, and the garden clubs in each state were invited to participate. Every federation president was asked to secure the collaboration of the state highway department before undertaking a Blue Star project, as this was considered requisite to the success of the plan. A uniform marker was adopted to show memorialization, the design of which was a gift from Mrs. Frederic Kellogg, founder of the National Council. By 1947 the project was ready to launch.

The garden clubs of Colorado were the first to undertake a Blue Star project and from then on it was a sisterly race among state federations for "firsts." The Rhode Island clubs were the first to memorialize, the Pennsylvania the first to introduce protective legislation, the California the first to memorialize both east-west and north-south Blue Star highways, the Vermont clubs the first to publish a descriptive folder about their project, and the Michigan clubs the first to have a marker complete with a model planting.

The project has been expanded to include roadside parks and rest areas, scenic turnouts and a safety program, with the National Council going on record with several resolutions opposing billboards. Indeed the organization is at the present time endeavoring to memorialize the new 41,000-mile highway system!

The Blue Star project was inaugurated under the presidency of Mrs. William H. Champlin, with Mrs. Vance R. Hood its first chairman. The original New Jersey project was undertaken when Mrs. Lewis M. Hull was president of the state federation. She succeeded Mrs. Champlin as president of the National Council and guided the project through its early years as a national undertaking.

Beautifying a Route to the National Capital

The road entries into our communities should be pleasantly inviting—like the doorways of our homes. This is particularly true, the garden club of Arlington, Virginia, believes, of the doors of the national capital. Virginia launched a state-wide project to clean up and beautify its roadsides three years in advance of its 350th anniversary in 1957. Arlington's share of the project was on Route 50, one of the entrances to the city and a main artery into Washington from the South. In carrying out its task, the club worked with the County Planning Board, State Highway Department, and the National Park Service. The planting was varied, consisting of native trees, dogwood, winged euonymous, forsythia, firethorn, Father Hugo roses, and ground cover.

Bermuda's Competition for the Queen

The garden club in Bermuda has 200 members and, like our own clubs, is particularly interested in roadside beautification. A few years ago the cedar trees on the islands began to die from a scale infection.

Members of the club realized that a replacement must be quickly
made to prevent erosion, protect birdlife, and maintain the beauty
of the islands.

Their first step was an educational campaign, alerting the public
to the threat and stressing the importance of each individual's help
to correct the situation. The conservation committee contacted the
heads of government departments, utility companies, chambers of
commerce, service clubs, and other groups, as well as the parish
vestries. (Bermuda is divided into nine parishes, similar to our counties. The vestries are the parochial authorities.) All agreed to help.

A series of meetings were held in each parish in conjunction with
the Department of Agriculture. Arbor Day societies were revitalized
or organized, and a contest arranged among the parishes for the
greatest improvement in the period of one year. An attractive bird
bath was to be the prize, awarded by the governor.

The next step was to work out with school authorities a program
for children. The children were told how loss of the cedars affected
the birds and brought the threat of erosion. Then they were taught
how to plant and care for young trees. Contests between the schools
were arranged with bird baths as prizes.

"Plant a Tree Week" followed, with the Department of Agriculture giving trees to all who would plant them. Merchants inserted
plugs in their advertisements and radio stations gave spot announce-
ments and air time for talks by the committee. The Department of
Agriculture undertook the removal of dead cedars along the roadsides and the replanting of denuded areas.

The committee next organized a roadside competition in which
color and arrangement were stressed. There are many quick-growing
and colorful shrubs and trees especially suited to the Bermuda climate, and people were urged to use these for roadside plantings.
Among those recommended were oleander, hibiscus, scarlet cordia,
casuarinas, bay grape, poinsettias, and palms.

This entire program has been carried on consistently since it was
organized and the garden club plans to continue it indefinitely.
"Thousands of trees are needed to replace Bermuda's lost cedars,"
says Mrs. J. J. Outerbridge, former chairman of the conservation
committee, "and to prevent erosion of her soil."

To commemorate the coronation of Elizabeth II, a special roadside competition was held among parishes. The winning parish planted 120 poincianas and ninety-eight royal palms.

In the Far North

Garden clubs in Alaska are also concerned with community and roadside beautification. There are active clubs in Juneau, Ketchikan, and Anchorage, all belonging to the National Council of State Garden Clubs, Inc. Though the growing season is short, the list of flowers blooming in Alaskan gardens is about the same as ours. Projects of the clubs are similar too in some ways, in others colorfully different. The Ketchikan club periodically conducts a cleanup-paintup campaign for totem poles and campaigns annually for window boxes along the waterfront. It also gives plants to rural gardeners for attractive plantings at their mail boxes and along the roadsides.

New Hampshire's Roadside Improvement Contest

There are many places for the philanthropic dollar, but a contribution toward a more beautiful country is an investment more than a gift, paying heavily in personal satisfaction. The New Hampshire Roadside Improvement Contest illustrates this. The contest, a most outstanding one, began in 1947 when Harold Ley of Melvin Village and New York City offered $1,000 in prize money for a project to clean up tent caterpillar nests along the roadsides. Since the caterpillars follow a seven-year cycle, he extended the prizes to all roadside improvements and backed the contest every year until his death in 1956. Mrs. Ley and her son then notified the New Hampshire Roadside Improvement Associates, Inc., sponsors of the contest, that the tradition would be continued in Mr. Ley's name.

The association is a volunteer unit whose officers and consultants are drawn from supporting organizations—state conservation groups, garden and service clubs, women's organizations, sportsmen's clubs, and industrial groups. The extension service of the University of New Hampshire, the Department of Public Works and Highways, and the Planning and Development Commission actively participate, backed stoutly by the governor.

Any group, person, club, organization, or community may enter the contest and no fee is required. The projects include roadside plantings, correction of "roadside blight" (dumps and litter), pest

control, the provision of roadside rests and parks, the restoration of
historic sites and landmarks; the beautification and improvement of
cabins, motels, filling stations, wayside shops, stores, and restaurants;
youth and school projects, and the landscaping of homes, farms, and
public buildings. Almost any project that would help make New
Hampshire more attractive is acceptable. An interesting feature of
this contest is that as much emphasis is put on *maintaining* an established project as in creating one, with prizes awarded on that basis.
The New Hampshire project has grown to such proportions that a
planting specialist now tours the state, assisting people with their
problems.

The entries are as individual as these "Down-Easters" themselves.
An entry for Franconia one year was the planting of window boxes
at places of business along the main street. Claremont and Newington restored the old watering troughs which are landmarks and
worked out unusual plantings around them. In Enfield, the Civic
Association sponsored an individual flower garden contest. The
Greenfield Improvement Association promoted a community working bee, and the Rumford chapter of the Daughters of the American
Revolution, in Concord, marked historic trails and beautified the
shrines tourists visit. A Claremont couple won a prize for bringing a
beautiful planting on their property down to the road to delight
passersby, and the Busy Bees 4-H Club in South Acworth contributed lawn mowing on public grounds and along roadsides. The Sand-
wich Woman's Club had a seven-point program in which each youth
group of the community carried out a civic project under its direction.

The famous old country store of New England is still in business
and the owners of one in Greenfield, and another in Short Falls, took
prizes one year for their lovely plantings of native material. In East
Andover the 4-H Club won a prize for cleaning up, improving, and
patrolling a town swimming pond. There is a special category in this
contest for school children, and in this their anti-litter drives win
prizes consistently. The schools conduct poster contests every year,
and some of the posters on wildlife protection have been so outstanding that other organizations now contribute prize money for
them. One child's slogan for motorists might well be adopted nationally: "Give wildlife a brake."

A top prize winner of special interest to conservationists is the project undertaken by the Stratford High School while George C. Zoulias was principal. A road bordering the school had been changed, leaving a slope that became deeply gullied. Mr. Zoulias suggested beautifying this slope as a science department project. The faculty liked the idea and so did the students. Consent was given by the school board and highway department, and the county youth extension agent agreed to help. The science classes studied the causes and effects of erosion, and slides and films on the subject were shown before the entire student body so that everyone would understand the project. The extension agent then organized a work party of ninety boys and girls from the seventh through the twelfth grades. The students brought their own shovels, picks, and rakes; the county conservation department furnished the plant material. After raking and filling in the gullies and removing rocks and boulders, the group staked chicken wire over the area. A sluice was built to take rain water safely down the slope and the seeding and planting were done. "Before," "work progress," and "after" pictures were taken, enabling future students to study erosion through this practical demonstration.

A three-time winner—once for the project and twice for maintenance—is the paper birch forest established in Shelburne as a memorial to service men and women. The forest is in the Androscoggin Valley, in the shadow of the White Mountains, an area noted for its beautiful scenery. It borders the road on either side, an outstanding example of the many lovely birch-bordered roads in New England. This forest is one of the most photographed scenes in New Hampshire. It would have been destroyed long ago if a handful of conservation-minded individuals had not become interested in saving it.

Originally the land was privately owned and in 1942 the trees were scheduled to be cut for timber. Lawrence E. Philbrook asked the owners to wait and give him a chance to see if the town would purchase the forest. Ralph Peabody, a neighbor who also loved the forest, joined forces with Philbrook and they contacted the town authorities. It took "some doing," as Mr. Philbrook says, but they finally succeeded and these two men, together with a third, were appointed a board to administer the town's new forest. Although a yearly appropriation is made for maintenance, most of the work is done by volunteers, including the 4-H Club. The "maintenance" money has been used to buy more land, to establish picnic areas, and to build a memorial.

The New Hampshire Roadside Improvement Associates enlarges its scope each year. It plans eventually to have a contest chairman in every county so that more and more people will compete. The present contest chairman is Mrs. James A. Funkhouser of Durham. Sponsors of the contest call it "traditional New Hampshire good housekeeping."

Modern Johnny Appleseeds

Texas garden clubs also have a unique project. They scatter thousands of packages of wildflower seeds, Johnny Appleseed fashion, along their roadsides from border to border of the state.

CHAPTER III

CREATING MORE
BEAUTIFUL COMMUNITIES

Charm and individuality in a community give pleasure not only to its residents but to visitors who take with them pleasant memories. Such qualities appeal to all of us, for in our travels we seek the most beautiful places. Who has not dreamed of Paris in the spring, of Washington at cherry blossom time, or of the fountains and pines of Rome?

Venice is enchanting, but it is not just its gondolas that one remembers, its fragile glass, or even St. Mark's. The potted plants and vines on the balconies of this narrow-streeted, almost gardenless city contribute much to its haunting beauty. And how could one forget the potted plants fastened to the walls of the houses in Seville? The Swiss Alps are magnificent, but the boxes of geraniums on the wooden bridges and the picturesque signs on the shops give Lucerne its story-book personality and cling vividly to the memory. New York is in the midst of an epochal slum-clearance program, but what are New Yorkers excited about?—the trees planted along Third Avenue where the old "El" used to be.

Most of our communities could easily have individuality, charm, and character, but few do. They are mostly a "dreary monotony of Main Streets." This is due in part to our fabulous growth. Across the country towns sprang up overnight, mushrooming into sprawling, shapeless cities, ragged at the outskirts. We have had little time since

51

to think whether they express the character of our country, or the individuality of the people. But the headlong rush of youth is over now and we have time for reflection. Most of us will not be satisfied much longer with the monotones of our home towns. We will want them to express the bold, clear colors that depict our nation's vitality, to catch something of that "rockets bursting in air" quality that inspires us. We shall unquestionably want our towns to be as varied as our landscape—and as beautiful.

Beautifying the community is like good personal grooming. Neatly cropped lawns and painted fences, tree-lined streets, well cared for public grounds and gardens are indications of people whose hearts are of today and tomorrow, not of yesterday. These may be little things, but as long as we keep doing them the star of the United States will continue to rise.

Beautification is often a step toward greater community improvements. It is a tangible accomplishment that makes people look at their town perceptibly and opens their eyes to other needs. One enthusiastic person can instigate it; any small group can carry it through. A gay spot of tulips at a corner of the square may make a businessman aware that his store front needs sprucing up or cause a town official to notice eroding soil along the sidewalks. When one man fixes up his place of business, others are likely to follow. Once people become interested in controlling erosion in a village, it is easier to stir them to action over a sick watershed. Apathy is the greatest stumbling block to improvement, but a beautification campaign will often arouse public interest when nothing else does. It will motivate many who would not be interested in conservation as such. Yet the two go hand in hand, in league with nature. It may be merely a matter of using clumps of dogwood to keep the soil from washing away.

Flower Features and Festivals

Petunias in Westminster

Westminster is a village of less than a thousand in southern California. It has an active garden club of seventy men and women, formed a few years ago for the purpose of improving the appearance of their community.

Since the club was open to everyone interested in its purpose and willing to help, the dues were only a dollar a year. This necessitated an inexpensive project. "We decided upon a petunia contest," Mrs. Thomas Richards, contest chairman, explains, "because petunias grow well here, and give a fast return of color for a small expenditure. We got the idea from Stayton, Oregon. The people there have an annual petunia contest and Stayton is known throughout the state as 'The Petunia City.'"

The Westminster club divided the contest into three classifications: homes, grounds of business houses and public buildings, and vacant lots. First and second prizes were offered in each category, with ribbons for third place and honorable mention. Prizes were hibiscus bushes. The rules of the contest provided that the entries must be in full view of the street so that judges could see them from their cars.

"We had thirty-five entries that year, which we did not think was bad for our first try," Mrs. Richards says. "We put posters and entry blanks in the stores and business houses and at the nurseries. The newspaper ran editorials and articles about the contest and kept reminding people to get their entries in. Then the winners and their plantings were photographed and featured in the paper so that more people would enter the following year. Our object was to get splashes of color all over town, so we judged mainly for display and drew no specifications as to the type of petunias to be grown or the size of the beds. One of our biggest obstacles was getting people to submit their entries because many felt that their displays were not sufficiently impressive.

"One of the winning entries was a 'symphony in pink.' The house is pink stucco with a curved walk from the driveway to the door. There are pink rose trees along the driveway and walk, and that year pink ruffled petunias were planted thickly under the roses. Another outstanding entry was a terraced yard with masses of white petunias trailing down over brick walls. The volunteer fire department had a large bed of white petunias with an 'FD' of red petunias in the center.

"The petunia contest has become a tradition in our town with more entries each year. Instead of hibiscus we now give checks payable to the nursery so that people can buy what they want. We are a small club in a small town and our project is small too, but the success we have had has encouraged us to try for bigger improvements."

Roses in Crows Landing

Crows Landing, also in California, has a population of about 500. It too has an active garden club with an interesting project, started a few years ago while Mrs. Walter L. Isom was president.

"I was visiting a friend in Palmdale, California," she says, "when I got the idea for our project. My friend was busy with a project she had started—planting hundreds of lilacs in and around Palmdale. Her town has so many lilacs now that thousands of people come there every year for the Lilac Festival.

"I kept thinking about her work and what we could do in Crows Landing. Roses came to my mind, Paul's Scarlet roses. They grow well here and make a beautiful splash of color, all blooming at about the same time. Then too, the Jackson & Perkins Company has rose gardens near here. I hoped that we could make our town so attractive that people coming to see their gardens would want to visit Crows Landing too. I came home with my dream and my plans. My thought was to use roses to cover unsightly fences, at corners, for public buildings, at service stations, just anywhere they would grow. I talked to friends, business men, fellow garden club members, anyone who would listen. Everyone liked the idea. The idea of red roses seemed to appeal especially to the men.

"We have only fifteen members in our club, but they are all workers. We sold fifty rose bushes in our first campaign, but I ordered a hundred from the nursery, taking a chance on selling the rest. By the time they arrived all had been sold and we could have used more. We didn't make a big showing the first year or the second, but by the third year the idea began to take hold. Every year our little town becomes more beautiful at Paul's Scarlet time, and we hope that some day Crows Landing will be known for its red roses."

Galveston's Oleanders

To most of us, Texas means big ranches, endless prairie, longhorns, and oil fields, but Galveston is famous for oleanders, and a yearly festival is centered around them.

The oleander was introduced into Galveston in 1841 by Joseph

Osterman, an old sea captain, who had packed some cuttings in tubs on his trading schooner and brought them to his sister from far away.

The oleanders flourished in the sand and salt sea air, blooming until late fall, despite summer heat and dust. Within a short time the captain's sister, Mrs. Isadore Dyer, was giving cuttings to friends and neighbors. Today every yard, sidewalk, street, park, garden, and esplanade is planted with oleanders, making Galveston "a sure enough Oleander City."

Galvestonians love to celebrate, responding to the call of sand, sun, and sea breeze at the slightest pretext. Shortly after World War I they held their first Oleander Festival, with a pageant depicting the history of the town from the days of the pirate, Jean Laffitte, who called the island his *Campache*. With a few exceptions, the festival has been held every year since. In it a special scene dramatizes the planting of the first oleanders.

Tulip Time in Pella

Pella, a little town in Iowa, has an annual Tulip Festival that attracts visitors from all over the state, and from neighboring states too. With its million or more tulips, scrub-brush cleanliness, its windmill, thrifty farms and famed Dutch cookies, Pella is "a bit of Holland in America."

The name means "the City of Refuge." And it was just that to its founders—between 700 and 800 Dutch who chartered four vessels and sailed for America in 1847 to escape religious persecution and tax oppression. The name was chosen long before these people left Holland. After two months at sea, they landed at Baltimore. From there they traveled by railroad and canal to St. Louis, by boat up the Mississippi to Keokuk, Iowa, and from there to what is now Pella in carriages, wagons, ox-carts, on horseback, and on foot. The three-day festival of today, held in the early spring, is a tribute to the original settlers. It was intended to be a local event, but outsiders like it too and these hospitable people always make them welcome at tulip time.

Chappaqua's Pink Dogwoods

Though the idea of a festival may not appeal, most of us would like our towns to have individuality. Many civic organizations are striving for this quality through their projects. Chappaqua, New

York, is one of the most charming communities in Westchester County, but that was still not quite enough for members of the garden club. They wanted their community to have a special personality as well, and decided to make it a pink dogwood village. They organized a house-to-house campaign, selling the dogwoods at special rates—over a thousand the first year, one to nearly every home. Next time they will include business houses, parks, and public buildings and try to persuade homeowners to have *three* pink dogwoods instead of just one.

Apple Blossoms in Dell Rapids

In Dell Rapids, South Dakota, the garden club is working to make the town "the hopa crab community." The members have asked all clubs in the state to join them in making the state known for these trees, in spite of "so MUCH wide-open space where there are no garden clubs and no trees of any kind." Mrs. George M. Jorgensen, chairman of the Hopa Crab Committee, explains: "Our club has been beautifying the community through tree planting ever since it was organized in 1932, but our first efforts were isolated projects. We planted weeping willows along the half-mile path to the cemetery, doing the actual labor ourselves. Then one year we got a hundred hackberry and ponderosa pine seedlings offered by the state for shelterbelt planting, and distributed them to homeowners who would care for them. Another year we planted weeping willows along the river bank where age and erosion had destroyed the original fifty-year-old trees. As another project we planted red elm and hackberry. Finally we got the idea of concentrating on the hopa crab, which Dr. N. E. Hansen developed especially for our state. We get the trees from the nursery at special rates and sell them to homeowners at cost."

Portland's Rose Festival

The first rose bush to reach Oregon territory was brought around the Horn in 1837—a gift for a bride. It was presented to Anna Marian Pittman upon her marriage to the pioneer missionary, Jason Lee, and cuttings from this bush are blooming today in various parts of the Willamette Valley. Sentiment for the rose is thus deeply rooted in Oregon history.

Every year since 1907, Portland, the City of Roses, has held a week-long festival in early June. A queen is crowned and there is a parade; the Navy has open house, and there are floral exhibits, garden tours, rose planting ceremonies, a ski tournament, and street dancing. Because of the climate and the International Rose Test Garden in Portland, the area enjoys a great abundance and variety of roses, and it is said that in Portland "roses bloom in more grandeur than in any other spot on earth."

How the Tournament of Roses Started

The Tournament of Roses in Pasadena, California, has been held every New Year's Day since 1890, but its origin is not widely known. In horse and buggy days, members of the Valley Hunt Club decorated their carriages with flowers grown in their own gardens, families competing to see who could produce the most original designs. Then they paraded down the main street, and from there went to the ball park where they spent the afternoon performing feats of horsemanship. The rest of the country learned of this mid-winter pageant when a Los Angeles newspaper reporter saw the parade and wrote a story about it that was picked up by papers in New York and Chicago. A wave of visitors came to see this unusual spectacle featuring flowers in mid-winter and within five years the parade had become so famous that the Valley Hunt Club relinquished its sponsorship to a committee of community leaders who formed the Tournament of Roses Association. The association is now a year-around organization, beginning work on the next tournament as soon as the last one is over.

Washington's Cherry Blossom Festival

Of all flower festivals, the one dearest to our hearts is the National Cherry Blossom Festival in Washington, D.C. The festival is held at different times every year because these beautiful Japanese trees around the Potomac River Tidal Basin do not bloom on a set schedule and the fragile blossoms last for only a short time. The Tidal Basin may well be festooned in a crescent of pink when March winds blow cold and spring seems far away. But the capital can always count on thousands of visitors. The festivities last for nearly a week and are highlighted by a coronation at the Cherry Blossom Ball, with a queen selected from among the Cherry Blossom Princesses of the states and territories by a turn of the wheel of fortune.

The cherry trees were presented by Japan to the United States in

1912, as a living gift in the interest of international understanding. The suggestion for the gift came from Dr. Yukio Ozaki, Japanese statesman, then mayor of Tokyo. Mrs. Howard Taft planted the first of the 3,000 trees on March 27, and Viscountess Chinda, wife of the Japanese ambassador, planted the second.

Window Boxes on City Streets

Lesson from Montreal

The lovely window boxes in Montreal, Canada, have delighted visitors for years, and the project is a splendid example of how a city of any size can be made more attractive.

The Montreal Window Box Competition, offering small prizes, was started eighteen years ago by the Parks and Playgrounds Association of Greater Montreal, a citizen's organization. It was to serve the dual purpose of beautifying the city and giving persons without gardens an incentive to grow flowers. During the first year several hundred people registered, in the second several thousand. This was more than the association could handle and the members sought help from the Quebec Horticultural Federation and the City of Montreal. "In consequence of this," says Henry Teuscher, curator of the Montreal Botanical Garden, "a new set-up was organized in which the City of Montreal, the Parks and Playground Association, and the Quebec Horticultural Federation jointly sponsored the project. I was made chairman of a committee of two to organize the contest, which actually meant that from then on, the Botanical Garden had charge. Every spring since then we have given a three-lecture course and published a free leaflet on window box gardening. My book, *Window Box Gardening*, is a result of the experiences gained in supervising the contest through the years.

"At first we had thousands of entries. But as people learned over the years that only the hundred best had a chance to win prizes and that a box had to be good to win, only those registered who thought their boxes exceptionally fine. This has worked out well because it saves the time and trouble of having to visit and judge large numbers of inferior boxes. However, interest and competition are still as keen as ever. Our city is full of window boxes, though during the last eight years or so only an average of 250 people enter the competition.

"The distribution of prizes takes place in November. The prizes consist mostly of house plants, though the first five get silver trophies. At that time our chrysanthemum show is at its best and those who come to that assemblage can at the same time visit this show. Kodachromes of the winning boxes are shown on a screen and it is explained why one box is better than another. The prizes are bought from a $300 annual grant from the city of Montreal, which covers also the expenses of the judges."

Neosho, the Flower Box City

Neosho, a small community in Missouri, likes flower boxes too. It has approximately 6,000 people and some 3,000 window boxes. Flowers bloom in these boxes from spring to late autumn in both business and residential areas. So attractive is this little city that it received nationwide publicity through a *Life* magazine article a few years ago and has been written up a number of times since by other publications. During the past season, every business house on the square had flower boxes in bloom, as well as all the churches, schools, industrial houses, the court house, and hospital.

There are four judgings—in June, late July, September, and at a fourth date decided by popular vote. Although cash prizes are offered, Neosho sponsors say that this type of prize is often less effective than a masonite plaque that the winner can display until the next judging. Where cash prizes are used, it has been found that numerous small prizes are better than a few large ones. The Neosho project is a continuing one. It is sponsored by service clubs, churches, schools, the garden club, and the Chamber of Commerce, with business and industry cooperating.

Beautifying Philadelphia's Slum Areas

Philadelphia, like every large city, has its slums. And, being one of our oldest cities, perhaps the decay is a little worse than in some places. Going into the city from her country home, Mrs. James Bush-Brown passes through the heart of one of these sections. As she looked down into the bleak littered streets from the train window through the years, she saw the squalor increase and kept wondering what she could do about it. Slum clearance was the answer, but that could be far in the future. What could be done here and now? It seemed to

her that when she looked into the people's faces she could see reflected the conditions in which they lived.

"There wasn't a vestige of green anywhere," she recalls, "not even
a flower pot in one window in those long, long rows of jammed-
together dwellings."

One day while gathering flowers in her garden, she thought of
window boxes. "There may not be room for gardens," she remarked
to her husband, "but there *is* room for window boxes. Just suppose
those people had some geraniums to look at, think what it would
mean to them. Even a few boxes here and there would help."

With the enthusiasm which is characteristic of her, this small, vital
woman began a round of settlement houses in the area the next day,
explaining her idea. The settlement workers were skeptical. They told
her about the vandalism and petty thievery in such areas, of the
hostility toward "do gooders." The idea was nice, they said, but it
just wouldn't work. Louise Bush-Brown is not a woman who gives up
easily. She finally made them believe that these people would respond
to beauty. She said she did not want to do everything *for* them, she
wanted to help them help themselves. Garden clubs, she thought,
would gladly furnish the plants, but the boxes were to be made by
the people who wanted flowers and planted by them too. Several
settlement houses and a number of other interested persons met with
Mrs. Bush-Brown to discuss the possibilities of the project and on
February 23, 1953, the "Neighborhood Garden Association of Philadelphia" was formed.

The next step was to start pilot projects. The settlement houses
distributed questionnaires asking the people if they would be interested and what kind of project they felt they could do—a tiny backyard garden, a window box, or perhaps a plant in a flower pot. As a
result garden groups were formed, each with a chairman. Mrs. Bush-
Brown then contacted the garden clubs and got just the response she
expected. Each club would sponsor a garden group, providing the
plants and volunteers to give instructions for building and planting
flower boxes.

People in seven city blocks took part that first year. They made 427
window boxes and several small gardens, using 12,000 plants from the
garden clubs. The boxes were made by the men and boys in each block
and the planting done by the women. Block leaders were chosen to

make sure the flowers were watered and cared for, and that they were not harmed. The youngest participant in the pilot project was a five-year-old boy who hauled dirt from a vacant lot in his wagon to make a little garden by his front steps. The oldest was a woman of ninety.

It was a cold drizzly day in May when the first boxes were planted. The streets and sidewalks were dirty and littered, vacant lots filled with refuse—a dreary scene. But the neighborhood women came out, eager to choose their flowers and learn how to plant them. By the time the first few were finished, people were coming from nearby blocks to see, in spite of the drizzle. By the time all the boxes were up in that block, the street was crowded, with people going from box to box to admire. One excited woman exclaimed: "I've lived on this block for forty-eight years and never seen a flower growing before." A little girl asked what a garden was, and not one child in all that area had ever seen a geranium.

That was in the morning. By noon the sun was out, and by mid-afternoon the fire hydrant had been opened and every man, woman, girl, and boy was helping to clean the street. Sidewalks and steps were being scrubbed, two families were painting the wooden trim around their cellar windows, and a woman was going from door to door, taking a collection to paint the curb white. "Nothing, absolutely nothing, could have done for this street what these flowers have done!" a settlement worker exclaimed.

Since its beginning this project has transformed whole sections of Philadelphia's slums. The second year 2,000 window boxes had been installed, covering thirty-four city blocks; in the next year there were 3,000 in sixty-three city blocks. Each year the project grows with more organizations helping. The 4-H clubs made Tom Thumb gardens for the children, then taught them how to make their own.

More important still is what has happened to the people themselves. Just as Mrs. Bush-Brown had foreseen a sense of neighborhood pride developed. Vacant lots have been cleaned up, fences whitewashed, flower boxes repainted, and on many blocks little brick flower bays have been built. The little touches of beauty outside have brought improvements within: fresh curtains, cleaner floors, painted walls, better homes. But Mrs. Bush-Brown is happiest of all with the leadership that has been developed, particularly among the teenagers.

The project is well organized. After a garden club has sponsored a block for two years, furnishing flowers and superintending, the block is on its own and the club sponsors another. The people buy their own flowers, usually at wholesale rates through the Neighborhood Garden Association, and are encouraged to sponsor another block. One of the most successful block organizers is a woman in her eighties who is totally blind. Another block leader is a girl of eleven.

Mrs. Bush-Brown continues to seek out new areas for her block projects, using color slides to show what has been accomplished. She has gone into some of the worst sections of the city where policemen warned her: "Lady, you're just wasting your time." But even though it sometimes takes her a year to create interest, this warm-hearted woman finally wins the people over.

Leadership from Business

A Beauty Contest for Industry

Industry is finding that beautification is "good business." A nicely landscaped site not only improves the general appearance of a community but attracts more customers and a better type of employee. In the past, a factory tended to pull a neighborhood down, but some of today's beautifully landscaped buildings set the pace for the neighborhood around them. Cincinnati, Ohio, encourages industrial beautification with an annual contest.

The contest was started on a small scale by the Garden Center in 1949, but the Chamber of Commerce and the *Cincinnati Enquirer* quickly saw its possibilities and became powerful allies of the club. "The first year just a few firms participated," George E. Cramerding of the Chamber of Commerce says, "but participation has increased steadily to the point where we have increased the number of categories and now award prizes for the best landscaping among large factories, medium-sized ones, and office buildings. The prizes are plaques for the winners and honorable mention certificates for outstanding entries.

The Fifth Avenue Association

It is said of New York's Fifth Avenue that no other street in the world can match it for variety, wealth of goods, and sheer excitement or equal its class, opulence, and year-round air of festivity. They also say it is one of the best-run business streets in the world. Credit for what the street is today belongs to the Fifth Avenue Association, whose members are known affectionately as "policemen in striped trousers."

Founded in 1907, the Fifth Avenue Association is a non-political, non-profit civic group with no legal powers, no legal connection with the city, and no authority to take punitive action against violators of its code. It relies on persuasion to enforce its rules, backed by "a consistent policing that depends upon vigilance, cooperation, and self-discipline." Its activities cover zoning, traffic control, architectural standards, and merchandizing.

The first major task undertaken by the association was to expel the garment industry from lower Fifth Avenue in 1911. Later it was responsible for legislation to prohibit projecting and illuminated signs and sidewalk obstructions, to ban hawkers, beggars, and hurdy-gurdies, to widen the street, and to increase police protection. By getting ordinances passed and awarding prizes, it has striven to achieve an architectural harmony along the main sections and has worked consistently to keep undesirable business off the street. How well it has succeeded is attested not only by the beauty, prestige, and financial soundness of the avenue, but by the fact that cities all over the world ask its advice and have set up similar organizations.

Historic Churches, Parks, and Cemeteries

Charleston's Historic Section Dramatized

Accenting its historical areas is one way a community can achieve individuality. The Garden Club of Charleston, South Carolina, has made such sections focal points. Charleston has a charm all its own, with its fine old homes, beautiful gardens, and the roadsides around the city lined with ancient moss-draped oaks. In 1930, to help celebrate the 250th anniversary of the city's founding, the club converted a section used as a storage place for trucks and automobiles into a park, the first civic project it had attempted. Because of the ten wrought-iron gates in its length the members named it "Gateway Walk."

In carrying out its project, the club persuaded the churches in the vicinity to beautify their grounds and cemeteries. The main problem of the club, then, was to beautify the interior of a large city block, the heart of this section. The Southern Railway donated a handsome fence with gates, which was used to set the park off as a unit. Then the area was landscaped, with a large lily pool in the center. Maintenance, however, became a problem as the years passed, and the park began to look neglected.

In January 1953 the club decided to restore the square to its former beauty. They engaged the original landscape architect to re-design the pool as a sunken garden, paved with flagstones and planted with azaleas. As the work progressed, the community became so interested that contributions and help came unsolicited from innumerable sources—nurserymen, business firms, individuals, the city council, and the mayor. Instead of the simple planting the club had undertaken, the plans were changed to provide bloom at all seasons, with a maximum display in the spring. The sunken garden is now planted with camellias, holly, cherry laurel, winter jasmine, dogwood, azaleas, bamboo, and many other beautiful and interesting plants.

Trees for Philadelphia's Old Colonial Churches

Charleston's Gateway Walk inspired "The Path of Faith" in Philadelphia, Pennsylvania. The idea of this project—to connect the old colonial churches in the region of Independence Hall by means of trees—was that of Miss Katherine Nevins Bradford, whose ancestors helped settle Philadelphia. She had seen the lovely dogwood-lined path between the Burying Grounds of old St. Philips and St. Michaels in Charleston, shortly after the original Gateway project was completed, and for years had dreamed of doing something similar in Philadelphia, where the old historic churches were lost among the great buildings around them. In 1948, when she was seeking the support of the Society of Little Gardens and the Society of the Colonial Dames of America, Congress became interested in restoring and protecting the historic buildings in this area as a national shrine. Both projects are now underway, with Miss Bradford and her Path of Faith Committee working with the Department of the Interior. All of the garden clubs in Pennsylvania, and many other organizations are contributing to this project.

"These old colonial churches," Miss Bradford says, "are the realization of William Penn's dream for his 'fair green countrie towne'—all faiths worshipping in freedom in a City of Brotherly Love. But as isolated churches, crowded in among other buildings, their significance is lost. Without trees to shade them and soften the marks of time, they look forlorn and neglected, as though they meant nothing to us. Yet it is here that many of our patriots came for inspiration in making the decisions that led to the founding of the United States.

"My original thought was a tree-lined lane, a continuous planting of trees along the ancient streets between them, with this whole historic section set apart, as in Charleston. But that was not too practical since this is a commercial area. We are following out the plan as closely as possible, however, although sometimes we can plant our trees only at intersections."

New York City's "Salute to Seasons"

New York's Park and Fifth Avenues are unforgettably beautiful at Christmastime, and Rockefeller Center is famed for its flower displays, particularly the one at Easter. "Salute to Seasons," a civic beautification program, was launched in 1957 to create a festive air throughout the year. Merchants and private-property owners cooperate with the Department of Parks through tree, shrub and massed-flower plantings, and the seasons are heralded with colorful banners.

Restoration of Patriot's Park by the Tarrytowns

The two Tarrytowns in New York may have put the cart before the horse when they tackled a big problem before figuring out a way to handle it. However, small public-spirited groups often accomplish miracles by this method. The Tarrytowns are in the Sleepy Hollow section of Westchester County made famous by Washington Irving. Three small garden clubs there, with the help of village authorities and the townspeople, recently finished a ten-year project—Patriot's Park.

The park marks the site where the British spy, Major André, was captured. It covers four acres adjacent to André Brook, the village boundary between Tarrytown and North Tarrytown. At one time this was a beautiful residential park with large shade trees and a lovely lawn rolling down to a brook crossed with bridges of native stone. A large curving driveway swung around eight old mansions, ramshackled and forlorn. Just before World War II a group of citizens purchased the property and presented it to the villages as a public park. The best house was used as a Community Center, the others razed. But no money was available to improve the property and it was a park only in name.

When the war was over the three garden clubs of the Tarrytowns met to solve the park problem. Each appointed two members to serve on a joint committee which was assigned the task of finding a way to restore the park.

The committee tried a flower fair and raised $300—not enough to begin the project. Realizing the magnitude of the undertaking, the committee ran a publicity campaign to enlist the support of the community. One member, a landscape architect, drew up a plan that could be carried out over a period of years. The plan was presented to the village authorities and they were asked to help. The two villages agreed to appropriate $1,000 each toward the park, provided the garden clubs raised the balance. Someone donated $1,000 as a result of the publicity drive, and in the first year the clubs built an eighty-foot retaining wall, bought and spread fifty cubic yards of topsoil against it, and landscaped this area. Four dead trees were removed and dead wood pruned. The next year the clubs raised $500 with another fair and the villages again appropriated $1,000 each. The committee bought fill to cover the foundations of the old houses, an area of 50,000 square feet requiring several thousand cubic yards of fill. This section was graded, covered with topsoil, fertilized, and seeded.

The following year they rebuilt a retaining wall and mended the bridge and walls surrounding the big pool. They removed more dead trees, planted dogwoods in the areas already finished, and landscaped the park entrance with red and white azaleas, laurel, ivy, and white dogwoods. One club contributed a rose garden.

Every year the program was carried forward according to plan, with the villages continuing to contribute the agreed amount and the clubs raising the difference. The paths, walks, and drives were black-topped. More retaining walls of native stone were built to correct erosion. The brook was widened at one point to create a reflecting pool with waterfalls. Landscaping was continued until the park finally became the beautiful area it is today.

The committee, still consisting of its original members, is now a permanent one, with the responsibility of supervising the maintenance of the park. The village authorities were so impressed by the way the committee handled the project that the chairman was appointed to the park board in Tarrytown and the vice-chairman to the board in North Tarrytown.

Restoration of a Colonial Cemetery

Westport, Connecticut, is in the heart of Revolutionary War country. But its beginnings go even farther back. At the crossroads of Kingshighway and Wilton Road, along which the British marched toward Danbury, is a little cemetery that predates the birth of George Washington by ten years. No famous person is buried there, just a few forgotten heroes of the Revolution, some unknown soldiers, and early settlers. But the people of Westport feel that it represents a page in the history of their town and their country. They have made it a beautiful spot, with flowers and shrubs of the colonial period.

Only a few years ago the cemetery was a tangle of brambles, so neglected and overgrown that few even knew it was there. Those who did would not have had the courage to penetrate the vines and weeds that smothered it.

The Westport Garden Club undertook to restore this cemetery in 1949, appointing a committee to plan the work. One committee member, a landscape architect, made a sketch; another browsed through rare old books and made a list of colonial flowers. Two others plotted the graves and sepulchres to make a blue-print for town records. Another gathered historical data. Each club member was instructed to bring either one large or two small steppingstones for a walk. Then the work began.

The day was set and club members, fortified by their husbands, turned out to clear away the century-old debris and straighten the headstones. When the truckloads of rubbish had been carried away, 132 graves were found and six vaults unearthed. One, dating from 1721, was the resting place of fifty-one early settlers. The men set everything in place, mended the stone walls, and remade the paths. Boy Scouts scrubbed the old headstones. Then the women sketched out their beautification plans.

A pair of old cemetery urns, the same age as the vaults, was purchased to mark the entrance. One member contributed a pair of ornamental iron gates to replace those that had disappeared. Two granite gateposts at least 150 years old were rescued from behind the town hall and put to use, as well as a 1,200-pound slab which made a fine bench for the colonial garden. Tree surgeons pruned and strengthened a tremendous 180-year-old maple. Then club members selected from their master list of colonial flowers and shrubs varieties that were inexpensive and easy to care for. These included *Vinca Minor*, ivy, syringa, strawberry shrub, barberry, laurel, boxwood, cedars, violets, primroses, day-lilies, plantain-lilies, and stars of Bethlehem. Along the banks they set out 2,000 ivy plants, filling the holes with leaf mold and carrying barrels of water daily through the summer to make sure the plants survived.

By this time the whole community was interested. A mason volunteered to repair the stone wall and also set the huge stone steps that lead from the road to the colonial garden. The town cleared out the poison ivy and undergrowth from the opposite corner and widened Kingshighway so people could park their cars and visit the cemetery.

The club received the Kellogg Medal for Civic Achievement from the National Council of State Garden Clubs, Inc., for this project.

Cemetery Entrance Landscaped

One of the most extensive renovations of this type is a project of the garden club in Kingfisher, Oklahoma, "Memory Lane," which also won an award from the National Council of State Garden Clubs, Inc. Working with the highway department, the club has landscaped as a memorial to the service men and women of Kingfisher County more than a mile of highway leading through the cemetery. The landscaping includes 260 elms, 476 Platte River cedars and pfitzers, and groups of shrubs. A stone wall has been built along part of one side which was badly eroded, and planted with 171 Paul's Scarlet roses. If you ever receive a post-card from Kingfisher, the picture on it will probably be of Memory Lane, for the whole community is proud of the project. "It's one of the nicest things that ever happened to Kingfisher," a highway crew member told Mrs. F. W. Gooden, then president of the Oklahoma clubs. He then asked if he could give $20 to help. The project was financed through contributions and a home talent play staged by the club. Former residents of Kingfisher donated generously.

National Cemetery Beautified

Willamette National Cemetery in Oregon is one of thirteen in the nation, and the only one in the Northwest. It is located in the Portland area and comprises 200 acres. Although there were plantings there, the garden club in Eastmoreland felt that the place looked barren, especially in the winter.

With the approval of the Memorial Division of the Army, the club initiated a beautification program, but soon realized that the undertaking was too much for their small group. They turned for help first to sister clubs in the area, then to The Oregon Federation of Garden Clubs. The federation agreed to help and in turn invited the Washington State federation to join the project. The clubs of the two states are now working together to "honor those who gave their lives for our country, by planting flowers, shrubs, and trees to comfort the living."

Togus at Lilac Time

A memorial project of unusual interest was carried out in the lilac planting of Maine garden clubs at the Veterans Hospital in Togus. Two thousand lilac bushes, both purple and white, were planted in the design of a huge cathedral window. The "panes" are eight plots of 107 graves each, framed by lilacs. Tall elms stand sentinel at the base. At the top is a granite monument with a cross, and in the background is a twenty-acre forest of white pines.

Working Together

Park "Work Days" in Niwot, Colorado

Many public-spirited groups with limited budgets have found the do-it-yourself idea very effective in carrying out community projects. The garden club in Niwot, Colorado, made a small park around an old bandstand, a town landmark. Landscaping was planned on a long-range basis with the area divided into four sections, and a chairman in charge of each. The husbands of club members do the heavy work while the women take care of planting and maintenance and raise money for plant material. Special days are set aside as "work days" and the participants have so much fun that the club can always depend upon a good turn-out.

The Rotarian Painting Bee

Tom Sawyer had nothing on the Rotarians of Garden City, Michigan, when it comes to handling a paint job. "At certain street intersections of the community are benches to accommodate people waiting for buses," the *Rotarian* reports. "To the tired housewife out shopping or the homeward-bound businessman, the sight of the benches has always been pleasing, but Garden City Rotarians thought they should look inviting even when a person was not tired. One year they decided to paint them, and they have been doing it annually ever since."

At first it was usually a two- or three-man job that required several hours. A new speed-up method brings out the entire membership and the annual job is done in no time flat.

Master Planning for Beautification

Irvington-on-Hudson's Long-Range Plan

Long-range community programs under a master landscaping plan are becoming increasingly popular with civic groups, and amazing results can be achieved in this way. Some years ago the garden club in Irvington-on-Hudson, New York, had a survey made of the entire village and a master plan drawn for a progressive beautification program. The Village Board allocates a specified sum each year to advance the program and the club contributes an equal amount. The conservation committee of the club works with the highway and park departments as the yearly plans are made. This program has been in operation for over twenty years, with such success that the village board has now adopted a master plan for community growth and building.

A Three-Year Plan for Bath, Ohio

Using the same idea, a small garden club in Bath, Ohio, adopted a project but carried it out in a somewhat different way. Its beautification plan was to be accomplished in three years. Two other clubs were invited to make a forum, the three working as a unit. Money for the landscaping is raised by card parties, and sales of baked goods and plants. All work is done by members of the clubs with the assistance of their husbands. As of this writing, 4,000 daffodils, 300 dogwoods, and 11,000 evergreens have been planted.

Master Plan for an Entire Valley

Fifty-one clubs in the third district of the Tennessee Federation of Garden Clubs launched a mammoth beautification plan which covered a valley with an area of 10,000 square miles. This tremendous five-year project, winner of the coveted Kellogg award among garden clubs, was directed by Mrs. Claude R. Givens.

The project originated in Chattanooga one autumn day in 1949. Three garden club members happened to meet while shopping and lunched together. They were soon talking shop and one remarked, "My club has just gotten a beautification program well launched and my term as president will be up before the project is finished. I'm terribly afraid the next administration may not be as interested in it as we are, and may even drop it for something else."

The other two women sympathized and expressed the same concern over projects of their clubs. "What we should do," Mrs. Givens said, "is work together. One club alone is limited in its accomplishment; combined there would be no limit to what we can do. But there must be a definite plan, so the project will be continued from one administration to the next."

This casual conversation resulted in a conference of all the district clubs. A master landscape plan was conceived which would include all clubs and communities in the area. The members realized that this was no small undertaking, that raising the money just to have a plan drawn would be a big job. But they voted unanimously to do it. It was decided to raise the money with one united project—a Christmas pilgrimage. Several women offered to open their homes for the pilgrimage and the most skilled flower arrangers were asked to decorate them. Two additional homes were to be opened for tea.

The pilgrimage was successful. Enough money was raised to employ a noted landscape architect and planning consultant, familiar with native flora, to make a survey of each garden club area and draw up a detailed blue-print. Every area and community having a garden club was surveyed, block by block, street by street. In each case the president of the local club accompanied the landscape architect. This insured a part in the plan for each unit. Blue-prints were prepared for each club, together with a time-table and specific instructions. Among places marked for treatment were the grounds of schools, churches, hospitals, city halls, libraries, court houses, tunnel approaches, hillsides and streets, unsightly spots along the streets, and unauthorized dumping grounds. Two years were required for the survey alone.

"This was to be no haphazard affair," Mrs. Givens says. "Our plan was to have every club know exactly what to do and how to do it. We knew well that the task ahead would not be easy—that it would take time, effort, and money—but we were determined to do it."

When the survey was finished another big pilgrimage was held, to raise money to launch the landscaping program. Half of the receipts were divided among the clubs for their individual projects, the other half was to beautify Chattanooga. Except for these yearly pilgrimages during the five years required for the project, each club raised the money for its own program. Yearly awards were made to clubs reporting the greatest progress. Members of the committee visited the various areas and selected the three best, basing their decision upon improvement (30 points), following the architect's plan (30 points), and maintenance (40 points). Each spring an Awards Banquet was given, with outstanding speakers.

"Many dollars were spent from private purses in this work," Mrs. Givens recalls, "for which no accounting was kept, but in the final report forty-two of the fifty-one garden clubs participating reported an expenditure of $50,000. Clubs reported planting 21,000 trees, 33,000 shrubs, 11,000 roses, 106,000 bulbs, and 14,000 plants. The newspapers cooperated wonderfully. We made a scrapbook from the clippings— one hundred pages measuring twenty-four by twenty inches. We have received inquiries about our project from all over the country."

A Professional Effect in Community Landscaping

Many garden clubs are now conducting landscape courses and clinics in an effort to achieve a more professional result in their programs. In Arkansas the courses are conducted throughout the state by the University of Arkansas Extension Horticulturist. The university furnishes master plans in connection with club projects, which may be carried out over a three-to-five-year period. Missouri garden clubs achieve a similar unity of effect by having each community choose some specific shrub or flower to keynote its plantings.

The Los Angeles Plan

The idea of organizing for community improvement is taking hold throughout the country. Many large cities have recognized the need for some plan or program whereby a pleasing general appearance may be assured. Los Angeles has handled this matter most effectively.

Several years ago a group of civic-minded citizens organized Los Angeles Beautiful as a working committee of the Chamber of Commerce. They realized that the rapid industrial and population growth of the city had changed its appearance to that of a bustling metropolis and were afraid that beauty of surroundings would cease to be important. Their purpose was to coordinate and promote projects which would make the city more beautiful. One objective was to enlist the support of individuals and community organizations in a city-wide beautification program, another was to extend organized support to approved projects developed by individuals or community organizations. Today more than 150 groups participate in Los Angeles Beautiful, representing every facet of community life. The program, carried out on a voluntary basis, is a continuing one, founded on long-range planning. It covers all manner of projects, integrated to create a harmonious effect and emphasize the city's personality.

An especially interesting feature of the program is the annual "presentation" to the city, which originated in 1950 as part of the 169th anniversary celebration of Los Angeles. At that time the executive committee of Los Angeles Beautiful held a city birthday breakfast in a large hotel, with more than 400 citizens attending. The city was presented with a huge package containing fifty-nine beautification projects, carried out during the year by community groups. "Many people were for the first time alerted to the tremendous volume of citizen activities going on in our city," Mrs. Valley M. Knudsen, chairman of the committee, says of the event. "The affair stimulated so much activity that a presentation to the city the next year was almost mandatory and has been part of the program ever since."

Why we respond as we do to beautiful surroundings is something most of us would have trouble explaining. In the last twenty-five years we have become the most beauty conscious people in the world so far as our homes are concerned. Surely our communities, almost as much a part of our lives as our homes, should be beautiful too.

CHAPTER IV

SPECIAL GARDENS AND SANCTUARIES

It is difficult to explain the charm of a garden, because charm it-self eludes definition. Sir James Barrie says, "If you have it, you don't need to have anything else." Large or small, a garden enchants us and the world would be a dreary place without trees and flowers.

Municipal Gardens

Tulsa's Rose Garden

Tulsa, Oklahoma, is one of our most garden conscious cities and, like Los Angeles, has a well organized plan for beautification which includes homes, industries, parks, and the grounds of public buildings. So extensive is its program that Tulsa is known as one of our most beautiful cities and hopes to become *the* most beautiful. It is already a leader in industrial landscaping, with one of its shopping centers, Utica Square, a prize winner in a national competition. Tulsa also boasts one of the finest garden centers in the country, the only one financed by a municipal bond issue. A host of garden clubs flourish in the city, known by such alliterative names as Till and Toil, Seed and Weed, and Sun and Shade. Each in its own way helps make the city more attractive. But the crowning achievement in garden club work is a project of the Tulsa Garden Club, the Municipal Rose Garden.

Here again is an example of what a group can do by means of a long-range plan, conscientiously followed over a period of years. Considered by rosarians one of the best in the United States, this garden is internationally known. It contains more than 7,000 rose bushes, representing more than 200 varieties. The garden is magnificently terraced and landscaped, with reflecting basins multiplying its enchantment. Around it is a wall of large trees. Skillful care of the plants has caused it to be chosen as one of the country's twenty-three rose-testing plots. Information as to varieties and their care is furnished to all rose growers. In 1937, the Tulsa Garden Club, in recognition of this garden, was awarded a bronze plaque by *Better Homes and Gardens* in its "A More Beautiful America" competition. From its inception in 1934, the garden has been a cooperative project. The Tulsa Garden Club furnishes all the roses and replacements and the Park Board provides labor and maintenance.

Roses in Tyler, Texas

The Municipal Rose Garden in Tyler, Texas, is a city project, developed by the Park Department. Although it was started in 1952, it ranks among the outstanding rose gardens of the country.

Tyler is in the heart of a rose-growing area, and the garden is being developed in a typically Texan large-scale fashion. It contains nearly 25,000 rose bushes, representing all possible varieties that are grown commercially. The garden is the focal point of a twenty-acre park, which permits unlimited expansion and provides a background of towering pines and oaks. There are winding walks and stairways, rock terraces, reflecting basins, and fountains. The design is formal, accented by water oaks, mimosas, azaleas, and camellias. Most of the beds are edged with polyanthus, and floribundas, and contain from twenty to sixty bushes of a single variety, a massing technique striking in its effect. Along the borders of the reflecting basins snow-in-summer has been planted in long, lovely drifts which glisten white in the sun.

A feature of the Tyler garden is the section devoted exclusively to miniature roses. This area is raised two feet and curbed with concrete to bring the Lilliputian blooms closer to eye level. It is developed in a formal design, with borders of alyssum and a miniature boxwood hedge, and accented with tree roses less than a foot high. The miniature rose bushes are only six inches high with blooms smaller than a dime.

Because the soil here is a hard clay, it was necessary to remove it completely and fill the beds with special earth and compost. The basis of the beds is a mixed composition of sewage sludge, a waste product of Tyler's sewage treatment plant, and leaf mold collected from the streets and parks of the city. The sewage passing through the treatment plant is chlorinated and undergoes a natural process of digestion. After dehydrating in open drying beds, it is free of dangerous bacteria. Fallen leaves are taken to a composting area and placed in long gullies, where they decompose into a heavy leaf mold which is chopped fine and mixed at the site. Since roses are highly susceptible to nematodes, microscopic organisms that cause root knot, this mixture is sterilized with steam.

Most of the plants in the Tyler garden are contributed by rose growers from Texas and other states. An experimental half-acre has been developed for a demonstration of rose growing, through cooperation with the Texas Rose Research Foundation. Tyler has a rose festival each year, and the Rose Festival Association, in cooperation with the city park board and the garden clubs in the area, has built a large garden center in the park. This building is used for the spring flower show, the festival, and for garden club activities.

A Community Affair in Kansas

The Municipal Rose Garden in Pratt, Kansas, is the dream-come-true of the garden columnist of a local newspaper. Mrs. E. L. Hilliard, a garden club member, says that so many people visited her rose garden that she began to think how nice it would be if Pratt could have a public one. She began to visit municipal gardens in other cities, wrote letters to rose growers, and sought information from every available source until she was thoroughly familiar with the problems involved and their solutions. After five years of paper preparation she began to look for a possible site, and chose a block-square piece of city-owned land already in the park system. It is a naturally sunken area, bounded on three sides by heavily traveled streets. The square, she felt, had three advantages: (1) being lower than the streets, high winds would pass over the plot without damaging blooms and foliage; (2) the heavy traffic would help prevent vandalism;

(3) the aged and infirm could look down into the garden without leaving their cars. With the site chosen, she went to the civic authorities for their approval. This was granted, provided that enough community interest was manifested and sufficient contributions were made to finance it. The plan which Mrs. Hilliard had drawn for the garden was accepted without alterations by the park board.

The plan called for forty beds, to be sold by subscription, either in part or whole. That is, an individual, civic group, business firm, or any organization could buy an entire bed or part of one. Prices varied according to the size of the bed and the type of roses used. Included would be the cost of the rose bushes, peat moss, bonemeal, and heavy metal liners to keep out the probing roots of Bermuda grass which had dominated the plot for years.

Mrs. Hilliard got the garden club to appoint a working committee of six members, and began to plug the garden in her newspaper column. She felt that if they could sell ten or perhaps fifteen beds the first year, they could add a few more each year until all forty were planted. Within six weeks after they had begun a canvass of the community, all the beds were sold.

The whole community, it seemed, was now enthusiastic about the rose garden. The metal, labor, and hauling for the heavy liners was contributed by a local tank company. A citizen contributed labor and machinery for breaking up the hardpan found in the bottom of some of the beds, since the soil had to be dug to a depth of from twenty-two to thirty-eight inches. After this work was finished, topsoil, mixed with peat moss and bonemeal, was hauled in. Here again, the labor was either volunteer or contributed by business firms and the materials sold at cost. Since this is a region of long, dry summers, the city water department ran lines having outlets flush with the soil surface so that fifty feet of hose could reach any spot. A resident then improved this by contributing traveling sprays which cover the whole garden. So it went. A tool house was needed and in short order was constructed by volunteers. For Dedication Day in June 1956 someone thought it would be nice to have a flag pole with Old Glory. Within a day or two, someone had contributed it.

The long-range plan Mrs. Hilliard had drawn up for the garden was accomplished in one year, and by that time the townspeople were thinking of enlarging the original concept of the garden. Mrs.

Hilliard has drawn plans for more beds. Almost any evening through the spring and summer, you will find a few businessmen, a housewife or two, and maybe half a dozen teenagers working in the Rose Garden. In a feature article about the garden for a Kansas paper, a writer commented: "All this beauty came about because one person dared to dream and then put those dreams into action."

Historic and Memorial Gardens

The Williamsburg Gardens

The growing interest in the preservation of historic areas is emphasized by the great popularity of the Colonial Williamsburg Restoration in Virginia. Fifteen eighteenth century gardens were restored along with the buildings, not only as a part of our past, but because they reveal so graphically, through their design and choice of plant material, the different tastes and economic positions of the people who nurtured them 200 years ago. The gardens range from a modest herb, or "kitchen" garden, to the extensive and magnificently landscaped "pleasure" gardens of the Governor's Palace, which include a maze designed after the one at Hampton Court in England and laid out in American holly. They reveal too, through the practical use of evergreens and imaginative topiary work, some of the basic characteristics of the people who settled this country.

Garden Projects of Garden Clubs

While the Williamsburg restoration, financed by John D. Rockefeller, Jr., shows what philanthropy can accomplish, small groups everywhere are contributing just as importantly in saving the rich heritage of American gardens. The garden club in Lakewood, Ohio, has restored an old garden around a pioneer stone house typical of early days, working with the Lakewood Historical Society. Garden clubs in Virginia have done remarkable work in restoring, or helping to restore, historic gardens, and their spring garden tour has become famous. The Garden Club of Lexington, Kentucky, undertook as a major project the restoration of the garden at Ashland, the home of Henry Clay. At a cost of some $4,000, the Garden Club of America created a beautiful amphitheatre at the Fairchild Tropical Garden in Miami, Florida, which contains the largest collection of tropical plants in the United States. And these are only a few of the many projects public-spirited groups in all parts of the country have successfully executed.

The Abraham Lincoln Memorial Garden

When the late Jens Jensen, internationally known landscape architect, was asked by the garden clubs of Illinois to design a garden as a memorial to Abraham Lincoln, he said: "I have received many honors . . . but to be asked to design a garden that will be a living memorial to Abraham Lincoln, I consider the greatest honor of them all."

That was in 1930. A year later he delivered the plans to the club with this note: "I know this has taken a long time, but no good work is done in haste. I have given you the best I have to give. This garden has been planned on a large scale, in keeping with the country of which it is a part. In centuries to come our descendants will enjoy and cherish this garden. Only the most fitting and enduring plants are to be used—trees that will give dignity and nobility to the garden in ripe old age and scatter their seed and produce their offspring as far as man's vision goes in the distant tomorrow. I know of no idea more noble or fitting as a memorial to our Great American than a garden. It is not to be an arboretum, or a collection of plants, but a pure symphony of living beauty and eternal youth. In fifty years, if cherished, this garden will be the outstanding planting of the Middle West. It will sing the song of America." Although he had achieved world fame for his naturalistic plantings and was in such demand that he could command any price, Mr. Jensen would accept no fee for designing this garden.

Today the Abraham Lincoln Memorial Garden in Springfield, Illinois, is a breathtakingly beautiful reality. It covers sixty acres of rolling prairie and wooded hills along Lake Springfield, with trees, shrubs, and flowers that were a part of the early Illinois landscape. The hills are planted with such trees as oaks, elms, Kentucky coffee trees, hickory, tulip, sycamore, beech, and sweet gum. Bordering the wooded areas are small trees native to Illinois: the redbud, white flowering dogwood, crabapple, hawthorne, wild plum, snow-drop tree, shadblow, gray dogwood, sumac, and fringe tree. In the "sun openings" are prairie flowers, while meadow blossoms nod at the water's edge.

The inlets are planted with water-lilies and water-grasses. Over the many little streams are foot bridges, each with its special planting of meadowsweet, columbine, marsh marigold, and small shrubs.

When this area was chosen as the site for the garden, it had been farmed for generations and few trees were left. Feeling that the oak best symbolized the character and personality of Lincoln, Mr. Jensen had included many varieties in his plans. To find some of them was a problem. Moreover oaks are difficult to transplant satisfactorily. If the taproot is injured the tree will always be a cripple. An appeal was sent out by the garden clubs for acorns—acorns of historical trees, trees located in places Lincoln visited, favorite trees of people especially interested in Lincoln. The response was overwhelming. With the advice and help of the Morton Arboretum, these acorns were planted in November 1937. They are now sturdy oaks.

A unique feature of the garden is the "council ring." There are nine of these great circular stone seats ringing paved areas, with a firepit in the center. They are scattered through the garden, in the depths of the woods, at the edges of sun openings, or near the lake shore. The largest, fifty feet in diameter, is in a grove of white oaks, the most stately and sturdy tree of Illinois, and is known as the Lincoln Council Ring. Later, rustic benches were added, each bearing a quotation from Lincoln. These are contributed by the garden club federations of the various states and the plan is to have every state represented.

The plantings were designed to attract and protect the birds, and the garden has become a sanctuary for them. Many species which had never been seen in the area before have established this as their habitat.

Like so many similar projects the Lincoln Garden began as one person's dream. Mrs. T. J. Knudson conceived it and has shepherded it through the years, inspiring others to work for it just as enthusiastically. At her suggestion it was undertaken as a project of The Garden Club of Illinois. It has had the support of the National Council of State Garden Clubs, Inc. from the beginning. But people in every state wanted a share in it, and it has thus become a national project. While the City of Springfield maintains the garden, it is supported by voluntary contributions from all parts of the country. The scope of the garden is such that, for years to come, plantings can be added to it constantly. The garden clubs of Springfield have an annual "Wild-flower Planting Day," when woodland flowers are planted in the ravines and along the many lanes. In places where the shade is deep, fern colonies are being established. This is all a part of Mr. Jensen's plan to keep the garden a living, constantly changing tapestry of the United States.

The International Friendship Gardens

Like music, gardens speak a universal language. Their message is one of peace and fraternity. This, in essence, was the creed of three brothers—Joseph, Virgil, and Clarence Stauffer—who founded the International Friendship Gardens just outside Michigan City, Indiana. Here, authentic gardens of sixty nations testify the desire for "a warmer relationship between all peoples of the world." As the location for these gardens, the brothers chose the site where the Potta-wattamie Indians held their pow-wows and Father Marquette made friends with them in 1675.

This section is in the heart of the Lake Michigan dune country, often called the "Land of Singing Sands." The setting for the garden is a 100-acre area in the valley of Trail Creek, where many streams merge. The tract had been left mostly in its virgin state, with wooded hillsides, springlets and waterfalls, bordered by native shrubbery. Some of the gardens are side by side along the extensive green paths, others in open spaces. Beside the Greek garden, which depicts an ancient legend, is the French Garden, a maze of formal hedges. The Canadian Garden comes next, with its sheared green wall of arborvitae, and beyond it is the Polish Garden. Each is as individual as the country it represents, with a special distinguishing feature. In the Chinese Garden a scroll conveys greetings from Teh Ching Kung, 77th descendant of Confucius. The Italian Garden is recognized by its columns, which might have come from the ruins of the old forum or from Pompeii, while the Scottish Garden is ringed with a cradle fence. The Dutch have sent thousands of tulips for their garden, as many as 200,000 bulbs in a single planting. The Persian Garden is planted with roses, from 40,000 to 50,000 bushes. Beyond them all is the beautifully landscaped Theatre of Nations, with its island stage. There is also a Symphony Garden Theatre, with the trees behind the stage arranged to give the appearance of a huge pipe organ.

The International Friendship Gardens are an outgrowth of the
"Old Mill Garden" at the Century of Progress Fair in Chicago in
1933, an exhibit planned by the garden-loving Stauffers. When it was
decided to hold the fair over for another year, the brothers contacted
presidents, kings, and the world's Who's Who with the idea of an
international friendship garden. King Gustavus of Sweden was the first
European to respond, and Jorge Ubico, then president of Guatemala,
was the first in the Americas. He sent orchids and other flora valued at
thousands of dollars. Queen Wilhelmina of the Netherlands sent a
carload of tulips and other countries responded with the same enthusiastic interest. This project had almost 300 participants, representing
nearly three times as many countries as were represented at the fair
itself. Most of the work was done by the Stauffers. At the close of
the fair the gardens were established at the present site, about fifty-
two miles from Chicago. They are visited by people from all over the
world—just as the three brothers had hoped they would be.

The International Peace Garden

The International Peace Garden was established in 1932 to memorialize the long friendship between Canada and the United States. It
spans the International Boundary at a point between Dunseith, North
Dakota, and Boissevain, Manitoba, and covers about 2,400 acres. The
site was chosen because of its natural beauty, because it comes within a few miles of being the geographic center of North America, and
because there are no natural barriers within the garden area to restrict the free movement of people from one country to the other.
It lies within the lake-dotted region of the Turtle Mountains—which
are really gentle hills—the formal area stretching along the boundary
for a distance of about a mile. In width it varies from 600 to 1,200
feet. The master plans for the garden were prepared by the National
Park Service of the United States, working jointly with the National
Park Service of Canada and the State Historical Society of North
Dakota.

The design consists of eight panels. The Peace Panel was the first
to be completed, the Terrace Panel is still under construction, and the
other six—the Sunken Garden, Cascade Panel, Turf Panel, Reflecting
Pool, Peace Tower, and Emblem Panel—await development. On a
turf strip near the entrance to the Peace Panel is the Cairn, bearing

the dedication pledge of the two countries: "To God in His Glory—
We Two Nations Dedicate This Garden and Pledge Ourselves That
As Long As Men Shall Live, We Will Not Take Up Arms Against
One Another."

The land for the International Peace Garden was contributed by
the State of North Dakota and the Province of Manitoba. The
United States and the Canadian Governments, as well as North
Dakota and Manitoba, are contributing financially to its maintenance
through appropriations and grants, but it is not exclusively a government project. Municipalities, business organizations, service clubs,
women's organizations, and individuals of both countries also have a
part in it. The International War Veterans Association presented the
steel flag poles which flank the Cairn, while the Federated Women's
Institutes of Canada and the Home Demonstration Council of the
United States landscaped the area around it. The Fraternal Order of
Eagles of the Dakotas and Manitoba placed in the Peace Garden a
stone monolith carved with the Ten Commandments. The Homemakers Clubs of North Dakota and the Federated Women's Institutes of Canada furnished the information booth, and the Boissevain
Chapter of the Imperial Order, Daughters of the Empire, provided
funds to stock a souvenir booth.

To the west of the Cairn is a large turfed area, bordered by an
Asiatic elm hedge and rows of lilacs, banked by American elms and
Amur maples. This turfed area was financed by the Junior Red Cross
of the United States and Canada. The Terrace Panel is divided into
seven parts. Each of the massive stone walls in the first two terraces
is topped by an iron balustrade, with flagstones forming the floor.
The Imperial Order, Daughters of the Empire, provided the iron
balustrades for the walls on the Canadian side and the flagstones,
and gave funds toward the construction of the upper pool and the
garden house on the Canadian side. The Manitoba Horticultural
Association is developing an arboretum on the banks of Lake Stor-
mon, while the General Federation of Women's Clubs of the United
States has financed the development of the Colorado Blue Spruce
Grove and is providing for its maintenance.

The Federated Women's Institutes of Canada, the Manitoba
Women's Institute, and the Order of the Eastern Star constructed
four kitchens and a cookhouse in the picnic area, among other con-

tributions. The Dakota Homemakers Clubs installed electric stoves
and hot water in the Lodge, and provided bedding for a number of
tourist cabins. The Woman's Christian Temperance Union of the
two countries has provided a drinking fountain and park benches,
with the Homemakers Clubs of Maine furnishing a second fountain.
And these are but a few of the many contributions that have been
made by individuals and groups toward developing the garden.

The idea for this garden came from Dr. Henry J. Moore of Isling-
ton, Ontario, gardener, author, graduate of the Kew Gardens in England, and a member of the Royal Horticultural Society of London.
The inspiration came from the warmth and friendliness he found at
a gathering of the National Association of Gardeners, held in Greenwich, Connecticut, in 1928. A year later, at its Toronto meeting, the
association approved his idea and was the original sponsor of the
garden, which is administered by a board of nine Americans and
nine Canadians.

The formal area of the International Peace Garden is so designed
that it is exactly duplicated on either side of the border, with the
flags of the two nations flying side by side. The garden is on a highway
that links the United States and Canada, and it is Dr. Moore's hope
that the same highway will eventually link it with the Christ of the
Andes, erected at their boundary line by the Argentine and Chilean
Governments.

Gardens for Therapy, Medicine, and Welfare

A Fragrance Garden for the Blind

There is perhaps no more heart-warming example of what civic
groups can do than their work for the blind. A comparatively new
feature of this type of activity, at least in the United States, is the
establishment of gardens designed especially for the sightless in which
emphasis is placed on fragrance and texture rather than color and
design. The Botanic Garden in Brooklyn, New York, created such a
garden in 1955, sponsored by its Women's Auxiliary and supported by
individuals, garden clubs of several states, and numerous other organizations.

This is a sunken, oval-shaped garden, bounded by a stone wall with
a guide rail. Most of the beds of fragrant plants are along the top of

this low wall, and at intervals there are labels both in Braille and Roman numerals that give a brief account of the plants. More than 150 kinds are featured here, some having delightfully scented flowers or foliage, others pleasantly textured, and still others whose leaves, twigs, or bark offer novel experiences in taste or touch. In the wall itself are planting pockets containing still other plants. But not all plants are smooth and friendly to the touch. At the request of the blind themselves, the plantings include coarse-spined cacti, thorny rose bushes and prickly holly.

The garden has many inviting benches and a flagstone terrace, but it is not primarily a refuge for the blind. Its purpose is to give those among them who are interested in gardening an opportunity to discover, or rediscover, the world of plants. According to authorities, 90 per cent of sightless people become blind after the age of twenty, so need only to recall familiar things. The fragrance garden has become so popular that the Botanic Garden has appointed Miss Theresa Wood, a blind teacher and former social worker, to take charge of visiting groups.

The Toronto Garden for the Blind

The Garden Club of Toronto, and its friends, recently presented the Canadian National Institute for the Blind with a fragrance garden, the first established in Canada. Both this and the Brooklyn garden were modeled after those in England. Since the institute is a residence for the blind, which employs blind workers, the garden is designed for recreation, exercise, and relaxation. It covers a one-acre tract framed with a rectangular exercise walk and intersected by two auxiliary walks. One of these passes through wildflower and fern plantings and the other through fragrant shrubs and small trees. Beds are raised by brick walls two inches above the ground, and provide toe space so that people may stand close to examine and smell the flowers. All plant material is labeled in Braille.

The beds are planted to give a succession of blooms; from the earliest spring crocuses, daffodils, and hyacinths through the scented annuals of summer, such as heliotrope, stocks, nicotiana, and petunias, on into the more pungent smell of chrysanthemums in the autumn. The plantings of scented flowers are separated in the beds by textured needle evergreens, small broad-leafed evergreens, and woolly-leafed

plants, while pungent herbs trail over the walls for bruising scent.
At the doorway of the library and dining-hall are flowering shrubs and
small flowering trees. Along one of the walks is a border of lilacs,
with a ground cover of English violets. To bring another dimension
to its fragrance garden, the Toronto club has created interesting
sounds. There is a pool, with water trickling and splashing into it.
Tall Canadian white pines have been planted where they will swish
softly with the wind, and a group of trembling aspens has been arranged so that they rustle with the slightest breeze. Shrubs and trees
that attract song birds have been planted extensively.

The Toronto club raised the money for its project through gifts
and memorials. Wherever possible, the donor was permitted to desig-
nate what was to be purchased with the money.

A New England Herb Garden

One of the earliest fragrance gardens in this country was a herb
garden established several years ago by the New England Herb
Society at the Sunlight Camp for the Blind in Egypt, Massachusetts,
cared for by members of the garden club in nearby Scituate. The
group tested the idea on a small scale, then enlarged it and made it
a permanent part of the camp program.

Montreal's Cutting Garden

Providing hospital wards with fresh flowers is a favorite project of
most garden clubs, but it is not always easy to secure a steady supply.
The Diggers and Weeders Garden Club of Montreal, Canada, over-
came this problem by planting a cutting garden on the hospital
grounds.

Their garden was created from hard, poor soil which had been a
pile of rubble. Club members, with the assistance of the Community
Garden League and patients from the Queen Mary Veterans Hospital, cleared the land and did the planting. The garden yields from
seventy to eighty bouquets a week and offers therapy work for the
patients.

A Five-Acre Cutting Garden in Toledo

The Garden Club Forum of Toledo, Ohio, has established a five-
acre cutting garden at a mental hospital. Like the Montreal garden,

it provides not only flowers for the wards, but therapy for the patients. Similar gardens have been created by garden clubs at correctional institutions, cancer hospitals, and homes for the aged, the deaf, orphaned children, and cripples.

A Medicinal Plant Garden

The activities of garden clubs are amazingly varied. The Garden Club of America, for instance, is largely responsible for the establishment of a medicinal garden at the Morris Arboretum of the University of Pennsylvana in Philadelphia. As long ago as 5,000 years Egypt had well cultivated gardens with flowers, fruits, and vegetables, and in the famous temple gardens were planted rare trees from distant lands. Through the ages there have been gardens in which horticulture was highly developed, among them the famous hanging gardens of Babylon. But although the healing properties of plants have been known from ancient times, there apparently were no important gardens devoted to drug plants until the sixteenth century, when the first scientific studies of plants for medicinal use were made. Whether the garden at Pisa or the one at Padua was the first is controversial. But these famous Italian gardens, both still in existence, were the first of many and the origin of the botanical garden as we know it today. They were used in connection with the universities, for the instruction of future physicians. At that time most medicines were derived from plants, either wild or cultivated, and it was essential for a doctor to know their properties.

Few gardens of drug plants exist today and nearly all are devoted to hardy species. "An interesting and, I believe, unique feature of our garden is that it contains tender as well as hardy species," says John M. Fogg, Jr., director of the Morris Arboretum. "In addition to such plants as digitalis, aconite, witch hazel, and cascara, we exhibit many tropical forms like nux-vomica, ginger, camphor, eucalyptus, and the Rauwolfias, which are the source of modern tranquilizers. These warm climate forms are, of course, in tubs or pots and must be shifted to the greenhouse before the coming of frost."

At the present time, the project is in its embryonic state, but Dr. Fogg expects to enlarge the area devoted to the garden and steadily increase the number of species. He has made expeditions to Mexico, Central America, the West Indies, and to many Asiatic and

European countries in search of valuable plants. The garden is available to the students of five medical schools.

A Garden Built at Night

A delightful project which aptly demonstrates the special gifts of a garden was carried out in Philadelphia, Pennsylvania, in connection with Mrs. Bush-Brown's window box program. Three women in a slum section, where few people knew each other by name, joined in creating a garden in a trash-filled lot, hidden from view by a tall fence. Slipping in at night through a back alley, they worked secretly for three months, clearing away the rubble. Basketful by basketful they took it away for disposal. Then they repaired and painted the back fence and trained scarlet runner beans over it on strings. On the other three sides they planted annuals, edging the beds with bricks salvaged from the rubble. In the center of the plot they made a flower bed, edged with white-washed bricks. They called it "The Secret Garden" because no one even suspected it was there.

When the garden was finished and blooming, the three women got up very early one morning and removed the fence. The people in the block were so impressed with the little garden that one of the men made a little picket fence for the front, while others supplied benches. It has become the gathering place for the whole neighborhood. At Christmas time a big evergreen is placed in the garden and the people in the block gather around it to sing carols on Christmas Eve.

Experimental Projects

For Dirt Gardeners Exclusively

The list of garden projects carried out by public-spirited groups is endless and those in this book are merely representative. All are interesting and many are very unusual. The garden clubs in New Orleans, Louisiana, promote civic improvement through a garden center which anyone can visit for information. In connection with it there is an experimental garden, where members test various soils, new plants, fertilizers, transplanting, and disease control. The information gleaned is passed along to others.

Nebraska's Plant-Testing Station

As a major project, the garden clubs in Nebraska contribute financially to the research program of the North Platte Experiment Station, conducted in conjunction with the University of Nebraska. Because of hot, dry summers and cold, dry, windy winters, many plants suitable for other sections of the country cannot be grown in Nebraska. The station is doing extensive work in rose breeding to develop winter hardiness and floriferousness in the better varieties. It also tests plant material for adaptability to the climate. Another goal is the development of new plants for this area. As a result of the work many new plants have been introduced, including hardy roses. Better chrysanthemums, pentstemons, dianthus, asters, lilies, and strawberries are sought. The research program was the idea of Mrs. Edgar Irving of Omaha, a garden club member who realized that only through a long-term project of this sort would the people of Nebraska have the kind of plant material they wanted for their gardens.

A Garden Club Committee of Ecology

Because of limited water, and climatic conditions in New Mexico, resource-minded groups do not have the problem of educating people to the need for conservation as in other states. They are more concerned with finding the best ways to use the land and supporting the methods found most effective. This is perhaps best exemplified by the program of the garden clubs in New Mexico. The State federation maintains a permanent Committee of Ecology, thought to be the only one among garden clubs. The committee studies the practical application of the cycles of nature, reporting the findings of research in this field to clubs throughout the state along with the results of their own experiments. At present it is concerned with the effects of chemical fertilizers upon the life of the soil and upon nutrition, and the effectiveness of blanket spraying as opposed to the control of pests by natural predators.

Botanic Gardens, Arboretums, and Sanctuaries

The Cherokee Botanic Garden

The Great Smoky Mountains are often called a botanist's paradise. Few spots in the world have a richer plant life and there are not as

many species of native trees in all Europe as there are in Great
Smoky Mountains National Park, an area of less than half a million
acres. In April and May more than 200 varieties of wildflowers bloom,
the most striking being the dense stands of phacelia that carpet wide
areas of the forest floor and look like snow from a distance. Several
species of trillium also grow in profusion. Dogwood, mountain laurel,
azaleas and rhododendron are everywhere, each in turn reigning su-
preme through a magnificent pageant of bloom.

With an outdoor laboratory such as this, the garden clubs in North
Carolina thought that the best conservation project they could undertake was the establishment of a botanic garden. They were making
plans for one when they learned that the Cherokee Historical Association had the same idea. The "Land of the Sky," as this section is
called, is the ancient home of the Cherokee Indians, who live on a
reservation there. This is the tribe of Sequoyah, one of the greatest
and best loved of Indian leaders. He created the Cherokee syllabary
through which thousands of Indians learned to read and write.
Tragically it was Sequoyah's tribe which was the victim of the in-
famous "death march" when gold was discovered in Cherokee territory. The famed pageant "Unto These Hills" is held annually in
this region.

Through an agreement with the Department of the Interior in 1951,
the Cherokee Historical Association was developing a botanic garden
and a replica of an old Indian village on a thirty-acre tract, located on
the reservation at the entrance to Great Smoky Mountains National
Park fifty miles from Asheville. The garden was to have nature trails,
and was to be used as an outdoor classroom by students of the
Cherokee Central School. Feeling that such a garden would be very
worth while, the garden clubs dropped their own plans and cooperated with the association's project.

"To date, more than 18,000 plants have been collected and
placed in the arboretum and along the nature trails," John Parris, an
association member and author of "Roamin' the Mountains," relates.
"Three trails with Indian names have been laid out. Each is up to one-
half a mile in length and features a different plant grouping. The
Squaw and Sachem Trail has been largely planted to wildflowers and
ferns. It winds below a pine slope, through hardwoods, past a mossy
spring, into an open glade, and on through a rhododendron jungle.

It crosses and recrosses a bouncing, icy mountain stream, and finally completes the loop through a natural bog. Great care has been exercised in relocating plants, with special attention given to drainage, exposure, shade, soil, and moisture. The Sequoyah Trail is planted to shrubs, vines, and trees. Two features give it unusual interest. It includes, in a cleared area, an Indian garden of 200 years ago, complete with a variety of vegetables and medicinal herbs. Many of the old varieties of squash, beans, maize, and yams were difficult to find and grow. The whole garden is enclosed by a stockade to keep animals from pillaging the crops. In another area the trail winds through a man-made canyon of large rocks, and many native rock plants and ferns are tucked into the crevices. A new Tsali Trail, named for the famed Indian martyr, has been staked out; it will wind along still another mountain brook and include a waterfall. It will be planted to special collections. All construction, planting, and maintenance work is done by the Indians and they are very proud of their garden."

The garden was designed by a landscape architect and a collector selected the plants. No attempt has been made to group the members of a family together botanically, but special emphasis is placed upon suiting the particular species to its best environment. The association plans to employ a full-time botanist, and hopes that one of the young Cherokees will make it his life work. The project is financed by the Cherokee pageant and garden club contributions.

A Contribution to the National Arboretum

One of the least known of the large botanic gardens and arboreta in this country is the National Arboretum in Washington, D.C. Established by an Act of Congress March 4, 1927, its development has been slow and even its partial completion will require years. Because it still lacks an adequate road system it is not yet open to the public on a full-time basis and most visitors to the capital do not even know it is there.

The National Arboretum occupies 415 acres in the northeast section of the District of Columbia. Its hills overlook the Capitol and Washington Monument to the south, with the Anacostia River bordering it on the east. Natural woods provide a backdrop for introduced plantings, which are being established upon a concentration of individual genera. On the eastern slopes above the river there is a planting of 100 varieties of *Camellia japonica*, which forms an extension of a planting of some ninety-two varieties of *Camellia Sasanqua* in the valley. The latter are part of the Garden Club of America plantings in Cryptomeria Valley. This section is devoted chiefly to oriental plants, and when complete will serve as an educational demonstration of the plant contribution of China and other parts of the Orient to the gardens of North America. Through the assistance of the American Nurseryman's Association, the arboretum has a superb collection of more than 200 crabapple varieties, their fragile beauty heightened by underplantings of daffodils contributed by the garden clubs of Washington. In a broad valley planting, magnolias, including many specimen trees, are attractively combined with about 300 species and varieties of holly.

The arboretum has a huge collection of azaleas, some 1,600 varieties. The most spectacular display is the planting of Glenn Dales, with 65,000 specimens included. These are color-massed in brilliant groupings of thirty or forty plants to a clone along the curving slopes of a hillside covered with oaks and tulip trees. This new race of large-flowered "Japanese" hybrid azaleas was bred at the Glenn Dale Station of the Department of Agriculture by B. Y. Morrison, former director of the arboretum. Other plantings include the fine collection of Ghent and Mollis hybrid azaleas, a gift from the Netherlands.

The plantings in the arboretum are arranged in varied patterns. The idea is to establish the collections in such a manner as to make an attractive landscape scene and at the same time contribute to the educational value of the arboretum. An interesting feature is the "synoptic" garden. This thirty-acre garden, when complete, will present in miniature the plant groupings in the arboretum. For technical reference, a herbarium with a collection of 470,000 dried plants is maintained. It is of world significance because of its large collection of economically important plants. The directors think of the arboretum as eventually becoming an institution which, in the field of living plants, will be a counterpart of the Smithsonian.

The arboretum offers an ideal opportunity for public-spirited groups to participate in a national project, and many are taking part in it. The Woman's National Farm and Garden Association, Inc., is establishing a dogwood planting on a long-term basis. It is estimated that some sixty-eight forms of dogwood could be grown in this area, and the plan is to include them all. To date about thirty-four varieties have been planted. The dogwood collection is a memorial to Mrs. Francis King, former president and one of the association's founders. It is laid out on a small plateau of about eight acres, in a semi-formal pattern designed by Mr. Morrison.

The New Castle Sanctuary

Like other modern museums, the American Museum of Natural History in New York features show-case scenes of our countryside and woodlands, with wildlife in its natural habitat. Every year thousands of school children make a tour of these sections. A group may be seen there almost any time, gazing wide-eyed at a butterfly resting in a mass of Joe-pye-weed, a blue jay perched on the limb of a birch tree, or a red fox half-hidden in the sumac.

To many New York children, looking at Joe-pye-weed through a piece of glass is about as much of him as they will ever know. To an extent this cannot be helped, but none of us would want the day to come when it would be true for all children. These exhibits are a fine way for them to learn more about nature, but they can never be a substitute for the feel of the woods and open country. Picking violets in the spring should be a part of every little girl's life, and discovering on his own the ways of birds and woodland animals should be every boy's right. Yet our countryside is vanishing so fast that, unless we do something about it, fewer and fewer children will have these experiences as part of their heritage.

In order to counteract such a loss, many far-sighted groups are establishing sanctuaries near their communities. A good example is the project of the garden club of Chappaqua, New York. These women wanted to combine a conservation project with their nature study program and found exactly what they were looking for in a sanctuary. It was a piece of swampland owned by the Town of New Castle which, from a commercial viewpoint, was idle land. As a sanctuary it would serve as a place to study nature, preserve a bit of the countryside in its natural state, and provide a bird habitat. But this was not all; in saving the swamp they would be helping to maintain the water table. They asked the town to turn it over to them and the request was granted. Then a prominent real estate developer, learning their purpose, gave them several acres of adjoining land, making a total area of thirty acres.

Doing all the work themselves, members of this small group cut their way through a jungle of weeds, underbrush, and fallen trees to make a trail through the woods and across a little stream shaded by willows. They laid a bridge of steppingstones across the stream, cleared other trails, and made a firebreak. Then they planted shrubs and small trees that yield the berries and fruits birds like. Several open areas were created for bird watching and plant study, and all plants, shrubs, and trees along the trails were labeled. School children, teachers, youth groups, and youth leaders were invited to share this little nugget of nature, as well as the townspeople. The children find the sanctuary an enchanting place and every winter make shelters for the birds and put up suet logs. In the spring they help plant more berried shrubs. This is strictly a sanctuary for birds and small animals, a place for nature and conservation study. There are no recreational facilities and hunting is not permitted.

The sanctuary was begun in 1951 as the idea of Mrs. John Pichetto. Later the work was carried forward by Mrs. Murray MacDonald. Mrs. MacDonald has created an active interest in countryside protection thoughout the area where she lives. She conducts nature classes and tours in the sanctuary, has an extensive wildflower garden of her own that attracts many visitors, and has for several years created arresting conservation exhibits at local, district, and state flower shows.

Kentwood Sanctuary

Almost every community has idle land, either privately or town owned, which can be made into a sanctuary. Often there is isolated land, not suitable for other purposes, which the town or private owner will gladly contribute for the purpose. In Kentwood, Louisiana, a former resident owned ten acres of high, creek, and semi-swampland on the outskirts of the town. On one side it was bounded by an old highway, on the other by a railroad. Because of its location it had become an unofficial dumping ground. When members of the local garden club approached him about the possibility of clearing it and using it for nature study, he gave them the land outright.

This too is a small club, but with the help of Boy Scouts, husbands, and others, the rubbish was cleared. An acre was made into a roadside park, another area into a community picnic ground, and the rest became a wildlife sanctuary with trails and added native shrubbery. The club raised the money for the picnic equipment and shrubbery through donations and cake sales. Mrs. Gurley Mixon, who super-intended the project, describes the former dumping grounds as it looks today: "In the background is a winding streamlet banked with wild azaleas, overhanging yellow jasmine, and gleaming smilax vines. Magnolias, flanked by sweet bays with their silver-backed leaves, grow in abundance. Beech and crimson maples intermingle with lordly pines. Hickory, poplar, and many varieties of oak overhung with silvery moss give a lacy appearance. Underneath flourish the snowy dogwoods. Trails of redbuds, crabapples, catalpa, and haws light up the land-scape. Lower down are banks of mallows—white, pink, and rosy red —that blend with beds of Louisiana iris of rainbow hues."

The Loda Lake Sanctuary

This sanctuary, named for an Indian princess, is a seventy-two acre tract in Manistee National Forest, located in northwestern Michigan. It was established as a project of the garden clubs throughout the state in conjunction with the Forest Service. The purpose in creating it was to save the plants that were there and to add more, so future generations would have some idea of how the original forests in that area looked. The tract consists of sandy soil that was originally covered with pine, some marshy ground, some that is quite arid—almost any kind of soil one could imagine—and a small lake. It had been part of a 1,000 acre estate owned by a Chicago family, and the ruins of old buildings were still there when the Forest Service purchased the land.

The project was actually begun in 1940, when the Forest Service invited the Michigan clubs to participate in establishing the sanctuary. Because of the war, it was delayed for several years. It is a continuing, long-range project of the clubs which will require several years. Trails have been laid out, native shrubs planted, and a complete survey of the flora has been made by a botanist. Maps of the trails and the approaches were distributed to all clubs in the state. Although the Forest Service provides maintenance and helps with the heavy work, no state or federal funds are used for the project. The necessary money is raised by the garden clubs and all plants are contributed by them.

An Arizona Area

The Alpine Garden Club of Flagstaff, Arizona, has also sponsored a sanctuary in connection with the Forest Service, at Mount Elden.

This 1,100-acre area has a permanent spring, an extremely important feature in this dry country, and an abundance of food for the birds. The club has cleared a trail along the foot of the mountain and set up permanent labels for plants and trees, giving the scientific name, the common name, and interesting facts about them. Mount Elden is covered with such trees as ponderosa pine, Colorado pinyon, Rocky Mountain juniper, mountain mahogany and cliff rose, small shrubs, and a wealth of wildflowers.

Bowman's Hill Wildflower Preserve

In the hills where Washington and his half-frozen men camped before the Battle of Trenton, there is now a 100-acre sanctuary. Sponsored by conservation-wise individuals, groups, and organizations in Pennsylvania, it is a living memorial to the men who crossed the Delaware on Christmas night, 1776. The project has won numerous awards, and is a model for similar preserves in several other states. It was a gift to the people of Pennsylvania from its sponsors, and was made an integral part of Washington Crossing Park through legislative action by the Commonwealth of Pennsylvania.

The Bowman's Hill Wildflower Preserve is not confined to flora indigenous to this section. The purpose in creating it was to gather together in one area as many as possible of the flowers, ferns, shrubs, and trees native to Pennsylvania, by simulating their natural haunts. This has been achieved; more than 800 species of native plants from all parts of the state are now well established along the trails. A drift of foamflower from the mountains, a clump of sweetbays from the swamps, and a colony of walking-fern from the forests are neighbors here, growing happily as in their own habitats. Delightful and informative as this may be for the visitor, it was a complicated and often perplexing task for those who accomplished it, since this was an uncharted field of horticulture. It involved miles of travel to collect the plants, many discussions as to their identity and care, and years of trial-and-error effort to establish them in their new home. However, it has proved that most wild plants, with care and diligence, can be transplanted and will adopt a new location if their requirements are met. It is the opinion of the committee in charge of this project that many of these plants may some day be rare specimens if the countryside continues to be destroyed at its present rate.

The preserve has twelve nature trails, two sphagnum bogs, a pond, and a fifteen-acre tract known as Penn's Woods, which is devoted exclusively to tribute trees, and other special plantings. There are, for instance, azalea, bluebell, evergreen, fern, gentian, laurel, marsh marigold, and medicinal plant trails. Another, the Mary K. Parry Trail, was planned for school children and young botanists, and is planted with common wildflowers, all neatly identified.

This nationally known project grew out of an "over the back fence" conversation. One day in 1933 Mrs. Henry Parry, then chairman of conservation for the Bucks County Federation of Women's Clubs, was planting daffodils along the old mill race when W. Wilson Heinitsh, who was doing special work for the Department of Forests and Waters, happened to pass by. They got to talking about how beautiful the wooded area was along the stream below the Memorial Tower, and what a pity it would be if it were destroyed. Soon they were discussing different ways of saving it. Finally, a sanctuary was suggested. Mrs. Parry suggested that Mr. Heinitsh call on Mrs. Clarence C. Zantzinger, the new president of the Council for the Preservation of Natural Beauty in Pennsylvania. He did, and Mrs. Zantzinger thought the idea excellent. She brought the matter up at the next meeting of the Council, and a proposal to sponsor such a sanctuary was voted on and approved. Attending this meeting was Mrs. Alan Reed, who represented the Garden Club Federation of Pennsylvania. She presented the sanctuary idea to the federation at its next meeting, and a similar proposal was made, voted on, and approved. Meanwhile Mr. Heinitsh had obtained the endorsement of the Washington Crossing Park Commission. By October 1934 the sanctuary was well on its way.

In 1950 the Park Commission, in cooperation with the Department of Forests and Waters, published a comprehensive catalogue of the plants in the preserve. Listed are more than 1,000 different kinds of plants, identified by Dr. Edgar T. Wherry of the University of Pennsylvania, who is actively interested in the sanctuary.

The Theodore Roosevelt Sanctuary

A twelve-acre bird sanctuary, Trailside Museum and Memorial Fountain in Oyster Bay, Long Island, New York, is dedicated to Theodore Roosevelt, a great conservationist. It is situated near Sagamore Hill, the Roosevelt home, and it was in this area that Theodore Roosevelt frequently walked and observed nature during his youth and through his mature years. It is here that he is buried.

The sanctuary features plants and animals characteristic of this part of Long Island and provides a year-round food supply, nesting sites, and cover for wildlife. Since 1935, when observation was established, 133 species of birds have been found there. This sanctuary is of more than ordinary significance in view of its importance to migratory birds as part of the Atlantic Flyway, and the tremendous loss of such areas on Long Island. It is administered by the National Audubon Society.

Hawk Mountain Sanctuary

Eagles within a hundred miles of the Empire State Building? That isn't possible. But it is true nevertheless.

Near Hamburg in eastern Pennsylvania, about a hundred miles from New York City, a whole mountaintop has been set aside as a migratory refuge for birds of prey, such as the broad-winged, red-tailed and red-shouldered hawk; the goshawk, rare gyrfalcon, peregrine falcon, osprey, golden eagle, and the powerful bald eagle, our national emblem. During the migrating season, from mid-September through early November, these "lords of the air" soar over this mountaintop in a "pageant of the sky" so breathtaking that many naturalists consider it one of the most dramatic shows on earth. Thousands of people come to see it every year. Perched atop a rocky promontory, a thousand feet above the valley and overlooking six counties, they sit spellbound as they study our amazing birds and witness "the mystery, the eternal wonder of migration."

The "Lookout" is such that, unless the birds are flying unusually high, the spectators may see them fairly close, look down upon them, or even see them at eye level. It may be one large flock after another of small, chunkily built broad-wings, pouring over the mountain ridge in a steady thirty-miles-an-hour procession as they fly south. Or it may be a magnificent pair of bald eagles, mated for life, gliding into the distance, their wingspread a good seven feet. Or perhaps it is a golden eagle, circling effortlessly high overhead, then dropping down obligingly close as it sweeps out over the valley with the sun shining on its powerful, broad-winged body and golden head. Then again, it might be a raven, doing aerial acrobatics with wing-overs, dives, and tumbles —apparently just for the fun of it—or engaging in mock combat with some other large bird and out-maneuvering him on every count. It could be a dizzy, zig-zagging chase through the treetops between a sharp-shinned hawk and a flicker, an often repeated drama in a sanctuary such as this. Or a huge osprey, materializing out of nowhere with a plaintive, shrill whistle, a fish clamped in its talons.

Perhaps they are listening to the cackling defiance of a goshawk as it fights off an enemy, the fearless courage of this spirited bird thrilling them as it once did medieval hawkers who trained it to fly from the wrist at flushed game. On the other hand, their eyes may be riveted upon the torpedo-like peregrine as it makes a spectacular 200-mile-an-hour power dive, plucking its victim from the air in a stroke. But then, it could be that memorable moment when a big, white gyrfalcon is making one of its rare appearances, flying low and leisurely with a slow, powerful, short wingbeat. As if aware of its breathless audience, it stops suddenly and hovers for a few seconds, or swoops and plunges at passing sharp-shins and red-tails before it passes majestically out of sight, amid a spontaneous burst of applause. If the season is late and there is a strong northerly wind, it may be the big day for red-tails—thick, heavy, short-tailed hawks. Well over a thousand have been known to pass along this mountain ridge in one day, coming singly, in groups of twenty or thirty, or in caravans of forty or more. Most hawk species take this ridge in absolute silence. But not so the red-tails. They advertise their coming with a characteristic squealing whistle, repaying observers at the height of migration with a day-long procession.

There are, however, other birds besides Raptores that follow this flyway. The curator of the sanctuary, Maurice Broun, quotes from his records of a day in late October "when red-tails were the order of the day," such extras going over as "1,300 crows, eighty-five bluebirds, 125 purple finches, hundreds of goldfinches, twenty-five pine siskins, 800 rusty blackbirds, 500 grackles, 200 red-wings, one wild turkey, thirty-six loons, seventy-five Canada geese, one Hutchin's goose, twelve herring gulls, and three ring-billed gulls." On the same day there were two bald eagles and nine golden eagles. He also tells of days when "thousands of warblers were in the sky," when wedge after wedge of white whistling swans passed by, calling as they went, and of humming birds "in bullet-like passage," zipping within inches of observers in this "school in the clouds." He speaks of one occasion when 12,000 broad-wings passed through during the day, with well over 7,000 passing in a single hour; of a red-letter day when countless thousands of blue jays passed along the mountain ridge in one of the most colorful migrations he has ever seen, and of 500 evening grosbeaks being in the air at one time. With binoculars and telescopes ready, competition is always keen among the observers to see who can first correctly identify the oncoming birds as they appear like specks over the knobs of the ridge.

People from all walks of life come to see these flights—ornithologists, physicians, truck drivers, artists, clergymen, housewives, admirals, and factory workers. They come from all parts of the United States and from other countries—Canada, Great Britain, Mexico, Venezuela, France, and Japan. A Japanese, on his honeymoon, hurried to the sanctuary with his bride as soon as they had cleared customs, taking a taxi all the way from New York. More than anything else in the United States, they wanted to see this unique refuge for birds of prey and to witness a hawk migration. The sanctuary has always been popular with children; about three-fifths of the adults who visit it are men.

And yet, not long ago, these splendid birds were killed by the thousands every year on this same mountaintop in what naturalists describe as "a senseless and appalling slaughter."

Predators are among the least understood and most maligned of nature's creatures. Only in the past few years have we begun to realize that they too are a necessary link in nature's chain, helping to maintain a proper balance between population and food supply. For many years the attitude toward all predators was somewhat the same as that once taken toward our forests—"the best thing to do with them is to get rid of them." And there are numerous instances where man has killed off predators only to find that it was to his own detriment. For instance, a bounty was placed some years ago on the puma, known in various regions as cougar, mountain lion, catamount, and panther. The puma preys on deer. So many were killed in the Kaibab National Forest of Arizona that the deer population multiplied far beyond the capacity of the forest to support it. As a consequence the deer depleted their food supply and seriously damaged the forest by over-browsing.

Many starved and others had to be destroyed to restore a working balance between the deer and their environment. Another example is that of Swainson's hawk, which feeds on grasshoppers, crickets, and rodents. So many of these hawks were killed in the West that many areas were plagued with grasshoppers and millions of dollars worth of crops were damaged.

"If all birds of prey, all predators, mammals, reptiles, and fishes were destroyed overnight," the Conservation Foundation states, "the long-range effects might be even more disastrous for the American people than if a number of hydrogen bombs were dropped on Chicago and New York."

Blue Mountain, of which "Hawk Mountain" is a part, is a long, continuous ridge. In their southward journey, the birds ride the ascending air currents, thus flying with minimum effort. The topography of the ridge is such that at the point where the sanctuary is now located there is something of a bottleneck. The razor-back ridge ends abruptly and its wooded slopes merge into a broad cross-ridge which zigzags southward. In order to gain altitude the birds often circle or mill about at this point. That is why the lookout affords such a wonderful opportunity for observation and study. But for many years before the sanctuary was established in 1934, it offered the same opportunity for irresponsible gunners who shot the birds merely for the sake of killing or from mistaken prejudice against hawks. The majority of these men were not true sportsmen—the type of man who is fair and, more often than not, a good conservationist. The birds were shot down indiscriminately by the thousands, with many wounded and left to suffer for days. Cruel practices too were not uncommon—such as tying a wounded hawk to a log, then jabbing it to make it scream and attract other birds within gunshot range. Protected birds, such as the osprey and the bald eagle, and song birds were often shot along with the others.

Sickened by what was happening, two conservationists—Richard H. Pough and Henry H. Collins, Jr.—took pictures of a week-end slaughter and sent them, along with articles of protest, to newspapers and nature magazines. The articles aroused shocked indignation among nature lovers, particularly those who knew the true value of these birds. One such person was a young naturalist in Boston, Maurice Broun, who was making a special study of hawks. Another was

Mrs. Charles Noel Edge, chairman of the Emergency Conservation Committee in New York, which works for the protection of wildlife. On an impulse, Mrs. Edge phoned the two elderly brothers who owned this land and succeeded in leasing the entire mountain top, with an option to buy it. Then she sent an S.O.S. to Mr. Broun, asking if he and his bride would consider spending a few weeks there during the migrating season, keeping hunters away—a rather stiff assignment, she admitted. Unhesitatingly, the Brouns accepted the challenge, insisting that it be "on their own," and hastened to what is now Hawk Mountain Sanctuary.

Persons of less courage would have been intimidated by the belligerent threats of gunners deprived of their favorite "sport" and the derisive attitude taken toward them as hawk lovers. But the Brouns held their ground, returning the next season and for several succeeding seasons. Meanwhile, Mrs. Edge had raised the money to buy the land and fulfill her dream of having the Brouns take up permanent residence on the 1,400 acres which comprise the sanctuary. When Mr. Broun returned from the service after World War II, he and Mrs. Broun moved in and they have been there ever since.

Hawk Mountain Sanctuary Association, a voluntary non-profit organization, is composed of less than 3,000 members. Yet it supports the sanctuary and carries on an extensive educational campaign in the interest of hawks and other birds of prey. It has succeeded in getting laws passed in the northeastern part of Pennsylvania which protect hawks during autumn migration so that they will not be killed after they pass beyond the sanctuary, and is working for the same protection throughout the state. Roger Tory Peterson, famed ornithologist, says of the epic of Hawk Mountain: "Like the drama of the egrets, it is one of the great heart-warming stories of bird conservation."

When the sanctuary celebrated its twentieth anniversary in 1954, Mrs. Edge received congratulations from well-wishers everywhere, including President Eisenhower, Jean-Paul Harroy, Secretary General of the International Union for Conservation of Nature and Natural Resources, and Naotake Sato, president of the National Parks Association of Japan. But perhaps the greatest tribute to her work is epitomized in a recent letter from a Boy Scout. In one of the "Lassie" television shows an uninformed writer had a red-tailed hawk put to death because it was a "hen hawk," although this bird is by nature a destroyer of rodents and not a poultry killer. By implication, all hawks were condemned, undoing years of hard educational work by the association in one brief half-hour. Letters of protest poured in to the sponsor of the program, most of them from children who considered the incident a tragedy. The association also received many letters, asking them to please do something about it. Among them was this letter from Stephen Cribben, aged thirteen, a Boy Scout in Weston, Massachusetts:

Many people think hawks and owls love to kill and devour chickens. They don't. Once in a while when food is scarce, they will. But not very often. The sharp-shinned, cooper's and goshawk, also the great horned owl, will do this on occasion. But that is the nature of these birds. Surely we could overlook this, for every year thousands upon thousands of harmful insects and rodents are taken by these birds of prey. Mice, rats, gophers, and rabbits are among the many that are killed. When a hawk is seen near a farmyard he is usually looking for rats and mice, not chickens. If these rodents were not killed by birds of prey, they would soon overpopulate. So please try to explain to others how helpful these birds are."

The sponsor had the matter investigated, and acknowledged its mistake.

CHAPTER V

COMMUNITY PLANNING

Gertrude Stein wrote of this country a few years ago: "In the United States there is more space where nobody is than where anybody is. . . . That's what makes America what it is."

This is indeed an interesting observation and one over which we could ponder at length, for certainly our "wide open spaces" have much to do with the kind of nation the United States is, and the kind of people we are. But while there is still plenty of space, many communities are bursting at the seams and many more are steadily approaching that precarious condition, particularly in the areas surrounding our large cities. The so-called "surge of suburbia" is one of today's most insistent problems. In any number of communities which certainly did not expect it, the population has doubled, tripled, and even quadrupled since World War II. And with the trend toward younger marriages, larger families, and houses rather than apartments, most communities probably will feel the effect of our expanding population.

Most of our cities grew haphazardly and the results in most cases have not been too satisfying, either from the standpoint of beauty or convenience. Add to this, mass-produced unrestricted housing on the remaining open land, usually by large-scale developers who have no real interest in the community, and the result is likely to be bulldozed trees, invaded privacy, crowded schools, higher taxes, lowered property values, and the mutual disappointment of newcomer and established resident. The seeds of blight are sown before the paint is dry on the new houses and the community slips into ugliness and a desperate race with the slums. On the other hand this same growth, if planned, can add to the beauty, character, and individuality of the community, protecting the value of old homes and providing for the new ones a landscaped setting which otherwise would take years to accomplish. The cost of new schools, sewers, roads, and public buildings can be apportioned as the community expands, rather than handled as a series of costly emergencies. With directed expansion, facilities can be located more conveniently, saving time and money. A community that has planned its future, that has planned what it will be like five years from now, ten years from now, attracts people with a future and industry with a future. In so doing, it provides jobs for its young people instead of forcing them to seek employment elsewhere. Most important of all, it brings a sense of civic pride, security, and well-being to its residents.

Planning is just as beneficial to the community that has no expansion problem. We are all aware that our cars depreciate, that our homes must be brought up to date periodically, that timely repairs and improvements are essential in the care of all our belongings. But we are inclined to go along from year to year without noticing that the community is getting shabbier, more inconvenient, urgently in need of improvements. Then one day we are jolted out of our complacency by an emergency, which probably means high expenditures and a sharp tax increase. And the tragic point is that we shall have to spend more than is necessary and may still not have the kind of community we want.

One of the most important factors in community planning, and the one most often overlooked is the wise use of open land. There was a day when there were endless acres of fertile land just for the taking, but this is no longer true. We have no fertile land to spare today, yet approximately a million acres of productive farmland are being diverted each year to such uses as suburban homes, highways, airports, and factories. If we are to keep the way of life that has made us what we are, we shall have to make better use of our land through planning.

Planning Commissions and Master Plans

Some communities have tried to protect themselves through stringent zoning, requiring new houses to have a specified amount of land. In general, however, either the Planning Commission or the Master

Plan seems to have worked out better. Where the two have been combined the results have often been unusually satisfactory.

Yorktown's Master Plan

Yorktown, New York, where the population more than doubled between 1950 and 1956, provides a good example. In 1950 it was a small rural community with large dairy and fruit farms, several large estates, and four small business areas. But it had good road and rail connections, an excellent municipal water supply, and many open and wooded areas. It attracted housing developers who began to buy the open land.

The community had a planning commission, but the problems encountered with the first subdivision brought sharply to its attention the need for revisions in the land division regulations and the zoning ordinance. Also, the spectacular increase in the subdivision plans filed with the commission brought even more sharply to its attention the need for a comprehensive town development plan if the community was to keep its character. The commission felt that such a plan involved so many factors that experts should be employed. The comparatively small cost of such advice, they were convinced, would be more than offset by the millions of dollars saved later and the mistakes that might otherwise be made in trying to cope single-handed with too rapid growth. Professional planners were called in.

The planners first made a thorough study of the community, taking into consideration the type of people who lived there, its past, present, and possible future growth, its general character; economic factors such as commuting, trade, and manufacturing; the trend of development in various sections and the desirable objectives of future development. Study maps were made, showing present land use, topography, drainage, population, zoning, land suitable for development, special districts, and the present road system.

A series of community meetings were then held, in which town officials and townspeople expressed their opinions as to the type and size of town they wished to have. These ideas were noted and later studied by the planners and town officials. A new set of subdivision regulations was drawn up and a new zoning ordinance drafted. Subdivision requests were reviewed and housing developments planned. Then a long-range master plan was worked out, incorporating all of these factors, together with a financing program. This plan was presented to the people in another series of meetings. Again comments were recorded. Changes and additions were made in line with major desires expressed at these meetings, until a plan was found that was acceptable to the majority of the townspeople. It was finally approved and adopted August 10, 1956.

The plan provided for enlargement of the central business area, for outlying shopping centers, future industry, future school sites, recreational areas, playgrounds, regulation of the size of residence lots, fire protection and water supply, flood control, and maximum growth. In carrying it out there has been close cooperation among the Planning Commission, the Town Board, and the Board of Appeals.

The Yorktown Master Plan has been so successful that it has become the model for communities throughout the country. Just recently, Supervisor John H. Downing sent out more than 200 copies of his report, "How We Use Our Master Plan," to other communities. Not only that, Yorktown is attracting the kind of industry its people want.

How De Soto Planned Its Future Growth

De Soto, Missouri, is a community of less than 5,000 people. Its problem was exactly opposite to that of Yorktown. It was attracting no outsiders and losing its young people at the rate of about 30 per cent a year. The community seemed lacking in civic pride; there had been no major improvements for years, and it offered its youth little opportunity. As one townsman said: "We were faced with a mathematical certainty of doom unless something dramatic was done to reverse the trend."

The "something dramatic" turned out to be the winning of a community improvement contest by the high school students. The students, after four months of work, submitted a report showing the strength and weaknesses of their town, its assets and liabilities, together with recommendations as to what should be done. They won first prize of $750 over reports submitted by twenty-seven Missouri schools.

The students' report woke the town up. An adult group was formed, representing all organizations in the community, some seventy-nine in all—from bridge clubs to labor unions. This group was subdivided into five major committees and three organizational groups. Each committee invited a teenager to participate. Then a "Planned Progress Program" was developed.

The most difficult problem the group faced was apathy. Before anything could be done, the townspeople had to be shown that they could work together and pull their community up by its bootstraps. Since that year, 1953, was the 150th anniversary of De Soto, the group decided to have a sesqui-centennial celebration with as many people as possible participating. A pageant was planned with 450 in the cast, all amateurs and volunteers. Others were included on committees and building crews and as solicitors or souvenir salesmen. Still others toured the countryside in old-time costumes for weeks in advance of the event, advertising the celebration.

The affair was a tremendous success. While the program was not planned to raise money, it netted $3,500, which was used for community improvements. More important, it created civic pride and, as the group had hoped, showed the townspeople what they could accomplish by working together. The Planned Progress Program in De Soto is now well underway. There is a full-time maintenance man who cares for the grass and shrubbery in the parks and around public buildings, a new fire house, and a Little League Baseball Club. Parking facilities in the business section have been improved, a street-lighting system installed, and the streets have been paved or blacktopped. These are only a few of the improvements. Business houses have been remodeled and new businesses have come into the community. Oddly enough, the improvements, instead of increasing taxes, have resulted in a 30 per cent reduction. The citizens themselves have pitched in and done most of the work, even to blacktopping eighty blocks of streets. Through other savings, increased business, a better understanding of town problems by the citizens, the community is more economically managed. Today its young people are happy to stay home and raise their families in De Soto.

How Abbeville Got Its Planning Commission

Community apathy and stagnation, which usually go hand in hand, are frequently as much of a problem as the threat of over-crowding. Civic groups are likely to find this combination more of a stumbling block than almost any other community problem, since there is no emergency or threat demanding action. However, there is always some way of arousing a community.

Abbeville, Alabama, was a "good town," but many of its citizens felt that it had not progressed with the passing years. Still, it went along from year to year without much being done about it. As is so often the case, all that it needed was for some group to take the lead. In this case it was the Matrons' Club—membership twenty-five.

After much discussion, the club decided that one of the main reasons why major improvements had not been made was the lack of coordinated effort and an over-all program. Other groups had tried to get things done but, working alone, were limited in what they could accomplish. There was indecision regarding projects and an overlapping of endeavor, since no central committee existed which could appraise the town's problems and work out a plan for action. The Matrons' Club decided that Abbeville needed a planning commission.

These women were aware that, while some of the other civic organizations might be willing to support such a project, arousing the interest of the whole community would be a problem. If they were to succeed, they must map their strategy carefully. They chose as their club project for that winter (1954-55) "Community Enthusiasm"— a working title used only among themselves. To the public the project appeared as a question: "What does our community need and what can we do about it?" The bi-monthly club meetings pivoted around this theme. Many of these meetings were held in the evening with the public invited. Capable speakers addressed these sessions and discussion followed. Each meeting was given full coverage by a cooperative, progressive newspaper, which staunchly supported the club. Thus the Matrons' Club planted the idea in the minds of the people and let it grow until the whole town was talking. Finally it arranged for a general meeting of community representatives at the City Hall, inviting all volunteer organizations as well as members of the city and county governments to participate. At this meeting the organization of a central planning council was discussed. By the time the evening was over, the Abbeville Planning Commission had been formed, with one of the town's leading citizens as chairman.

Having gained its primary objective, the Matrons' Club stepped aside, content to be just one of the nineteen voluntary groups serving

on the "Pan Council," as it was now called, together with representatives of official agencies. The first step of the Council was to
pinpoint the immediate needs of the community and work out a long-
term program for the others. Five areas of action emerged: civic, cultural, recreational, economic, and educational. Each organization and
agency was assigned definite responsibilities for specific improvements,
according to its preferences and capabilities. As a result of this teamwork, the community has had a rebirth, is planning its future growth
and development, and has found a unity and strength it never knew
before. *And things are getting done.* Gas lines were run in, twenty-six
miles of rural telephones strung, over-due paving laid, water lines installed, a zoning ordinance passed, and a mile-long airstrip laid. As for
the Matrons' Club, its project was considered a typical demonstration
of citizen leadership. As such it won a top prize in the "Community
Achievement Contest" of the General Federation of Women's Clubs
for 1956.

A Master Plan to Save Vanishing Farmlands

While lack of progress is still a problem in many communities, most
of them, like Yorktown, are facing the problem of overwhelming
growth. In many cases such growth has serious consequences not only
to the community but to the entire country. In certain sections of
California, to cite an example among hundreds, the most fertile farmlands are being swallowed by housing developments at such a staggering rate that a San Francisco newspaper featured a series of articles
about it which resulted in a state law to help protect this fundamental
resource. This rich agricultural land which is succumbing to the "ten-
tacles of steel and stucco," as the *San Francisco Examiner* expresses
it, is the source of our food—truck farms, dairy farms, orchards, fields,
and vineyards. The articles were not written to indict developers but
to arouse the people to the need for planning the best use of the land.
One farmer, whom the newspaper quoted, said, in speaking of the
necessity to hold on to our good farmland: "The soil is the basis of
existence. Destroy California's farms, one by one, dozens by dozens,
hundreds by hundreds—take away the best land—and some day you'll
have no farms."

For this farmer's words substitute United States for California and
the picture comes into sharper focus. Most of us have seen only frag-

ments of the picture. When the fragments are fitted together, the result is sobering. For this indeed is happening all over the United States to our countryside, woodlands, and farms. We are losing each year approximately a million acres of productive farmland to housing developments and other non-agricultural purposes. No family should be denied the right to a home, nor would anyone want to deny it to them. The very fact that our young people are seeking homes instead of apartments, as in the thirties, is a healthy sign. But there is no need to destroy the beauty of the country, its security, and the source of our sustenance in filling either need. There is still plenty of room, but the land should be used properly. That is a matter of planning, which is to the interest of developers as well as communities. *We don't need rich farmland for asphalt pavements.*

Will Stevens' graphic articles in 1955 showed Californians the picture on a state-wide scale, adding up the lost acres county by county. "With subdivisions being created anywhere and everywhere in California, willy-nilly," he protested, "the good earth—the same good earth that made California great—is slowly ceasing to exist." He then gave examples of how matters could be handled through the intelligent use of a master plan, giving Napa County as a classic illustration. Certain areas in Napa, zoned for agriculture and grazing, are protected from further encroachment by industry and housing and left unhampered for farming. The zoning order also protects the underground water supply from pollution and eliminates other conflicts between community and farming needs. The same zoning makes newcomers welcome by providing homes in areas designed for community living, creating harmony instead of hodgepodge. Urging every county to evaluate its position in relation to current trends, Stevens quoted from Karl Belser, planning director of Santa Clara County: "Soils are a fundamental resource. The concurrence of soils, climate, water, and other factors producing ideal conditions for agriculture is a rare phenomenon. When it is destroyed by improper utilization, the entire social complex is irreparably harmed."

In ten years (1945-1955), California lost 400,000 acres of farmland in this way. As Mr. Stevens said, "Every year for a decade an area of sixty-two square miles—approximately a San Francisco and a half—has replaced much of the richest farmland in California."

The situation in California was aggravated by what Mr. Stevens referred to as "something called the 'uninhabited land' law" under which a city could annex any such land provided there were no more than twelve persons residing within it. As city populations swelled and spread farther and farther into the farming areas, many sought to protect themselves through this law, which left the farmers virtually helpless. All the city had to do was pass an ordinance that certain "uninhabited" land was "annexed" to the city, whether the farmer liked it or not. Farmers who sold to real estate developers got fabulous prices for their land. Those who wanted to keep their farms found themselves "residents" of the city and their land taxable as such, even though they were still farming.

In each case a city was perhaps taking only a small bite of farmland compared to the total area of such land in California. What no one realized, of course, was how many bites had been taken until Mr. Stevens added it up for them. Nor did they realize how the continuance of such a trend could imperil the future of everyone—even the cities themselves, which are dependent upon the farmers.

This series of articles brought a flood of requests for reprints from counties all over the state. As the result of an aroused public a bill was passed and signed by the governor on July 6, 1955, which states: "Any territory which is, by the consent of the owners, zoned and restricted for agricultural purposes exclusively, pursuant to a master plan for land use in any county, shall not, while it is so zoned, be annexed to a city . . . without the consent of the owners."

Many counties in California now have master plans, and others are in the process of working them out, with "green belts"—voluntarily zoned agricultural areas—becoming more and more common. The development of such plans takes time, because many factors must be considered, but the necessary work can often be done by citizens and civic groups on a voluntary basis. For example, it was necessary to incorporate five villages in Alameda County as the City of Fremont, in order to work out a master plan for that area. A planning commission was formed, with an accompanying board of appeals. Then a careful study was made of the area and a preliminary plan worked out. This does not cover the entire county, but does include great stretches of fine farmland which will be protected. After public hearings have been held and necessary changes made, a permanent master plan will be made, with proper zoning. All this, which has required many months, was accomplished through citizen leadership, with the active support of voluntary groups.

The Community Ecologist

Good land use is a complex problem. As the preceding project demonstrates, an undertaking designed to meet the needs of one group may work unexpected hardship upon another and actually become a detriment to the whole community. All too often the harm is discovered too late. This usually results from a failure to evaluate properly the long-time effects of policies, projects, and enterprises from an ecological point of view—the interrelationships of man and his environment. As a solution, scientist F. R. Fosberg of Falls Church, Virginia, suggests the "community ecologist," a man with a special type of background who would act as consultant to the planning commission.

"The community ecologist is, so far as I am aware, a phenomenon that does not yet exist," Dr. Fosberg says. "However, it is clear that there is a place and a need for an official in a community government whose function is to foresee the ecological consequences of projects and activities sponsored or sanctioned by the community."

There are hundreds of instances where such a person's knowledge would have been invaluable in avoiding unforeseen detrimental consequences, but one example will illustrate Dr. Fosberg's point. "During the first quarter of this century," he says, "melon culture was a source of great prosperity in the Turlock Irrigation District in central California. The production of high-quality melons in that area depended upon a relatively high water table and 'sub-irrigation' or a capillary water supply from below. Demands from a small group of peach orchard interests caused the irrigation district authorities to install deep drainage pumps and ditches to lower the water table. This benefited the peach growers but forced the melon growers to surface-irrigate their melons. The quality of the melons then declined and melon raising dropped to the status of a relatively minor and not very profitable activity in the area, certainly not the aim of the authorities."

Training for such a position would include, in addition to courses in ecology, botany, zoology, and bacteriology, such subjects as chemistry, geology, soil science, agriculture, economics, and geography, along with two or more foreign languages. "An absolute essential would be a fluent and effective command of the English language to enable the ecologist to express his ideas in a clear and convincing manner," Dr. Fosberg insists. "In addition to academic training, demonstrated ability to work out a detailed problem in interrelationships would be equally a requisite."

The experienced man, accepting such a position, would have a comparable background. He would familiarize himself with every aspect of the community and develop an understanding of its interrelationships and functioning. His purpose would be to consider the proposals of the departments and agencies in terms of their effects on all aspects of community life, with his opinions a matter of public record. Thus the planning commission and the public alike could evaluate suggested projects more accurately.

Thus we have a community project looking for a sponsor. Public-spirited groups could share in such a program by providing scholarships to train such men or by sponsoring a qualified person in the community. They could promote the idea, volunteer to work with such an appointee, and possibly raise money for part of his salary on the condition that the community contributed the rest.

Visual Projects in Community Analysis

A Traveling Illustrated Lecture

Most of our cities are outdated in efficiency, and the problem of congestion is acute and complicated. They must either keep on sprawling and absorbing surrounding land or make better use of the land they have. The type of planning required cannot be done by any one person, group, or by the elected officials alone. It must be done with widespread citizen support and coordinated action. This is not simple, but neither is it impossible. Again, civic-minded groups can help.

A project along this line originated with *Life* magazine and is now being carried on by Action, the American Council to Improve Our Neighborhoods. It is a visual presentation called "Our Living Future," narrated by David Hardy, a sort of traveling show on a giant panoramic screen with black and white and color pictures, cartoons, and movies. In a dramatic and stimulating way it takes you across the country, showing you the beauty of America's cities from the "eagle's eye vantage point of a night pilot on the transcontinental airways." Then dawn breaks, the darkness lifts, and you are taken down into the cities to face the realities of slum and blight and the social evils they nourish. You see the complexities of city life: transportation, parking, zoning, the move to the suburbs, downtown congestion, schools, and the maze of metropolitan problems. Then you are shown how people across the country are mobilizing in a rebirth of community spirit. You are shown how "a city, any city, your city, can mobilize its people and its resources—and unite to build a better community for the future."

The *Life* presentation has been shown in communities throughout the country, and is followed up with practical help from Action. In its aims, Action might be compared to a giant paint brush swishing across the country, offering a "do it yourself—how to do it" program for communities. Working with public officials and responsible groups, this public service organization provides information and technical assistance to communities for improvement on a planned basis and helps them get started on long-term programs in a practical way. Its board of directors is composed of leaders from business, industry, labor, civic groups, government, and other fields.

Action's objective is to make the community itself a better place in which to live so that people will not be forced to move from the city in order to find suitable homes. Its program encompasses the conservation of basically good homes and neighborhoods, the rehabilitation of neighborhoods where buildings can be salvaged, and the clearance of slums. It is perhaps in the conservation of middle-aged homes and neighborhoods that Action makes its greatest contribution, preventing once fine homes and streets from becoming blighted. For, it reasons, when a neighborhood goes down, surrounding business houses, schools, parks, and other facilities go down with it and must be rebuilt elsewhere. These same homes and neighborhoods, if cared for properly and *in time*, could mellow with age, remain in keeping with community standards, and add to its charm and character. This, Action feels, is good community management and economy as well. It can be accomplished through a planned program of civic improvement, with which Action is prepared to help. In a number of instances the organization has conducted information centers for the townspeople in connection with these community programs. The centers are manned by volunteers, leading citizens who are specialists in fields relating to the home and can supply home owners with factual information concerning improvements.

Community Improvement in a Movie

Another interesting project of this nature is an inspiring twenty-seven minute film called "Your Community," presented as a public service by the General Federation of Women's Clubs and the Sears-Roebuck Foundation. It tells how active groups in seven communities solved typical community problems, ranging from swimming safety to a fight against blight. The film has been shown to civic groups in all parts of the country and, like Action, is responsible for many community programs.

Adult Recreation Areas

Communities have many problems but the matter of adequate recreational facilities is one of the most perplexing everywhere. For elected officials it is difficult because, due to unplanned and too rapid growth, there are few suitable places available in most communities and taxpayers are not always willing to assume the added expense. The projects which follow show how some communities have managed to establish recreational areas.

A Dilemma in Vacation Land

Many communities today are creating family recreational areas, rather than specialized ones which take members of the family in different directions. An instance is the project in Brattleboro, Vermont.

Although Vermont is famed as a vacation spot, the people in Brattleboro found themselves in the paradoxical position of having no community facilities for recreation. "Ours," said a member of the Woman's Club, "was a town starving in the midst of plenty." In all the community's lovely wooded sections, there was not one picnic spot equipped with a table or fireplace. To picnic a family had to drive five to twenty-five miles to crowded state parks. There is a picturesque river, but it was a dumping ground for upstream sewage. The chlorinating system made the water reasonably acceptable, but it invariably broke down on the hottest days, making swimming unpleasant. Ice skating in the winter and day camp activities in the summer were dependent upon the generosity of individual property owners. Yet this typical Vermont community is a beautiful place, its gabled white houses and tall church steeples in harmony with its dairy farms, its apple and maple sugar orchards, and its forest-clad hills.

The idea for a community recreational area originated with a fund in war bonds purchased during World War II with the idea of building a town swimming pool as a memorial to service men and women. When the bonds matured in 1955 it was impossible to build a pool for the amount on hand, $35,000. Trustees of the fund used the money to buy a fifty-three acre tract of land which they presented to the town, saying in effect: "You take it from there."

"The town did take it from there," Mrs. Ethel May, a club member, recalls, "a little doubtfully at first but before long with almost unanimous participation."

In one year the community created a play area with a recirculating swimming and wading pool large enough to accommodate seventy-two children, a pitch-and-putt golf course for iron shots, a large pond for fishing and sailing model boats in the summer and for skating in the winter. The park has a large picnic area with tables and fireplaces, a ski slope, baseball and softball diamonds, and courts for tennis, volleyball, and basketball. There are places for table tennis, shuffleboard, and horseshoes, as well as a playground and climbing forest for children, a concrete slab for roller skating and dancing, a camping site, and an outdoor theater with an auditorium which accommodates 2,500 people. In addition, there are several reforested areas for conservation purposes.

How did Brattleboro do it? A recreation board, appointed by the selectmen, had a Bennington firm draw plans for the area, complete with an estimate of the cost. Then each of the community's thirty civic organizations assumed responsibility for some part of the plan. The Rotary Club took the ski center, with one of its members assuming responsibility for the pond; the Exchange Club chose drainage of the ski tow; the Lions Club agreed to clear away the old buildings and build a park road; the Kiwanis took over the group picnic shelter; the Grange contributed four tables and built two fireplaces; and the Veterans of Foreign Wars, Red Men, and the Fraternal Order of Eagles, working as a unit, built sixteen tables and eight fireplaces. The landscaping was done by the garden club; the American Legion laid

out the softball diamond; the Woman's Evening Club gave lights for
the skating pond; and a lumber company contributed the outdoor
theater. The B. P. O. Elks, Masons, and other groups participated in
similar projects. Contributions also were made by individuals and
business firms. Units too large for groups to handle were financed by
the town.

Most of the physical labor was done by the men in the community,
with the women raising funds and doing the lighter work. Everyone
helped, including children and older people who did baby-sitting.

A Rural Play Area

Lowndesboro, Alabama, a rural community of forty families, also
has a family recreational area that would put to shame the facilities
of many towns of far greater size. The garden club, which has eleven
members, was the motivating force behind this project. In fact the
project was the reason for the club—there was no place for community
activity.

The women chose a site on a hillside, with a spring, and got the
town to lease the land. Then they went from house to house and collected $3,400, of which $1,500 was in cash and the rest in pledges. The
whole community worked to clear the land, with a local contractor
lending his machinery to level it. They made a double tennis court
and, with some outside help, a swimming pool. Picnic tables and
fireplaces, as well as other recreational facilities, came next. The landscaping is now being done and more facilities will be added gradually.
Meanwhile, the people in Lowndesboro are having fun. They did not
waste time discussing whether the community could afford a recreational area; they simply got together and created one.

Relaxation in the Desert

To communities fighting for elbow room, it might seem that there
would be no recreation problem in the western states with all those
wide open spaces. But the people in Glendale, Arizona, found themselves in somewhat the same position as the people in Brattleboro.
Arizona, one of our most scenic and colorful states, attracts tourists by
the thousands, but its very assets create a problem for residents.
Seventy-three per cent of the state's total land area is in federal ownership, consisting of grazing land, Indian reservations, and national

parks, monuments, and forests. The climate is dry with vast stretches of range and desert. Therefore it does not have the state parks and recreational facilities most states provide. While old mining towns, painted deserts, mesas, buttes, and canyons are interesting and often awe-inspiring, they are scarcely play and recreation areas.

In Glendale a community playground was claimed from a desert wasteland. It consists of nearly 1,000 acres, originally owned by the Federal Government, part of which is mountainous and part flat desert. When the members of the Woman's Club, who initiated the project, first went to work, they leased the land from the government. Later it was purchased.

To create interest, Mrs. Kenneth Cotts, chairman of the club's recreation park committee, offered a $25 savings bond to the boy or girl who suggested the best name for the proposed area. There were 1,900 entries in the contest and the winning name was "Thunderbird Park." A map of the area was submitted to each of the community's church, youth, and civic groups, and they were asked to give suggestions as to how the area could best be adapted to community recreation. High school students wrote a radio play about it which was broadcast. Members of the Dramatic Club addressed luncheons and meetings of various groups, telling how the recreational area would benefit the community, and asking for support. In the meantime, the newspaper supported the project with articles and editorials.

The men's service clubs responded quickly. This encouraged women's organizations to equal participation. As in Brattleboro, each group shouldered a special responsibility. The Woman's Club teamed with Rotary and contributed two ramadas, two barbecues, two game and picnic tables, and built a foot bridge across a ravine. The Lions Club developed a five-acre area for sports and gave a barbecue. The Carpenters Union and Farm Bureau built two rest rooms and contributed a steel ramada and a picnic table. The Fraternal Order of Police cleared an area for a target range, while the P. E. O. gave a fireplace and a picnic table. The Girl Scouts cleared a camping area, made a hiking trail, and supplied a flag pole. Four-H Clubbers made a trail to the mountain peak, the Boy Scouts built barbecue pits. And so it went. A cement slab for roller skating and square dancing was given by a private donor, the city built two and a half miles of dirt road and cleared eight acres for a playground. To launch the project the mayor proclaimed a "Thunderbird Park Work Week," and everybody turned out, bringing potluck suppers and jugs of water. Boy and Girl Scouts planted hundreds of packages of wildflower seeds, furnished by the Richfield Oil Company, along the slopes of the mountains to blend with desert flowers. Thus the people in this land of "saddle and suntan" carved out of the desert a recreational area typical of their way of life.

Inspired by their success, the Woman's Club, with $250 and a prayer, set out to raise $5,000 for an amphitheater, but by now everyone was a little tired. Refusing to give up, the club plugged along valiantly though not too successfully. Then one day Mrs. Cotts asked the editor of the Glendale *Herald* to help. He wrote an editorial, putting the matter squarely up to the men. Within a few months Thunderbird Park had an amphitheater, and at 6 A.M. on April 16, 1954, the first Sunrise Easter Service was held there.

Better Swimming

The Ol' Swimmin' Hole Replaced

Although none of us like to have our taxes raised, most people will go along with a bond issue if they feel it will provide a facility definitely needed by the community. The women in Lisbon, a small community in North Dakota, wanted a safe place for the children to swim and began by getting the facts, *all* the facts, before the people.

Lisbon is one of the scenic spots of the Sheyenne River, but as a place to swim most of the children were on the outside looking in. The only place for a dip was the traditional "ol' swimmin' hole" in the river and the river had become so polluted that it was neither pleasant nor safe. As far back as 1927 algae and leeches were bad and through the years the situation had become worse. There were so many cases of eye, ear, nose, and throat infection that most parents refused to let their children go into the water. The women had appealed repeatedly to the town officials to do something about it, but although the situation was "studied" nothing was ever done. They finally decided to make the problem their own and in exactly two years Lisbon had a fine swimming pool—one that has served as a model for neighboring communities.

The project was carried out jointly by the Woman's Club, Mother's

Club, Lisbon Study Club, and the Business and Professional Club. The four groups formed a committee which spent three months gathering data and comparing the costs of different types of construction. When the members had decided what kind of pool would be best, they studied the tax records and figured the cost per taxpayer. Then they arranged a community mass meeting. Every organization was contacted and asked to send representatives. Speakers included the mayor, ministers, the school superintendent, a Scout master, a doctor, and a river expert, as well as private citizens. Over 200 people attended. As a result, the City Council agreed to put the question of a bond issue to a vote.

The next problem was to raise money for circulars. This was done by means of cake sales and contributions. A questionnaire was sent to school children, asking if they could swim and, if not, whether they would like to learn. Over 90 per cent of the forms were returned, the major portion stating that the child could not swim but wanted to learn. The committee then asked the men's service clubs if they would underwrite the tickets for children who could not afford to pay. This they readily agreed to do. The candidates for mayor in the coming elections were asked to state their position on the swimming pool issue. Both parties endorsed it. Having secured the necessary data, the committee now prepared a question and answer pamphlet presenting the facts, and explaining how the proposed pool would be operated.

Members of the four clubs now formed teams and canvassed every home in the community. Not only were the pamphlets delivered personally, but these women went over the issue in each case, answering further questions and explaining details that were not quite clear. The canvass is largely credited for the overwhelming vote in favor of the swimming pool. The day after the bond issue passed, the committee ran a box in the local paper thanking the citizens of Lisbon for their cooperation.

The Fargo *Forum*, North Dakota's largest newspaper, became interested in the project and sent a reporter to Lisbon to cover the pool opening. He interviewed children having their first dip. One little boy, covered with goose pimples, his teeth chattering, listened silently to the reporter's questions, then turned and shivered up to the lifeguard. "How long," he asked, "do we have to stay in?" "You can leave

anytime," the guard replied, "but everybody has to be out by five."
The lad dived promptly into the water where he stayed until closing
time. He had no time to be interviewed on how he liked it.

Irrigation Ditch Swimming Abolished

Riverton, Wyoming, is a ranching and farming center principally,
but shortly after the war, oil developments and government irrigation
projects doubled its population within a period of ten years. Although
one or more children were drowned every year in the swift running
waters of the irrigation canals, a swimming pool was out of the question because of the pressing need for schools, sewage systems, paving,
and other necessities.

The Ponderosa Club, a group of twenty young women, decided to
try a fund-raising campaign for a pool. They put up a candy, soft
drink, and hamburger concession at a nearby softball park, and ran it
four nights a week. In the first summer they cleared $1,000 and an-
nounced that the money would be set aside toward a community
swimming pool. This statement made front page news and aroused
the interest of other civic organizations, which joined the project.
Within a year $15,000 had been raised.

But Riverton, just east of the Continental Divide, has very cold
winters. When the temperature dived, interest in an outdoor swimming pool went with it. About this time the General Federation of
Women's Clubs announced its annual "Community Achievement
Contest" and the Ponderosa Club entered, giving impetus to the campaign. Then the school board announced its plans for the long-awaited
construction of a high school gymnasium. It was decided to combine
the two projects and build the pool indoors. This was the spark that
was needed. Within a few weeks over $40,000 was raised, enough for
a fine pool. As for the Ponderosa Club it won an award in the Federation contest for spearheading the project.

Children's Parks and Playgrounds

Oakland's Fairyland Park

Many communities today are establishing play areas with equipment that kindles the imagination and invites creative play. Lakeside
Park in Oakland, California, has one taken directly from a child's

world of fables and fairy tales. "Fairyland Park" has an official post office, the tiniest in the world. The magic wand that created it is the Lake Merritt Breakfast Club, supported by individuals, groups, and organizations, in conjunction with the Oakland Park Department. A child enters the park through the door of the "Old Woman's Shoe" and from there on it is fantasy all the way.

He goes to a puppet show in a little theater shaped like an open story book, climbs into a cuckoo clock tower to a spiral slide, telephones in a child-size booth that is a clown's head, and rides on Alice in Wonderland characters when he goes on the Wonder-Go-Round. Hickory, Dickory, Dock is there, with a mouse on his way up the clock. So is Humpty Dumpty, the Crooked Man and Crooked House, Robinson Crusoe's island home, the Little Red Hen, Pinocchio, Mary, Mary, Quite Contrary, Little Miss Muffet, and all the rest. A tiny whale is a drinking fountain, giraffes hold lights neck-high over the pathways, and elves look down from the trees.

Among the many groups contributing to this project, in addition to the Lake Merritt Breakfast Club, are the Kiwanis, the Lakeview Junior Woman's Club, the Oakland Telephone Company and its employees, employees of the local post office, Local 302 of the Milk Drivers and Dairy Workers Union, the Pilot Club, the Wreath Club of the Oakland Park Department, Aahmes Temple, the West of Market Boys, and the West of Market Girls. The idea for the playground, which has attracted interest in all parts of this country and in foreign lands, was that of Park Superintendent William Penn Mott, Jr., and Arthur Navlet. The designer was W. Russel Everritt.

Pocket-Sized Playgrounds in New Haven

A number of counties and communities have had surveys made of existing recreational facilities, only to find that they do not meet the demands of the present population, without even considering what future plans may be. They are often far below the standards of the National Recreational Association. When New Haven, Connecticut, a community which already had 2,100 acres of park land, took an inventory of its facilities, the Park and Recreation Department decided that a recreation renaissance was necessary if the leisure-time activities and needs of its citizens were to be met.

The most urgent need was for small neighborhood playgrounds. To supply these, New Haven has provided pocket-sized playgrounds in heavily developed neighborhoods. These are modern, easily accessible play areas with colorful and imaginative equipment such as a spiral slide, a giant concrete turtle, a miracle whirl, shower spray, and sprinkler pool. Where the area is large enough there are softball diamonds for older children and facilities for adults, with shade trees to zone separate areas for each age group. Inviting benches in shady places are provided for older people.

CHAPTER VI

COMMUNITY FORESTS

The American people own an empire in trees. About one-third of the total land area in the United States is forest land. Our national forests alone—181 million acres—would be considered great tree wealth by some nations, yet they represent only a portion of our holdings. Including commercial and noncommercial areas, publicly and privately owned, we have more than 650 million acres of forest land, exclusive of interior Alaska, with about half a billion acres classified as commercial.

It would seem that with such a vast acreage our timber supply would be inexhaustible, but people once thought the same of the mighty cedar forest of Lebanon. This forest furnished the timber for Phoenician ships and wood for treeless Egypt and adjacent countries. So many trees were felled to build the temple of Jerusalem that King Solomon supplied Hiram, King of Tyre, with 150,000 lumberjacks to work in the forest and skid the logs to the sea. David's palace was so highly embellished with cedar wood that it became known as "the house of the forest of Lebanon." Today only four small groves remain and probably even these would be gone if a little church had not protected them as a sacred grove. Throughout that whole denuded area today a tree is highly prized—any tree, anywhere.

When the colonists settled here, virgin forests covered over 800 million acres, almost half the land area of the country. To them the forest was a nuisance, making farming impossible. It was something to be cleared, gotten rid of—burned if necessary. There was so much forest in proportion to the population that they thought they would never come to the end of it. Most people continued to think of the timber supply as limitless long after we became a nation, and even after we became a world power. In fact, it was not until 1956 that we began to replace trees faster than we were cutting them and the United States Forest Service warns that we are still cutting useful grades of timber faster than it can grow. In spite of our holdings we have no forest land to spare, for our demands for wood are exceedingly heavy. The trees our forebears considered "in the way" are an essential part of our economy and security today.

"Nearly all of the products used by the American people, whether vegetable, animal, or mineral," says the Forest Service, "use wood somewhere in the process of production, distribution, or utilization." More than 10,000 wood products have been listed and more uses are being developed constantly. "Each of us," the Forest Service has estimated, "uses twice as much lumber as a Russian, four times as much as an Englishman, and six times as much as a Frenchman."

However, we should bear in mind that, although the United States uses more wood than any other country, we are not the most richly endowed in forest land. We now have about four acres of forest land per capita, while the U.S.S.R. has about nine and Canada about sixty-six. Our holdings are about 8 per cent of the world's forest area, with Canada, the United States, and Mexico together having approximately 19 per cent. We should take into consideration too, our rapidly increasing population, which creates a greater demand for wood while sacrificing additional woodland to industrial and urban expansion. Even though we do have an empire in trees, we dare not be complacent about the situation.

Forest land is important to everyone in ways other than as a timber source. The forest is essential for watershed protection and the regulation of stream flow. When the ground is bare the soil cannot absorb and hold water as it does when carpeted with trees, grass, and other vegetation, and this is a factor in both floods and water shortages. The thick crowns of the trees break the fall of the rain and, when it reaches the forest floor, the leaf litter absorbs it, letting it seep gently into the soft spongy soil beneath. The excess filters into springs and streams, tending to make the flow of water regular and continuous throughout the year. Melting snow is absorbed in the same way. When snow is protected by unbroken expanses of forest, it lies on the ground from one to five weeks longer than on exposed land. Thus it has a chance to melt slowly and enter the streams and rivers a little at a time, instead of rushing into them with such force that they overflow. Good forest soils can hold 50 per cent or more of their total volume. By holding the rain where it falls and the snow where it melts, the forest helps to restrain floods while helping to maintain our water supply. Since a watershed may be only a few acres in size, or cover several states, a forest in some remote region can influence the lives of community dwellers hundreds of miles away. Tree roots, too, anchor the soil—a factor that helps prevent topsoil from being washed or blown away.

Grazing is another contribution of the forest. Grass and shrubs that provide good pasturage grow in open timber stands, in the meadows, and other grassland openings of forest areas. Grazing is permitted in our national forests, particularly in the West, through the summer months, complementing home ranges or ranges that provide pasturage only part of the year. However, it is controlled carefully so that the number of livestock does not exceed the capacity of the range to support them and thus damage the grasses that protect the soil.

The forest also provides an ideal habitat for wildlife, an integral part of our economy and a source of healthful sport for those who like hunting and fishing. And to all who love the out-of-doors, the forest has its own meaning. With so many wooded areas near our towns succumbing to housing developments and other uses, forest land assumes new significance as a place of recreation. But, lest we forget, the forests are a part of the natural beauty of this land of ours. Take away trees and the world would become barren, wither, and die.

Because we have abused so much of our land and destroyed so much of our virgin forests, there are millions of acres today which need to be planted in trees. The Forest Service refers to such areas as "problem land that nobody wants"—areas too small for the government to manage, too unprofitable to interest private enterprise. It may be cutover land, submarginal farms, spoil banks remaining from mining operations, eroding mountain slopes, deep gorges and gullies, or sand dunes.

Some is exhausted land, land that has had the life sapped out of it by unwise agricultural practices. This is particularly true in the South.

When land was plentiful it often paid a southern farmer to abandon worn-out farmland and move on to fresh land, since the staple crops grown—cotton, corn, and tobacco—draw heavily on basic soil minerals. As we have learned, planting the same crop in the same place year after year, without proper use of fertilizers, tends to use up these minerals. As the fertility of the soil decreases crops become poorer. As the minerals are exhausted the soil becomes dry and sandy, more subject to erosion, and the plants too become deficient in the minerals our bodies need. Animals that feed on such plants also deteriorate, producing less nourishing meat and milk. Sometimes it is more practical to plant trees on such land than to try to restore it to agricultural use.

Many communities are converting their waste land into public forests. Such wooded areas beautify the community, shelter wildlife, provide a haven for wildflowers, furnish a source of recreation, serve as classrooms for nature study, provide watershed protection and erosion control, and ease the burden of taxpayers. In size they vary. The nearly 4,000 in existence today cover approximately 4,500,000 acres.

As community property, these plantings of trees can exert a much needed influence on forestry generally, for most of the forest land in this country is privately owned. While forestry practices on federal-owned land can be controlled, on privately owned land they cannot be. It is the consensus of conservation authorities that the greatest advancements in forestry and the best conditions on commercial forest lands are to be found in publicly owned forest land and in forest industry ownerships. However, about 60 per cent of the potentially commercial forest land in this country is owned by people with holdings of less than 5,000 acres, and a large percentage of these owners do not depend upon timber for their livelihood. Though these lands may be the main key to America's future timber supply, the conditions on them are generally not good. The community forest that is properly managed can be important as an example of approved forestry practices.

Forestry experts at the various government levels have helped several thousand communities to establish such forests. "What we do in the next ten or twenty years," says Richard E. McArdle, Chief of the Forest Service, "will determine whether we shall grow enough timber to enable our children and their children to enjoy the abundance that we ourselves know."

Town Forests

A Progressive Law in Massachusetts

The first community, or town, forest in Massachusetts was established in 1914 by the City of Fitchburg under a newly enacted law providing for the acquisition of land by municipalities for growing timber. This law resulted from a study of the communal forests of Europe, especially those of Germany and Switzerland, made by the former secretary of the state's Forest and Park Association, Harris A. Reynolds. It is said that some of these small European communities have not levied local taxes for centuries because of their forest income.

The original concept of the Massachusetts law was to encourage the growth of trees in the state, and to return idle land to productivity, thus providing municipalities with a cash income through the sale of forest products. But today, as the population continues to expand, the community forest is becoming increasingly important for watershed protection. In many sections of the state, water shortages are already limiting industrial growth. Massachusetts is more than ever encouraging community forests in order to help insure an adequate water supply. One out of every three towns in the state now has a forest and thousands of acres of once idle land have been brought back to usefulness in this way. The state provides 5,000 trees, free of charge, to any community willing to establish a forest of 100 or more acres.

Pembroke's Forest

The land which Pembroke, Massachusetts, uses as a community forest was once described as "hardly fit to hold down its weeds." When the forest was established in 1924, the entire 100-acre tract probably would have sold for about $1,000. Today it is valued at approximately $50,000. It brings this community of less than 4,000 people a revenue of about $2,400 at the regular five-year cropping of trees and has become a model for such forests in Massachusetts and other states.

"But it isn't the dollar value that is important," Melvin B. Shepherd, head of the forest committee explains, "it's the fact that everybody in Pembroke knows that there is one piece of woodland where he can walk without trespassing. And with the boom in housing developments that is something every community must consider."

"The J. J. Shepherd Memorial Forest" was named in honor of Mr. Shepherd's father, a selectman for many years and a dedicated conservationist, whose foresight was responsible for its establishment. Originally a part of the poor farm, the forest was created through an article in the Town Warrant sponsored by Mr. Shepherd under the state Town Forest Law. When it was authorized, the Massachusetts Forestry Association furnished 5,000 white pine seedlings and volunteers planted them. Through the years the forest has been a community volunteer project. The high school manual arts classes make signs for it, the Kiwanis help plant trees, veterans' organizations help; indeed it is everybody's forest and everybody contributes to it. So highly do the people prize it today that they have authorized the town to buy several additional tracts to be used in the same way. The new forests will be in different sections of the community, making it possible for all residents to be within easy walking distance of a forest area.

The town forest is Pembroke's favorite recreational area, a community center for many types of activity. Ten acres were cleared and left as open fields, a part being used for the Little League baseball diamond. Another part is for rodeos, clam bakes, horse shows, and the annual carnival staged by the veterans. Scouts use the forest for camping trips, cook-outs, and nature study. Picnics are held in the pine groves and, at the forest's edge, there is a pond with good fishing. Most of the forest, however, is in its natural state. Not only is it beautiful, adding to the attractiveness of the community, but in it an area has been set aside as a nursery where shade trees are grown for Pembroke's streets.

Melvin Shepherd has helped many communities in the county establish similar forests. "Whenever good business methods are applied to land management," he says, "the town has in its forest an investment which will pay dividends in the sale of forest products, watershed protection, recreation, wildlife propagation, education, and beautification."

A Depression-Born Forest in Troy

"We call ours a town forest," Seavey A. Piper, town selectman, says of the forest in Troy, Maine. "A town up here in Maine is an organized area, usually six miles square. The people living within this area elect their own officials as provided by law. They assess and collect taxes on real estate and personal property to maintain highways, provide education, and support the poor. We are strictly an agricultural area in Troy. We have no village, no commercial or industrial enterprise. Our taxable area outside of lake and bog is about 21,000 acres. The population of 580 is nearly all native born, many of them descendants of the early settlers."

During the depression of the thirties many were unable to pay their taxes. A number of families left their farms and the town was forced to take them over for delinquent taxes as provided by state law. Ultimately 13 per cent of the taxable land became town property. In 1939 a study of land use was undertaken by the county agricultural service. From this study emerged the fact that much of the town-owned land was not adapted to modern farming. The county agent and the state forest commissioner showed the selectmen how this land could be forested. Twelve farms, totaling 963 acres, were chosen as adaptable to forest development and the selectmen were advised what it would cost for seedlings and planting.

"There followed local meetings with the townspeople—in kitchens, the school house, the Grange hall," Mr. Piper recalls. "There was opposition to the idea, plenty of it. But at the annual town meeting it was voted to establish the forest and the selectmen were authorized to use $400 for seedlings and planting."

Each of these twelve farms contained some woodland, some open fields. The old houses were sold and torn down, and as soon as the frost left the ground, 50,000 red pine and white spruce seedlings were planted in the open-field land. Altogether 200,000 forest seedlings were planted in the next ten years. At first this planting was done on days when the local people could help. Later, much of it was done through the National Youth Administration program. The town employed a foreman, who worked with the boys and local unemployed labor in selective cutting. Under the guidance of a state forestry specialist this was extended to include thinning and pruning.

The project has attracted much attention. Letters of inquiry have been received from all parts of the country and from Canada. There have also been many visitors, including a group of Icelanders who were here to study farm conditions.

"Our early plantings are now a beautiful young forest," Mr. Piper says. "The project has put to profitable use idle and abandoned land and furnished employment for local people. The products sold—pulp, fuel wood, logs, birch bolts, and plug wood—help supply Maine industries. These operations have yielded thousands of dollars and earned the town a net saving of $4,000 which, five years ago, was used toward the building of a new four-room consolidated school. Only last year, at the annual town meeting, the voters set aside a sum from the forest fund for a town office. Through modern forestry practices, we have put 200 acres of field land back to forest and improved several hundred acres of woodland. Several years ago the town voted to place the management of this project in the care of a board of trustees."

How the Schools Benefit

School Forest on "Land Nobody Wanted"

The project of the Wisconsin Garden Club Federation is particularly interesting because it covers so many phases of conservation and accomplishes so many purposes in a single project.

"Our clubs have always been interested in the wise use of our natural resources," Mrs. George L. Swearingen, former president, says. "In autumn, 1934 we concluded that good conservation practices would never come into general use in our state unless the subject was taught in the public schools. We campaigned actively for this and in spring, 1935 the state legislature passed our bill, requiring every school in the state to teach conservation. We were resting on our laurels when we were confronted with the fact that the law could not be put into effect because the teachers had no background for teaching conservation, and no study materials were available. Here indeed was a challenge greater than getting our bill passed. Out of this need grew our Wisconsin School Children's Forest project."

The idea for a forest which children could plant and use for study was that of Mrs. Frank K. Quimby, then conservation chairman of the federation. The Forest Service cooperated by setting aside for the forest a 1,200-acre tract of burned over, cut-over, eroded land. For each penny the children contributed, the Forest Service, with the help of the Civilian Conservation Corps, planted three pine seedlings in the school forest, a part of the Nicolet National Forest.

An analysis of this tract was made by Forest Service personnel. "Their report showed that every bad forestry practice known to man had been used," Mrs. Swearingen recalls. "Mrs. Quimby used this research material as a basis for conservation lessons which she wrote and the Forest Service had printed. The material was sent to every school in Wisconsin. As the seedlings were planted the children received first-hand information about the trees, plants, animals, and soil in their forest. The teachers were grateful for such help because it gave them first-hand, up-to-date information on good conservation practices which they could pass on to the children. The flood of pennies was overwhelming.

"In 1941, when the project was finished and the forest dedicated, it was gratifying to ride through the acres of pines which the children's pennies had planted. The governor, state superintendent of public instruction, and many other dignitaries participated in the event. Everyone present planted a tree in 'Quimby Grove' as a tribute to Mrs. Quimby, who had devoted five years to the project. It is even more gratifying to drive through the forest today and see the acres of towering pines. It was agreed that this forest would be treated as a crop, with selective logging at the proper time, but it will always remain a forest where good conservation practices are the watchword."

Three School Forests Established by a Garden Club

Garden clubs, particularly those in the South, have been among the most active civic organizations in planting trees. The Georgia clubs planted 1,500,000 seedlings in 1955, while the record of the Kentucky clubs almost equalled it. Many of these plantings are school forests, such as the three established by the Hollywood Garden Club in Birmingham, Alabama, a project carried out under the leadership of Mrs. T. M. Francis, as the club's 1955 conservation program.

A total of 7,600 seedlings were planted in the three forests in 1955. Others were given to students to plant at home. The seedlings were purchased by the club, and land owned by the three schools was used for the forests. A course of instruction in conservation was given in the schools with posters, displays, and reading and teaching material provided. Films depicting good forestry practices, the uses of the forest, and the plant and wildlife to be found there were shown in classes.

The seedlings were planted by the students under the supervision of the State Division of Forestry and the forests were dedicated on Arbor Day with a celebration in which all school children participated. These forests are the property of the schools and when the trees are grown they will be maintained on a sustained yield basis, providing forest workshops for school use.

The school forest movement is spreading rapidly. Michigan, for instance, has an extensive program launched under an act passed in 1931 by the state legislature. The law provides for county, township, city, village, and school forests. It has enabled communities and school districts to acquire 65,000 acres of state land. More than 600 school forests have been established.

The Natick Natural Science Park

One of the most highly developed forests for educational use in Massachusetts is the 100-acre tract in Natick, a portion of which has been set aside as a natural science park. The land was willed to the town for park purposes with the stipulation that no building should be erected on it. It was left in a relatively natural state. When the Lilja elementary school was built near it, specimens from the area crept into the classroom, openly or otherwise, so consistently that the teachers decided that the children's interest in natural history should be encouraged. However, they soon found that they themselves needed help in identifying and interpreting what the children found. As a result the "Natick Natural Science Park" organization was formed to compile information about the area. It consists of people in the community who wanted to help—teachers, students, parents, and others.

A comprehensive guide manual, pocket-sized, has been prepared, together with a map showing the locations of permanent study plots. The manual covers such subjects as "aquatic and land animal life; soil, including the geologic history of the area and the role of primitive plants in forming soil; the tree societies of the region and their economic importance; and the effect of the town forest on local climatic conditions." It represents the combined and coordinated efforts of a number of local residents who feel that "if we can develop in the youth of today—the landowners and policy makers of tomorrow—a deeper appreciation of the role of our natural resources in the economic and social welfare of the individual, community, and world, future generations will be prepared to cope more intelligently with resource problems as they arise."

A motion picture, made in connection with the manual, shows field trip techniques and classroom committees at work. This was used for study, with discussion following. Many stories have been written about the park by the students, such as: "The Lore of the Rotting Log," "Who Brought the Boulder?" and "The Saga of the Swamp." The superintendent of the Natick Public Schools, E. Davis Woodbury, says of such areas: "Today we consider the community as a laboratory for the school. The environment of the school site itself is a very effective stimulator of student interest. Young people get very little benefit from studies which are meaningless and distasteful."

A School Woodlot Project

The Cleveland Hill High School of Cheektowaga, New York, has won two awards for its woodlot project—a cash award from the New York State Conservation Forum and a bronze plaque from the Western New York Science Congress. It was carried out by seventh grade students under the direction of their science teacher, Miss Grace Heacock.

The project could be placed under any of several headings, but is included here to show how a community forest, or even a small wooded area, fits into the school curriculum. In this instance, a wooded section of the school grounds was used to teach natural science and to promote good citizenship. At the time, the school was new and this 100 by 195-foot area was infested with poison ivy and littered with trash. School authorities had the ivy removed, the underbrush cleared out, grass seed planted where practical, then turned the lot over to the seventh graders.

The class split into various committees, each with a specific job to do. One group had charge of the cleanup campaign, another the construction of bird houses, another wildflowers; one did tree labeling, another built a fireplace for the picnic area, and still another was to make "before" and "after" models of the woodlot.

Some committees were subdivided. The cleanup group had sub-

committees on signs, publicity, and recreation. The sign committee
wrote and designed the posters, making sure there were anti-litter
reminders in strategic places, along with warnings against tree climbing and other detrimental practices. The publicity committee did a
splendid job of publicizing the anti-litter campaign, using posters
provided by the garden club, writing essays, and making sure every
class member wore his litterbug badge. The third group wrote, cast,
and produced a conservation play. This was given before the school
assembly and later was mimeographed by Keep America Beautiful
for distribution to Parent-Teacher Associations all over the country.

The wildflower group, officially titled "Science Flower Committee,"
made paper flowers for the play, the setting of which was a reproduc-
tion of the woodlot. It was also the responsibility of this group to
identify the wildflowers in the woodlot, and plant the bulbs and
flowers given to the school by the garden club. Each member of the
committee was assigned a flower or plant to study and report on
before the class. In the same way, the bird committee studied the
birds to be found there, listed them, and made a chart of their appearance, food preferences, and nesting habits. The model class made
two scale models of the woodlot. They were so well done that they
won an Award of Excellence in the Junior Division of the Western
New York Science Congress. As for the tree committee, its members
not only labeled the trees in the woodlot but reported on other types,
where they grow, their importance in the community and to the
country, and the many uses of wood.

An interesting feature of this project is that all thirty-one members
of the class participated actively, and eventually the entire school
became involved, as well as parents and others. The class made a
scrapbook of its project which has become a permanent part of the
school record. "While small children are almost invariably interested
in nature, many lose that interest somewhere between the fourth and
ninth grades," said one educator, who uses a school forest in connection with his classes. "Sometimes this is because pupils do not have
sufficient opportunity to study *living* things."

School Project for Uses of Wood

Our generation has made tremendous strides toward solving the
mysteries of outer space, but we still cannot make a tree grow faster

than nature intended. We can cut a tree in a matter of minutes, where it may have taken early man hours, but it still takes the same number of years to grow a replacement. Like bread, wood is a necessity of life. And if our children are to have enough wood to meet their needs, we must plant trees and teach them to do the same. Perhaps, even more important, we must teach them the *value* of this precious resource.

To impress upon her pupils the importance of our forests, Esther E. Henning, a teacher in Eastmanville, Michigan, encouraged them to do a "uses of wood" project in connection with their 4-H Conservation Club. She has a one-room rural school and the twelve members of the club were in the fourth, fifth, and sixth grades. The project consisted of scrapbooks. These include reports of nature trips, films about trees, descriptions of important native species, questions and answers about trees, a spelling list of tree names, free-hand sketches, poetry, booklets, and pictures and articles from newspapers and magazines. The covers are of cork with original designs burned in.

The uses of wood are featured under such headings as household, buildings, furniture woods and finishes, sawdust, shavings, school and office, toys, shop, and firewood, with special emphasis on unusual uses such as film, rayon, chemicals, synthetics, and paper. In addition to the scrapbooks, each youngster collected ten leaves, ten samples of bark, and ten samples of wood. These were mounted on wooden plaques and shellacked. In recognition of the project, every member of the group received an "A" rating in 4-H, and the club was awarded a plaque by the county, as well as $25 from the Percy J. Hoffmaster Memorial Fund. Another $25 was added to the prize money and a movie, "Your Friend, the Forest," was purchased for the county film library.

Junior Forest Clubs

The Junior Forest Club idea originated with the Miller Park School in Omaha, Nebraska, and is based on a combination of guided practice and demonstration. Since the organization of the first club in 1941, hundreds of thousands of trees have been planted in Nebraska by these groups, both on private grounds and the grounds of public buildings. The idea became so popular that it spread to schools throughout the state, to other states, and to every continent with the possible exception of Africa.

Memorial Forests

"There is no danger," the Forest Service says, "of timber becoming a surplus crop." In fact, it warns that if the nation is to meet future demands for wood we must plant *billions* instead of millions of trees.

The Louis J. Taber Forest Memorial

The Grange, a national farm organization with nearly a million members, has carried out many fine community and conservation projects. It is a family fraternity, with a large youth membership. The Juvenile Grange—the five to fourteen age group—has a very active program. Typical of what the young Grangers are doing is their reforestation project in honor of Past National Master Louis J. Taber. The memorial is part of the Wayne National Forest near Columbus, Ohio.

The project was launched in 1941 with an agreement between the Juvenile Grange and the Forest Service. The children wanted to honor Mr. Taber, a strong conservationist, in an especially appropriate way. Through their programs they knew of the tremendous reforestation task facing this country and decided to honor Mr. Taber by taking part in it. Ohio was chosen because Mr. Taber served as Ohio State Master and had long been associated with Grange work in that state.

Much of the abandoned and idle land in Ohio resulted from strip mining prior to the passage of laws requiring mine owners to restore the surface after operations cease. The young Grangers undertook the restoration of 200 acres of badly treated land, a part of which was scarred by mining operations. To restore the area 52,000 pitch pines and 137,500 shortleaf pines were required. To purchase these the children contributed $1,122.16, collected in pennies, nickels, and dimes. The Forest Service planted and cared for the trees and agreed that this section of Wayne National Forest should be a memorial to Mr. Taber. It is marked by a bronze plaque mounted on a field stone from his farm. The project is a continuing one; each year the Grangers add to their memorial by reforesting more idle land.

Macon's Scout Forest

In 1923 the Boy Scouts of America established a forest on 235 acres of abandoned land in Macon, Georgia, which had been given them by the Al Sihah Temple of the Shrine.

"Several Scout leaders of that day, led by Dr. C. C. Harrold, of Macon, who was the Council Commissioner, had a tremendous interest in conservation, a virtue then very scarcely and sparsely practiced," V. Carl Sullivan, Mason and Scout executive, remembers. "Under Dr. Harrold's leadership the Forest Service aided us in making the first plantings of pine seedlings in this area of the country. This was done in the winters of 1923-24 and 1924-25. Natural reseeding and protection soon covered the old abandoned farm fields. The property was used by the Forest Service for many years as a demonstration area for good forest practices and, after the organization of the Georgia State Forestry Service, they too cooperated in the development of the area. Soon after we acquired the property we discovered that it would not be suitable for its original purpose, a summer camp, but it has been developed as a wilderness and overnight camping area for the Scouts."

This forest was the first area designated as a tree farm by Georgia when the state launched such a program. Only marked trees are ever removed. The first cutting was made in 1939-40, when 800,000 feet were harvested. About 400,000 feet were cut in 1948, and another 400,000 feet in 1957. After these cuttings more timber—of better quality—remained standing than when the original cutting was made in 1939. Income from sale of the timber is used to expand the camping facilities of the Scouts in that area.

"The Scout Council now has 600 additional acres of land which it is using for camping and forestry purposes," Mr. Sullivan says. "Experiments conducted in these forests by our Scouts under the supervision of the various forest services have been the subject of several pamphlets. They are also featured in the picture, 'A Scout in the Forest,' developed some years ago by the Visual Education Service of the Boy Scouts of America. Working in cooperation with governmental forestry agencies, the Scout Council has conducted conservation camps since 1923 when the first plantings were made. In recent years commercial forestry interests in this section have also cooperated. From fifty to 400 Scouts attend these camps each year."

The Forest of Fame in Wisconsin

Strictly speaking, the Forest of Fame in Dane County Village near Madison, Wisconsin, cannot be classified as a community forest, although it is a memorial forest. But the trees hold the soil in place and help maintain the water table, nevertheless.

This forest, started on Arbor Day, 1916, by John S. Donald, a professor at the University of Wisconsin, is planted with trees which have a special association. They have been transplanted from the homes of many presidents, famous generals, and leaders in religion, science, music, and commerce. Some are from historic places such as Sherwood Forest in England. The first trees planted there were from George Washington's home, Mount Vernon.

Among Our Older Forests

A Church Forest in Danville

Some of these forests date back to the early days of our country. One of the oldest, a church forest in Danville, New Hampshire, was established in 1760, when the town itself was founded. "It was the custom in New England, whenever a new township was granted, to set off a parcel of land for the use of the ministry," explains Agnes H. Collins, of the parsonage committee which has charge of the forest. "The deed for the forest in Danville (then called Hawke) reads 'for the use of the ministry forever.' From 1760 to 1789 this land was in the hands of the selectmen, but at the town meeting in 1790 it was voted to elect a parsonage committee of three members to have charge of the land and funds 'and to examine into the matter.' Every year since that time, at town meeting, this committee is elected and a vote taken 'to expend the income and interest for preaching.'

"The established church was Congregational. Each year, in the early days, they held a vendue at which time they sold at auction anywhere from one tree to a clump of trees. They also rented land for pasturage. The money was used toward paying for preaching. After passage of the Toleration Act, people could have their share given to different denominations. Now most of it is given to our local church, which is

Baptist. Since its establishment these seventy-five acres of forest land have provided the church with nearly $43,000.

The Newington Forest

Oldest of all, it is believed, is the forest in Newington, New Hampshire, established in 1710. Paul Revere is said to have been paid for recasting the bell in the meeting house from earnings of this forest. The forest also helped build the village church, parsonage, town hall, school, and library. Although it was recently taken over as a bomber base by the Air Force, it still contributes to the welfare of the village, for the money that Newington received for it has been used for a community center.

CHAPTER VII

"YOU NEVER MISS THE WATER . . ."

In Madagascar it is a common sight to see women with large clay jugs on their heads, carrying home the daily supply of water across the hot desert sands. Along the routes of travel in parts of the Egyptian Sudan, water is sealed with wet clay into the trunks of large hollow trees. In Asia Minor, India, Africa, and South America, millions of people still scoop up water from shallow pools and foul streams or haul it up from wells. Millions more live in appalling poverty in areas where the lack of water makes agriculture difficult to impossible.

By contrast, authorities estimate that the public water supply systems in the United States serve almost 150 gallons of water to each person every day. When agricultural and industrial consumption is included the daily average rockets to 1,475 gallons per person. A large paper mill uses in a day more water than a city of 50,000 people. Sixty-five thousand gallons are needed to produce a ton of finished steel, 15,000 to make an automobile, and from six to ten gallons to refine one gallon of gasoline. As a nation we use 250 billion gallons of water a day. At our present rate of population increase, this figure will probably reach 475 billion gallons by 1975. By then public water systems are expected to supply 175 gallons a day for each person. When this is compared to the eight gallons a day used in the 1800's and the five gallons per person which is considered average for primitive living conditions, one begins to understand why we are having water shortages. We drink about as much water, and use about as much for cooking as in the old days, but our way of life has changed.

Water has always played a dominant role in our economy. Without our wealth of streams, rivers, and lakes, our standard of living would not be possible. Water has helped to shape our destiny, just as it has controlled the destiny of all nations since the earliest civilizations of Egypt, India, and Babylonia. But the days have passed when we could take for granted a limitless supply of fresh water. Industrial expansion, high living standards, and the increased use of water for irrigation have imposed such a terrific drain upon water resources that many communities have water problems today. As the demand continues to soar, more and more communities will be faced in the future with water shortages, a poor quality of water, or both. The United States Geological Survey found that in 1953 a thousand cities of fairly good size up to big municipalities had to restrict the use of water. In many instances industry has been forced to alter or curtail expansion because the available water supply was not adequate.

Most of us do not realize until it is called to our attention that there is a *limit* to the amount of water available to us. The earth's fresh water supply depends upon a gigantic circulation system called the hydrologic, or water, cycle. This is an unceasing operation, with no beginning and no end. Water is evaporated from land and ocean surfaces, held in the atmosphere as vapor, transformed into clouds, then condensed to fall back upon the land and sea as rain, snow, or sleet. The amount of water involved in this cycle is believed to be as constant as the character of water itself. There is no way known to increase the earth's fresh water supply unless ocean water is desalted.

This country, as a whole, is blessed with abundant rainfall, an average annual precipitation of more than thirty inches. Approximately 70 per cent, or twenty-one inches, returns to the atmosphere by evaporation and the transpiration of plants—part of the water cycle. The remaining nine inches, from which we draw our supply, flows into streams and infiltrates the ground. Precipitation is not uniformly distributed, however, over our country. The seventeen western states receive only 25 per cent of the total, although they comprise 60 per cent of our land area, and the southwestern states suffer the greatest water shortages. But in recent years nearly every section has faced at least one major water problem: scarcity, floods, or

pollution. Some regions have been plagued with all three. The range
of precipitation in this country is from more than a hundred inches
annually in the rain forests of Washington to less than two inches
in Death Valley, California.

The Department of the Interior is engaged in research to find an
economical way of converting ocean water to fresh, and the National
Science Foundation is studying "cloud seeding" for the inducement
and control of rain. But, in line with Federal Government policy in
major flood control and other programs, no process would be considered practical unless benefits exceed costs. Thus, even though
these processes may be *possible*, they may not be *feasible* for some
time. Even if they became realities tomorrow, it is doubtful if they
would provide a cure-all for our water supply problems. "The conservation and use which we make of the water resources of our nation
may in large measure determine our future progress and the standards
of living of our citizens," President Eisenhower said recently. "If we
are to continue to advance agriculturally and industrially we must
make the best use of every drop of water which falls on our soil, or
which can be extracted from the oceans."

In 1955 the Secretaries of the Interior, Agriculture, and Defense
made a detailed study of water problems facing the United States.
The report of their findings in January 1956 emphasized that we have
no national water problem as such; there are, rather, nationwide water
problems which vary in different parts of the country. The problem
may be flood control, navigation, community and agricultural supply,
scenic and recreational value, or fish and wildlife preservation, along
with property and priority rights. We must also take into consideration the fact that some of our most important cities are located on
large rivers where major floods are most likely to occur, that large
industries vital to our prosperity and to national defense are dependent
upon this proximity to water. We think of floods as disasters but, to
an extent, they are a natural phenomenon. And the flood plain belongs to the river. In using it we are taking a calculated risk, as man
has done for centuries. When we build homes, factories, and bridges
on the flood plain, or use it for farmland, we increase both the fre-
quency and violence of damage. And yet the use of these flood plains
is essential to the nation's economy. How to use them wisely is a
challenge.

We must also consider the mobile nature of water, its disregard for man-made boundaries; the conflict of interests which arise over use of the same stream, river, or other body of water; the fact that we still know little about water; honest difference of opinion on the handling of our water problems; the gigantic cost of big power dams and other flood control projects; and the number of departments in local, state, and federal governments that have some relation to water use.

The Federal Government has a certain responsibility in the matter of leadership, research, and technical assistance, but cannot be expected to assume the entire burden. Most of the problems can, in fact, be handled best on regional or community levels.

Conservation does not mean *hoarding* our national resources, nor does it mean locking them up. It means wise use, with a regard for future as well as present needs. The early conservationists perhaps had the best definition when they called it "the kind of resource use which results in the greatest good, for the largest number of people, for the longest time."

Conservation measures, however sound, cannot solve all of our water problems, but they are an important part of the program necessary to overcome them. Experts believe that most water shortages arise, not from an absolute lack of water, but from failure to plan for the optimum use of the water that is available. Grave as our water resource problems are, they are not insurmountable. They can be solved, this report to the president concludes, through the organized efforts of the nation, with every citizen accepting a share of the responsibility.

Watersheds

The term watershed largely defines itself. It is the drainage area from which water moves toward a single channel. Expressed in another way, it is an area that sheds water into a given stream, river, lake, pond, or other catchment. A watershed may comprise a few acres or, as in the case of the Mississippi River, cover several states. The Nile, which flows 4,000 miles from the heart of Africa to the Mediterranean, has a watershed of more than a million square miles and extends into six countries. Such large areas are more frequently referred to as river basins.

"The greater part of most watersheds is made up of farm, grazing, or forest lands, although some may contain wild lands or badlands," D. A. Williams, administrator of the Soil Conservation Service, explains. "Most watersheds also include towns or cities; and usually they include considerable areas devoted to roads, highways, railroads, factories, mines, and other structures. And the stream, lake, or pond that serves as the catchment must also be considered a part of each watershed. Furthermore, the plant life that grows on the land forms an integral part of the watershed—the trees, grass, cultivated crops, and all other plants. Also a part of the watershed are the animals that live upon the plants and water, both domestic and wild. Finally, we should bear in mind that the people who live there and use and manage all these resources are a part too—the most important part."

A Small Watershed Project

Since a watershed is a water drainage and geological unit, the smaller watersheds serve as natural areas for tackling local soil and water problems. How a local watershed can be improved is well-illustrated by the Stony Brook–Millstone River project in New Jersey, now being carried out through local, state, and federal teamwork.

The Millstone watershed is a 300 square mile area, including five counties and more than two dozen municipalities. Stony Brook, a tributary of the Millstone River, has a drainage area of fifty square miles. There are a number of problems in the two watersheds which are common to many communities. Floods are a menace in the piedmont, or hilly, sections, while the people in farming, industrial, and residential areas are frequently troubled with drought. Land abuses have wrought severe damages to soil, water, forest, and wildlife, and poor natural drainage has limited the productivity of farms. Heavy sediment in the streams has decreased fish populations, clogged ponds and lakes, and made the water unfit for many recreational and economic uses. Poorly planned housing developments too have overtaxed water supplies and made sewage disposal a health problem.

The project to improve the situation originated with the conservation committee of the Princeton Garden Club, which saw the problem as one involving the entire stream valley, not just segments of it. As this group of women hoped, the project soon outgrew the garden club and was taken over by the Stony Brook–Millstone Watersheds Association, Inc., organized in 1951. This is a private, non-profit, non-political, educational corporation, formed by and for the people living in this area. The association believes that conservation is a community responsibility and its purpose is to conserve, restore, and improve the area's natural resources. The organization derives its financial support from membership dues and contributions and is composed of residents in both rural and urban areas. It has an active policy-making board of twenty-one non-salaried trustees, a number of special committees, and employs a full-time professional conservationist. One of its functions is to serve as a liaison between residents of the watersheds and the local, state, and federal agencies concerned with natural resources and planning.

The association did not attain its present status and influence overnight. It grew gradually, through education and persuasion, from smaller to larger projects. Whenever a landowner is receptive to its ideas, it lends a hand. Periodic news releases are sent to newspapers and magazines; progress reports are made to members; lectures and films are provided for schools, civic groups, and other local organizations. Field trips are also arranged to show interested persons the condition of the watersheds, explain what is being done and how the work is progressing. Everybody enjoys these trips, which usually end with a picnic. By means of them the association shows how private individuals, institutions, and business houses can work with governmental agencies to overcome local water problems. As the *Princeton Herald* said, the project now has "a public not only sympathetic to, but almost clamoring for, means of conserving and increasing the water supply and, conversely, of coping with too much water."

For convenience, the conservation measures undertaken in these watersheds are treated here as one project. All minor and local projects are part of the conservation program developed for the whole region, though they have been carried out as specific projects. Such a plan has its advantages, the association believes. Definite progress can be shown periodically, thus sustaining interest in the final goal. Also it is easier to arouse public interest in a concrete, rather than a theoretical or general, conservation problem. The associaton feels that this practicality is the key to its success in winning public support.

"It is very important to bring this picture of conservation down to specific problems or areas of study," Malcolm P. Crooks, executive director of the association, says. "Everyone is for conservation, as they are for peace, but it is difficult to get action on an appeal to help the general conditions in an area. The same people who are apathetic on that basis become concerned and willing to help when you talk about measures to stop pollution which is endangering the public water supply, fishing, and the community's aesthetic value."

The program adopted by this public-spirited group is extensive. A host of "minor" projects have already been completed. These include stream bank stabilization, operation of a community composting station, and the improvement of hundreds of acres of eroding farmland by sound land practices. Among major projects, it is sponsoring a rainfall and sediment study in the Stony Brook watershed. The purpose of this research, which will require several years, is to determine the effectiveness of soil conservation practices in reducing flood peaks and sedimentation, to study the effects of rainfall on erosion, and to evaluate the effect of conservation lakes, now being built in this area, on the sediment load of Stony Brook. We can appreciate more fully the importance of this project when we consider that topsoil carried away in our streams not only reduces the fertility of the land, but aggravates downstream flood problems, pollutes the water, makes the dredging of navigation channels necessary, and silts up reservoirs and other engineering projects so that their usefulness is impaired. The project is financed jointly by Princeton University and the U.S. Geological Survey of the Department of the Interior. "As our soil and water problems increase, we need more basic soil and water information to serve as a tool for the elimination of these resource ills," the association points out. "Farmers, municipalities, and conservationists can all benefit from this type of research."

Another of its major projects centers on a regional plan, undertaken in cooperation with Rutgers University. A study of the area is being made which encompasses land use; topography and slopes, stream flows and potential building areas; agricultural, residential, and industrial potentials; population trends and prospects; park and recreational facilities; an inventory of present zoning ordinances in the various municipalities; highway and traffic circulation; and water use and water potential. Base maps are being prepared by the university and the findings of the workers will be summarized and studied. An advisory plan will then be worked out, containing "broad out-line-type proposals" which the municipalities may use as a guide in their planning. Thus the region can plan its growth in relation to its resources, including water potentials and limitations. And each municipality can plan its own growth in relation to that of the whole region. Municipalities with mutual water problems can work together to overcome them.

The most outstanding project the association has initiated is a conservation program to control floods, soil erosion, and water waste. The program, now under way, was developed with the technical assistance of the Soil Conservation Service and other specialists. Approximately ten years will be needed to complete the program and the cost will be slightly more than half a million dollars. Included in the program are the construction of conservation lakes, the building of earth dams (less costly than concrete), tree planting and forest management projects, and the widespread use of modern farm methods such as contour plowing on sloping land to hold water and topsoil. The program has met the necessary requirements for financial assistance from the Federal Government, which will share the cost with those benefiting from the project (all those living in these watersheds) under the authority of the Watershed Protection and Flood Prevention Act. This act is administered by the Department of Agriculture as a part of the national soil and water conservation program. "By holding more of the water where it falls, encouraging it to soak into the ground rather than letting it run off," the association reports, "we will be eliminating a major source of waste of both soil and water. The water thus saved will serve us in good stead now and in the future for potable use, fire protection, and recreation. The reduction of erosion will make our land more productive; hence the economic value of our communities will be enhanced."

In recognition of the work members of the association are doing, the *Princeton Herald* ran a feature article about them which concluded: "For refusing to stand by while their community's natural resources are wasted and abused; for bringing into being a characteristically American grass-roots organization devoted to the betterment of the area; for giving new meaning to the time-worn expression 'For land's sake;' these far-seeing citizens are Town Topics' nominees for 'men and women of the week.'"

Applying the Principle of Multiple Use

The multiple-use principle under which such resources as the national forests are managed is perhaps not well understood by United States citizens. This may account, at least in part, for the fact that many communities do not derive full benefit from their own natural resources.

The principle of multiple use underlies a method of management whereby federal lands are made to yield to the public, without impairment, the maximum number of benefits. This principle is applicable to some of the people's property, but not all. For instance, the national parks are maintained for the *preservation* of outstanding features. If they were managed on a basis of multiple use, the very purpose for which they were established would be defeated. By contrast, the national forests are maintained for the *production* of the resources they contain. They are administered for the protection, development, and use of timber, water, range, and other resources in the public interest. A surprising number of people are not aware that timber is logged in our national forests and sold. Our national forests, in addition to their many other uses, also serve as a demonstration of good management to private timber owners and operators who study them. They yield a sizeable income, 25 per cent of which is paid to the states in which the forests lie, to be used for roads and schools. Ten per cent is used for forest road maintenance, and the rest goes into the United States Treasury. The forests on a small watershed cannot be expected to serve the multiple purposes of our national forests, but neither do the trees need to be "locked up," as the people in Waynesville, North Carolina, discovered.

Throughout the southern Appalachian region many municipalities depend solely upon a supply of unfiltered water from mountain watersheds. In 1915, far-sighted town leaders in Waynesville, to insure a supply of sanitary water for a growing population, purchased 8,244 acres of mountain land as community property. The headwaters of Allen Creek, which supplies the water for Waynesville and two neighboring communities, are on this forested land. The water is chemically treated, as is usually the case, but for more than thirty years timber cutting in the area was prohibited. Health officers of Waynesville and the general public were apprehensive about harvesting timber and using water from the same area.

In 1945 town officials requested the North Carolina Department of Conservation and Development and the TVA Division of Forestry Relations to help them determine the feasibility of managing the timber resource of this watershed while at the same time using it as a source of water supply. The two agencies made a joint reconnaissance and prepared a prospectus for forest management, developed on the basis that the water resource is of paramount importance, but that the timber could also be utilized, *provided it was harvested according to recognized watershed protection standards.*

By 1948 selective logging was being done. Mature trees, slower-growing trees, and trees with defects are now marked for cutting, while a reserve stand of high-quality, vigorous trees is constantly maintained. At no time does an individual sale area extend over more than a few hundred acres. Timber sales are scheduled for the various tributary watersheds, so that sufficient water can always be taken from areas where logging has been finished for at least one year. Sale of this timber has added substantially to the general economy of the community, providing jobs and improvements. In 1954 a new filtration plant and chlorinating system were installed, with a capacity of 2,500,000 gallons of water a day. A $300,000 bond issue was needed to float the project but the tax rate in Waynesville remained the same. It has been the same since 1943.

Despite steep mountain topography, logging activities have caused a minimum of erosion. "New logging methods were devised on this project for the conservation of water and prevention of erosion," N. J. Tucker, executive vice-president of the Waynesville Chamber of Commerce, says. "Ordinarily, in mountain logging, the trees are cut and pulled by horses *down* the mountainsides to the loading ramps along streams or in valleys where roads have been built. When it rains, water rushes down these logging trails into the main roads and larger streams, carrying sediment with it. Over a period of years this creates an erosion problem. And it constitutes a loss of water with every rain. On this watershed, the bulldozers build the roads *around* the sides of the mountains, and the logs are pulled by power-driven logging equipment *up* the mountainsides to the ramps. Earth scars made by the dragging logs create a pattern just the reverse of the old method. Water, dispersed through natural leaf litter, trickles down the mountainside to streams, carrying little or no sediment. We believe our project to be a fine illustration of dual resource use. Mountain logging methods that protect the watershed are demonstrated here for all loggers in the region to see."

A "Show-Me" Trip in Utah

Conservation is an integral part of garden club programs today. Most clubs are affiliated either with the Garden Club of America or with the National Council of State Garden Clubs, Inc., and an objective of both is to further the conservation cause in every possible way. Usually at least one regular meeting a year is devoted entirely to this subject. Since these programs must necessarily be educational, it is sometimes difficult to keep them interesting. The members of the garden club in Fillmore, Utah, consider this no problem at all; they simply arrange a "Show Me" trip every year.

The club learned how engrossing an on-the-spot study of land use can be when fifty of its members took a watershed show-me trip in 1955 with Forest Service and Soil Conservation Service experts. This is range country with a flood history. In 1946 overgrazed lands above the town of Mount Pleasant gave birth to a flash flood that sent several feet of mud, boulders, and other debris down the main street and over surrounding farmland. The purpose of this trip was to learn why such floods occur, and to see how conservation measures can control them. Many of these women were ranchers, so that the damaging effects of uncontrolled grazing was of special interest.

Their destination was the source of the community's water supply atop the Pavant Mountains. "Fifty of us left Fillmore in a caravan at dawn," relates Miss Ilene Cooper, then club president, "driving with the sunrise as far up the mountainside as our cars could go. We were met by Forest Service trucks which took us to the top, a steep seven-mile climb. The open seating was ideal for sight-seeing and the mountainside, ablaze with wildflowers, was a gardener's delight.

"At Indian Springs we had reached an elevation of 10,000 feet. We could look down into fertile Pavant Valley on one side; on the other we could see Sevier Valley. To think that way up here was where the water came from for both!

"At the ranger's cabin we had a 'skyline breakfast'—orange juice, hot cakes, ham and eggs, with a choice of buttermilk, hot chocolate, or coffee. Then a member of the Soil Conservation Service explained Public Law 566 and showed us how it applied to our watershed."

Public Law 566 is the Watershed Protection and Flood Prevention Act of 1954. It provides a program for rehabilitating damaged watersheds—small ones, of less than 250,000 acres. The projects are *local*, carried out with federal assistance. The responsibility for starting a program lies with the people living in the watershed. When the Federal Government shares expenses, benefits must always exceed costs. The program does not take the place of big dams and other major river flood control projects, but supplements them, because many floods start in small tributaries, building in size as they flow down the creeks and rivers. This law is based on wise land use as the *foundation* of watershed protection and flood prevention. It is administered by the Department of Agriculture.

"After this instruction," Miss Cooper continues, "we began our tour, seeing for ourselves the condition of our watershed. We were told that watersheds can be healthy or sick and were shown what to look for in determining whether a watershed is in good condition."

Except in semidesert areas, a healthy watershed has a good protective covering of thick grasses, shrubs, and trees; the soil is spongy and well littered with dried grass, leaves, and twigs, which help absorb the water until it can sink into the ground. When the soil is protected in this way, there is a good water flow. In a sick watershed the litter is scant, the soil poor in humus, and nine times out of ten there is evidence of fire damage. Bare or weedy areas remain where once forest or grass grew, and the slopes are scarred with gullies. Stream banks are bare and eroding, channels choked with gravel and silt, and the stream is muddy when it rains. Fish like the clear streams of a healthy watershed, but are seldom found in the polluted waters of a sick one.

Protection is needed especially on the higher and rougher portions of watersheds. Here slopes are the steepest and the soil shallow, and here more rain and snow fall than on the lower land. "We saw how terracing controlled the water on these slopes," Miss Cooper says, "holding it back so that it could soak into the ground instead of running off. Recent storms had caused no run-off on the terraced slopes, but on those not terraced there were deep new channels.

"After a box lunch," Miss Cooper continues, "we drove for miles. We were shown overgrazed areas and noted the lack of vegetation— the bare, trampled, eroded ground, the deep gullies and cattle tracks. 'The number of animals in any area must be limited to grazing capacity,' our guide told us. 'When there are too many the grass is cropped to the roots and can't reseed itself. The soil is exposed to erosion— robbed of its power to absorb water. Most people living in communities don't realize that they may have water shortages and floods because, far away in the hills or mountains, a watershed like this has been damaged by overgrazing, improper logging, a forest fire, or some other abuse. That's why the Forest Service and the Soil Conservation Service are always glad to cooperate with citizens' groups like this one.'

"We were taken to an overgrazed area that had been reseeded in the autumn of 1948. It was encouraging to see the grass slowly coming back. In some places where damage was less severe, the land had been left idle to make a natural recovery. Where the forage was thoroughly re-established we saw cattle grazing in tall, thick grass. In beautiful Chalk Creek Canyon we sat on the rocks while the shadows deepened and heard a talk on range management by the Soil Conservation Service representative. He impressed upon us the necessity for stabilizing our soils, using our ranges within reason. 'Grass is a crop, much like any other,' he said. 'Harvest it, but don't destroy it.'

"When it was time to go home, we felt that the tour had been the highlight of our year's program. We learned a lot, had a jolly good time, and found out that conservation is fun."

Our Water Resources

A Water Resource Study

The president of the League of Women Voters said recently that the modern woman "suffers from the common complaint known to all democratic societies—apathy and inertia. But when she gets stirred up she gets things done." There can be little doubt about that, as many of these projects prove. It is too soon to expect tangible results, but the League has undertaken a long-range study of water resources that should be of immeasurable help in giving the public factual knowledge of our pyramiding water problems and the urgent necessity to do something about them. League members throughout the country are holding study and discussion sessions of both national and local water problems, led by well informed committee resource chairmen. The impact will unquestionably be felt in community projects to conserve water and in support of legislation to protect our natural resources.

A Community Pond

To many people, New York means subways, traffic, Broadway shows, and night life, but the State of New York covers nearly 50,000 square miles and includes many rural communities. Jacksonville is such a place in the heart of the beautiful Finger Lakes region, a friendly community like thousands of others all over the United States.

A few years ago Jacksonville had abundant water for general use, but townsfolk were not confident that there was enough in case of a major fire. One day in 1953 Merrill Curry and Fred Frazier, Grange members, were talking about farm ponds and how they had saved several farmers in the county from disastrous fires. Soon they were talking about a community pond and within minutes they had moved on to a discussion of the possibility of building one on the back lot of the Grange Hall—an idle, brush-filled field.

Curry, a farmer and director of the soil conservation district, knew there would be technicalities. "You can't put a pond *anywhere*," he said. "There must be water, a tight soil bottom, and good engineering construction." Frazier, a carpenter, was concerned about cost and labor. "It's a big job for a community as small as ours to tackle," he remarked, "especially with every man having heavy responsibilities of his own." For a while the two men were silent, then they looked at each other and laughed. "We both knew full well the pond was as good as built right then," Frazier said afterward.

Curry requested help from district Soil Conservation Service specialists. A short time later a representative was measuring the slope and dimensions of the field. "People from the city are astonished when they learn that a handful of villagers financed and built such a big project," Bernhard Roth of the Soil Conservation Service says.

"They insist that it couldn't be done. But it was. Without fanfare, Frazier negotiated with a contractor working on a new highway. Soon mammoth machines scooped out a basin and pushed up the earthen dike. Whenever money was needed association members, Grangers, and others dug into their pockets. Furthermore, there was always a ready crew for the hard manual jobs—installing the drain, trickle tube, and flood spillway; for fertilizing, liming, and seeding the big areas of raw ground. Nearly everyone helped, simply because they believed it was worthwhile."

The pond covers more than an acre, and Jacksonville now has two million extra gallons of water on hand for fire protection. An improved road circles the pond, and a ramp runs out on the dam for the convenience of fire fighters. Not only that, this is a multiple use project. On warm days children splash along the shallow shore line, while parents relax nearby or fish from the miniature fleet of rowboats. In the winter there is skating, and twice a year migrating birds rest on the pond. Still, you cannot blame outsiders for saying it couldn't be done. It *was* a big project for such a small group—nine men, four women, and six children.

Protecting Bogs, Sloughs, and Other Wetlands

What are wetlands and why are they important? The term "wetlands" applies to the shallow and sometimes temporary or intermittent waters of the lowlands, as opposed to the permanent waters of streams, rivers, reservoirs, and deep lakes. Marshes, swamps, bogs, wet meadows, potholes, sloughs, river-overflow lands, and some shallow lakes and ponds comprise our wetlands. They are often referred to as shallow water or water-logged lands. Though most communities consider them wastelands, they hold a responsible job in nature's "water factory." When we get rid of them, we pay a heavy price, for they are not expendable. Among other duties, these small reservoirs hold the water where it falls, which is essential in maintaining the water table. They also help to hold it back from a headlong rush to the sea. This is important in preventing floods.

In regard to floods, wetlands are like safety valves. New England more than once in recent years has seen raindrops become raging torrents. In each case the spotlight was thrown upon the damaged areas and the streams that overflowed, in an effort to learn what caused the flood and how a recurrence could be prevented. "More could be learned by studying the areas that received just as much rainfall, but escaped," says Richard Pough, well known conservationist. "Every stream that did its job without seriously overflowing shared one outstanding characteristic. Somewhere along its course it flowed through or past extensive areas of swamp and marsh—lowlands that played the role of a safety valve. Before such rivers could rise even a foot, they had to feed millions of gallons of water into these 'natural' flood control basins. Tremendous as the rainfall and run-off were, these basins were able to absorb and store the water until the river could safely carry it off." When we drain these wetlands indiscriminately, we work *against* nature, instead of *with* her. We take away the "blotters" she uses to control water.

Another penalty could be a lowered water table and water shortages. The water table, it should be understood, is the level of the water present in the earth. This level is maintained by the downward seepage of rain water. Like litter on the forest floor, these small reservoirs give the earth an opportunity to absorb excess water, a portion of which eventually finds its way into storage underground. By thwarting nature's plan for getting water into the ground, we help lower the water table and increase the danger of floods, since run-off is increased. A small run-off here and there becomes important when it is multiplied many times through the sealing up of large surface areas.

The Department of Agriculture estimates the total annual flood and sediment damage in the United States to be slightly more than a billion dollars. The loss of topsoil through water erosion is difficult to measure in dollars, but is even more sobering. Before the Soil Conservation Service was created, our annual loss of soil by water erosion was estimated at about three billion tons a year. It is perhaps difficult to grasp the significance of such losses, but Russell Lord, in the government bulletin, "To Hold This Soil," has done it for us graphically. "If this amount of soil were loaded in coal cars," he says, "it would make a train approximately 476,000 miles long, long enough to girdle the globe at the equator eighteen and a half times." As our country developed, the annual loss of topsoil mounted steadily until it reached this astounding figure. Perhaps it would still be mounting, had it not been for the dramatic dust storms of the depression period which shook us out of our lethargy and forced us to recognize what was happening. It will take a long time to cure our water and soil ills, even with proper treatment. In spite of the healing measures of the Soil Conservation Service, Forest Service, and other agencies, millions of tons of topsoil are *still* being washed away every year.

Another service of the wetlands, perhaps the most important, is to the waterfowl and fur-bearing animals that depend upon them as breeding, wintering, and migrating habitats. By draining these areas we forfeit irreplaceable wildlife. Geese and ducks once bred in the wetlands of Minnesota, Montana, and the Dakotas in such countless millions that they "darkened the sky." Indeed the prairie pothole region in the northern Great Plains and Canada is called a great natural "duck factory," producing three-quarters of all wild ducks hatched in the United States and about 10 per cent of the continental duck population. The American section originally comprised 115,000 square miles, dotted with a myriad of marshes, potholes, bogs, and meandered lakes. But, as farm settlement progressed, much of this land was drained. During World War II the Federal Government offered subsidies for drainage to create more land for crops. The subsidies were continued after the war, and the practice of wetland drainage in this region became general—and controversial. Between 1943 and 1954 so many thousands of acres were drained that sportsmen and many conservationists became alarmed.

Many of the drainage projects were ill-advised, they warned, "practical" only because of subsidies. Some areas cost more to drain than they yielded in crops, these men said, while others proved worthless as cropland. Once drained, the land was valueless as a habitat for waterfowl and the fur-bearing animals that breed in the wetlands. We cannot change the habits of a wildlife species, they advised, and if we destroy its home, we are in danger of losing the species. Wildlife is not just a recreational resource; it is an important resource economically, a vital national asset. It is as much a product of the soil as grain, livestock, or timber, and should have the same consideration in a proper balance of land use. "The most desirable lands for agriculture have been drained," they stated, "and further drainage in this rolling, shallow soil country is not likely to be economically sound. In addition to the erosion problem and possible water shortages created, continued drainage at the present rate would cripple, possibly eliminate, duck and geese production there, destroying the best water-fowl producing region in the United States."

These thousands of small, shallow, temporary water depressions, many containing water only in the spring, are ideal for ducks when they court and pair off to breed, as they like privacy at that time. Later, after the young are hatched, the little family returns to the community life of larger waters. Also the vegetation there is just right, providing suitable cover during the brood-rearing period when the young are flightless and particularly vulnerable to predators. Banding has shown that ducks hatched in this area contribute to the waterfowl population of most states, as well as Canada, and Central and South America. As part of the Pacific Flyway, this region is also of critical importance to migration. Indeed, the United States has assumed a statutory obligation to protect and enhance migratory waterfowl through treaties with Canada and Mexico. Thus conservationists are deeply concerned over the effect of further exploitation of all wetlands in this country, 75 per cent of which have already been destroyed.

Another demonstration of how the loss of wetlands affects wildlife, as well as the public welfare, occurred in Manitoba, Canada, following the searing drought of the mid-thirties. At the turn of the century the trapping grounds along the Saskatchewan River marshes contained thousands of muskrats, minks, and other valuable fur animals. By 1934, the combination of over-trapping, drought, and drainage had reduced this area to dried-out reed beds, virtually empty of wildlife. Several thousand people, mostly native Indians, who depended upon these animals for their livelihood, faced starvation and became dependent upon provincial relief. The Province of Manitoba, as an experiment, undertook marsh restoration and a controlled fur harvest program which included the construction of thousands of small dams to stabilize water levels. Through several years of rigid trapping controls, the animals had an opportunity to breed in sufficient numbers so that they are once again supporting these people. The experiment was so successful that by 1942 it had been extended to 3,580,000 acres of marshlands in Manitoba alone.

The "Save the Wetlands" movement in this country originated in Minnesota in 1951 with the state Bureau of Wildlife Development of the Department of Conservation. The "Land of the Sky Blue

Waters" is popular as a vacation spot, particularly with sportsmen. In the heart of the prairie pothole section, it has a wealth of waterfowl, and the revenue derived from vacationers and sportsmen is important to the state's economy. Like the rest of the region, Minnesota's wetlands were being drained at an alarming rate, and this business, as well as the water level, was threatened. The bureau initiated a program to acquire such areas by outright purchase. The project gained national recognition and influenced action in Canada. As a result of the efforts of sportsmen all over the country, Congress passed an amendment to the Duck Stamp Act in August 1958, whereby the U.S. Fish and Wildlife Service is permitted to obtain adequate amounts of breeding, wintering, and feeding grounds to insure perpetuation of waterfowl populations. However, efforts to safeguard our wetlands have been far from successful, and indiscriminate drainage continues at a tragic rate. The reason undoubtedly is because so few people are aware of their importance, especially in relation to flood control and water supply. The program most urgently needs the support of public-spirited groups everywhere.

Assuring Canadian Waterfowl Habitats

Some conservationists may feel that the interests of sportsmen have no place in a book of this nature. However, America is what it is because the rights of every individual are guaranteed. As an ecologist recognizes the importance of each of nature's creatures in the scheme of things, the interests of all groups must be considered in dealing with our natural resources. Aside from that, the true sportsman is a conservationist himself. He has learned from experience that the balance of nature must be recognized and that if he kills indiscriminately he will soon deprive himself of sport. Because of their great number and the tremendous amount of money they spend, sportsmen can undertake projects beyond the capabilities of the limited number of conservationists in this country. "Ducks Unlimited" is an example.

When, in the late twenties, sportsmen began to realize from numerous observations and disappointing days in the blind that the migratory duck population was decreasing at an alarming rate, a group of them, in 1929, formed an organization called "More Game Birds in America." The purpose was to determine the causes of the decrease and to set up a program for combating those causes. More than a million dollars was contributed by sportsmen all over the country and a long-range program of research was undertaken—one that required ten years. It was discovered that at least 65 per cent of all North American waterfowl originated in three western Canadian provinces—Manitoba, Saskatchewan, and Alberta—and that the decline in ducks was due to drought, and to drainage of the potholes where they bred. Countless thousands of mother ducks and their broods were trapped in waterless areas, dying as they tried to waddle across parched country in search of water and food.

Two problems faced the sportsmen: no federal funds could be spent outside continental United States to rehabilitate the breeding grounds, and a depression existed in Canada as well as in this country. If anything was done, the sportsmen themselves must do it.

United States sportsmen took the responsibility. They formed a Canadian corporation, called "Ducks Unlimited," charged with investing funds raised by sportsmen in the United States. Since its formation almost $5,000,000 has been raised and sent to Canada to rehabilitate the breeding grounds. Over 400 "duck factories" have either been created or restored, with 1,500,000 acres of marsh habitat provided. This has resulted in a 300 per cent increase in ducks. The sportsmen operate a banding station in connection with Ducks Unlimited and bands are sent by the hunters to the Fish and Wildlife Service in Washington, D.C., where records are maintained and flight patterns studied. Some of the wildfowl bred in Canada are recovered as far south as Central and South America, but most of the bands returned are from hunters in forty of the United States.

The Water Pollution Problem

Stream Adoption

We have said that sportsmen are among our most active conservationists. They have carried out many worth-while projects, but none could be more worth-while than their appeal for sportsmen's clubs, communities, and groups to adopt a stream. "Many streams are orphans," says Dr. Charles A. Dambach, former chief of the Ohio Division of Wildlife. "Belonging in part to many, their total welfare is accepted by none." The following is the stream's story, as "translated" by the League of Ohio Sportsmen, sponsors of the adoption movement:

My home is in the heart of the valley. I am a part of the valley.

I owe my existence to the rain which falls on the valley lands, and in turn I protect the valley by carrying away the water which it does not use. I am a stream.

Many years ago my waters flowed clear and cool. Fishes darted from the shade of trees to snatch insects from patches of sunlit surface. Animals came to drink, and some to live in my waters. Grass and shrubs lined my banks. I laughed, for the soil of the valley was rich, and heavy with vegetation. I did not flood when it rained. Even in long periods of drought I did not dry up, for the water which had filtered into the loose earth during the rains slowly and steadily made its way to me and kept me alive.

Then man came. At first I was glad. There was more food for the animals and birds used my waters too. Often he would come to swim or fish, or take bucketsful of water to his house. He even put down a pipe and pumped water.

But gradually a change began to take place. I think I noticed it first when my waters turned brown during a rain. I realized then that many of the trees and shrubs had been cut from the valley and even for stretches along my banks. Earth was coming from the valley lands to cloud my waters, and choke the gills of the fish. Soon I noticed that each rain brought an avalanche of water which flooded my banks and filled my bed with silt. When the rains ceased I was all too soon reduced to a mere trickle. Stagnant pools in my bed covered the few rough fish that still remained. Animals and birds seldom came to drink now. It was small wonder, for I could see in almost all directions to the valley's rim, and a good part of the year it was practically barren of food or cover. Man no longer came to swim or fish, and the pipe which had once extended well into the water was now high and dry except at flood stage.

Then man went to work. At first I thought he was going to help me. But he cut the remaining trees from my banks, ripped out my bed, and left me but a ditch with mud banks in the sun. When the rains came I became a raging torrent, ripping at my earthen walls trying to get at man and wreak my vengeance on him.

At times I wonder why the animals and birds and fish, and man and I, cannot all live in this valley together. Some grass and shrubs in that barren eroded gully where those two slopes come together, a grove of trees on that old gravel pit that is no longer used, some berries along the fence rows, and some grass and trees and shrubs along my banks. It wouldn't take much. Mostly a little common sense, and a little effort. Put a small dam up there where that low spot is and make a pond of it —it doesn't grow anything anyway. It could be done. And it would surely be nice to know that the soil was staying on the land and my waters were clear and cool again, that animals were coming to me, and that man could swim and fish in my waters. I'm willing!

Does anyone want to adopt me?

When a group "adopts" a stream it takes over the responsibility of cleaning it up, planting shrubs and trees along its banks, and doing whatever is needed to restore its beauty. This is done, of course, only with the permission and cooperation of the landowners. The project requires guidance, available through local, county, and state conservation departments, agencies, and districts. It is not a matter of advising landowners as to what is needed, but a roll-up-your-sleeves-and-pitch-in program.

When this idea was launched in 1953, the League of Ohio Sportsmen developed it in a delightfully illustrated booklet, recently reprinted, from which "I Am a Stream" was taken. "Getting things done which need to be done by simply doing them is distinctly American," the writers point out. " 'Adopt a Stream' will work if we make it work. If we wait to pass a law, it will be just another faded idea. If we roll up our sleeves and assume responsibility for its success, it will succeed." The "Adopt a Stream" idea has spread throughout this country, into Canada, and even to foreign countries.

There are neglected streams everywhere. Want to adopt one?

The Brandywine Creek Story

In big-brothering a stream, Dr. Dambach suggests starting with a small one, or part of a larger stream—some project that can be handled easily—and go on from there. The Brandywine Creek story, however, is about a large stream that was adopted. The adoption took place even before the Ohio sportsmen launched their idea, but it illustrates effectively how the community benefits from such projects. Even though it is on a larger scale than most groups would be likely to undertake, it has features that are applicable to a project of any size.

The Brandywine Creek valley takes in parts of Pennsylvania and

Delaware. Two hundred thousand people live in the watershed, which includes 1,500 farms, several towns, and the City of Wilmington, all dependent for water supply upon the creek. A few years ago the Brandywine was an abused, orphaned, polluted stream desperately in need of a friend. Then Clayton Hoff, a chemical engineer, moved to Wilmington from Ohio.

Hoff is an outdoor man and the condition of the stream troubled him. It was laden with silt, sewage, and factory wastes. Unsightly dumps littered its potentially beautiful banks. Along its course old-fashioned farming methods and outdated forestry practices muddied it with topsoil, forcing it to carry away as much as 1,500,000 tons in one year. The topsoil lost to the farmland was deposited in Wilmington's reservoirs and harbor. Both land and water suffered as rainfall ran off the ground instead of soaking into it. During a two-day rain in May, 1947, a billion and a half gallon run-off carried 4,300 tons of silt into Wilmington harbor. The flood problem was not serious but it was bad enough to cause considerable damage, mostly to industrial plants. In 1942 there had been a gully-washer that caused well over $1,500,000 worth of damage.

Hoff talked with hiking friends and landowners. They too were disturbed by the situation but there seemed to be nothing anyone could do about it. Then Hoff got an idea. He took color slides of the creek, showing what was happening to it, and invited fifty influential valley residents to see them. Only thirty-five came, but they were impressed. As a result, the Brandywine Valley Association was formed with Hoff as executive vice-president. Expenses for the first two years were to be underwritten by the group. Edmund Du Pont was elected president.

Two tasks lay immediately ahead—determining what measures were needed to correct the situation and educating landowners and the public to the need for them. For the first, Hoff relied on forest and soil specialists and sanitary engineers. For the second he trusted in his camera and good public relations.

This watershed covers an area of 300 square miles, but Hoff believed that if he could get enough people to examine the facts shown in his color slides, something would be done about the polluted river. He was right. The entire valley now thinks and acts as one community about common water problems, with individuals, industries, and local, state, and federal agencies all working together. At least 90 per cent of the pollution has been cleaned up, and the Brandywine Valley Association is working for an even better percentage.

The first step was to have cleanup crews clear away stream-side dumps. Soil and forest experts then showed farmers how to hold their topsoil through contour planting, terracing, improved pastures, and other scientific soil practices. Many farm ponds were constructed. Municipalities and industries cooperated by installing waste disposal plants. Delaware passed a pure stream law, and Pennsylvania put teeth into an existing one. As a result, agricultural production and income have increased, new industries have been attracted, flood damage alleviated, and the whole valley has benefited. In several instances industries have paid for the cost of waste treatment with recovered by-products. Once again the stream is a clear, sparkling thing of beauty.

All this was done through an intensive, long-range educational program. When the association undertook the project it was pioneering grass-roots watershed protection. Because of its scope, Mr. Hoff and his assistant were paid on a full-time basis. Since the association was formed in 1946, the two men have averaged five talks a week, addressing every organized group of significance in the area. Hoff estimates that the Brandywine's plight has been presented to over 75 percent of the valley residents outside Wilmington and to more than half of those in the city. The tools are a camera, a projector, and the human voice—nothing more. At the time Delaware was considering its pure stream law, Hoff gave, at the request of one of the senators, an illustrated lecture titled "The Brandywine: Stream or Sewer?" before the assembled legislators.

The association has advanced its educational program through the establishment of a Soil Conservation District in Chester County, and conservation courses for teachers, financed by Granges, garden clubs, and other groups. Several farmers said they became interested in scientific farm methods by conservation essay contests their children entered at school. Mr. Hoff's goal is the establishment of such practices on every farm in the valley. "Practices developed in the name of soil conservation promise a solution for most water problems," he says, "and build fertility instead of wasting or drowning productive land."

The Brandywine Valley Association project has been the inspiration for similar projects in other communities.

Industrial Wastes in the Kalamazoo

The troubles of the Kalamazoo River in Michigan were caused by industrial waste. Fifteen paper mills dot its banks and because 35,000 gallons of water are required to make a ton of paper the river is important to the lives and the livelihood of the people in this area. But industrial wastes from these mills and sewage from the communities along its course had created a pollution problem so acute that the odor from this once beautiful river had become unbearable. Rivers usually become more highly industrialized downstream, but the reverse was true of the Kalamazoo. More hardship was experienced in communities that got no benefit from the mills. They were losing the potential assessed valuation of thousands of building sites along the river and, where it wound through forested areas, people who were trying to develop vacation resorts were finding conditions that made their plans practically impossible. The river had not grown through the years, but the size of its load had. There were just too many people and too many mills for such a small river to support.

To city officials who were trying to find a solution, the problem was far easier to state than to solve. The original mills came into the area during the depression and provided badly needed jobs. At that time industrial wastes thrown into the river were insufficient to constitute a public problem. As the region prospered, the mills grew larger and more numerous, increasing the load of the river. Yet to curtail production to ease the load would have meant unemployment. If some of the mills were to move away, the economy of the whole area would be upset. The only alternative was to find a way to treat the wastes. A further complication was the fact that the mills were of various kinds so that no single solution could apply to all. This in turn meant research, experiment, higher production costs, and an increase in the price of paper. Even so, there was still the matter of municipal sewage which contributed equally to pollution of the river. It costs money to treat sewage. Would the taxpayers be willing to pay for it, even though they had demanded that something be done?

This was the situation in March 1951, when a delegation of indignant citizens from downstream communities called upon Milton

C. Adams, chairman of the Michigan Water Resources Commission, insisting upon action. Adams was aware that if all the communities along the river had worked together years ago in planning their growth, this problem would not have arisen, but there was no point in going into that now. How could a fair and reasonable solution be worked out? Calling in the mill owners, he put the matter squarely up to them. They were responsible for industrial wastes, and theirs was the responsibility for reducing this load on the river. As a consequence the mills installed filters, clarifiers, chemical washers, settling basins, and whatever means were feasible to relieve the situation. Meanwhile the mayor of Kalamazoo had appointed a commission to study sewage disposal, with Dr. Harold Taylor, director of the Upjohn Foundation for Economic Research, as chairman. When the committee made its recommendations to Mr. Adams, he put the matter of sewage waste squarely up to the people, realizing that any plan must have the support of the voters. A $3,000,000 bond issue would be needed to construct a sewage disposal plant, and the voters would have to approve it.

To keep the people informed, an interesting public relations technique was used. The mayor appointed a committee of twenty-two men and women to review Dr. Taylor's report and, if they approved it, to recommend a "yes" vote. On the committee were representatives from labor, business, minority groups, the board of realtors, and the board of education. It included the president of one of the largest concerns in the city and the janitor of one of the smallest. After a month of study, the committee recommended a "yes" vote. This, together with the commission's findings, was highly publicized. On election day the people approved the building of a sewage disposal plant by an 80 per cent majority.

The pollution problem in the Kalamazoo River is not completely solved and may never be, but conditions are greatly improved and both industry and the community now realize the value of cooperation. Construction of treatment plants, the Public Health Service states, has not kept pace with the increasing amount of sewage and industrial wastes being discharged into our rivers and lakes. If such pollution is to be controlled, the Service advises, municipalities must build additional sewage treatment works or improve existing facilities, and the public must be willing to pay for this. Industry also must do its part by constructing waste treatment plants and by using good housekeeping methods to reduce the amount of waste that enters such plants. Such improvements are costly but, where public health is concerned, is cost the most important factor?

The Federal Water Pollution Control Act (Public Law 660), passed in 1956, provides financial aid, research, consultative services, and other federal assistance to state and interstate agencies and municipalities in an effort to encourage control of water pollution. A Water Pollution Control Advisory Board, appointed by the president, has been set up with "authority for enforcement against pollution of interstate waters, where such pollution endangers the health or welfare of persons in a state other than the one in which the discharge of pollution originates." The act is administered by the Surgeon General of the U.S. Public Health Service, who is also chairman of the advisory board. A progress report in the fall of 1958 listed 1,203 municipalities in all fifty states, the District of Columbia, Puerto Rico, and the Virgin Islands, as having sewage treatment projects under way, approved, or completed. The total expenditure amounts to about forty-five million dollars a year, with the Federal Government paying about 30 per cent of the cost. This is encouraging, but of course it is only a beginning. The real problem is truly staggering.

El Pumpo

Because of its size, varying climate and topography, and the blending of so many different peoples and interests, the United States has a tremendous diversity of problems. One is that of reaching people who cling to traditional living patterns and view with suspicion the efforts of government or private groups to help them. Instead of cooperation such groups contribute apathy, extravagant hopes and demands, ridicule, and often downright hostility to improvement projects. *Giving* them things is usually a mistake and it has been found that doing things *for* them is also a mistake. A better living standard may be within the scope of their resources, but the question is how to bring it to them. Like all of us, they judge the country as a whole by the community in which they live, but it is important to the United States that they share in general improvements.

The Department of Public Health in New Mexico was faced with this problem a few years ago in irrigated areas. New Mexico is arid and the lives of the people in many sections are governed by the quantity, quality, and availability of water. With water so scarce, it became only natural to establish villages along streams and in river valleys. As irrigation ditches were constructed, the farmhouses were built along the ditches, which became the source of the family water supply. They were used also for stock watering and the disposal of waste, including barnyard manure and sewage. The family laundry went into the ditch too. Indeed the ditch became well known in many parts of the state as *Acequia Madre*, "Mother Ditch," supplying all water needs of the family.

Historically, New Mexico has had one of the highest infant death rates in the United States and has been plagued with high morbidity rates. Contaminated water contributed to both.

"We were wondering how to handle such a tremendous problem," recalls Charles G. Caldwell, Director of Environmental Sanitation Services, "how to change the customs of people who had been using ditch water in this way for generations. Attempts to explain bacteria were useless since they had neither the background nor the education to understand. Also there was to some extent a fatalistic attitude that people die when their time comes, regardless of other factors."

About this time (1946) a New Mexico senator who understood the problem called upon the Department of Health, saying that he would like to do something for these people. The state did not have enough money for the whole job, he explained, and for that matter he did not think it should assume the entire responsibility. On the other hand, he realized that the per capita income in the area was small and that the people could contribute little. "But they do have the muscle needed to build a safe water project," he pointed out. "They can dig ditches, erect structures, and supply some of the local things necessary if we can get the state to put up the money for materials that must be purchased."

"We discussed the matter back and forth," Mr. Caldwell says, "and wrote several pieces of legislation, trying to arrive at the best answer. Finally we had the rough draft of a bill which provided essentially that any community in which there were ten or more families could incorporate as a Mutual Domestic Water Consumers Association. If they would agree to do all the work and supply all local material, the state would provide the funds for drilling a well, buying a pump, a storage tank, and the pipe to which it would be connected, together with all valves and appurtenances. We would then run the pipeline to the village plaza or community square where people could take home buckets of safe water instead of using water from contaminated irrigation ditches, rivers, or ponds.

"The association must agree that its members would do all the work, maintain and operate the water project upon its completion, and collect dues to maintain the equipment. People moving into the village must be permitted to join the association upon payment of a membership fee. Members must also agree to hold regular monthly meetings and to handle all affairs in an orderly manner."

The bill was passed but, instead of the $300,000 appropriation asked, the department was granted $40,000 for a test run. The legislators said, in effect: "We will wait and see. If the project is successful, we may give you more." It was estimated that four projects could be built with the amount, which was to cover a two-year period.

The problem now—and the major one—was to sell the idea to the people. "These communities had never had any type of political organization," Mr. Caldwell explains. "They were unincorporated farming communities. Because of the low evaluation most of them never paid property taxes. They were deathly afraid to enter into any agreement with the state, even for a water project, because they thought it might mean losing their homes or being obliged to pay huge sums which they could not afford."

In spite of its efforts the department could interest no one. Days, weeks, and months passed. The men had become so discouraged that they were almost ready to forget the whole thing when a minister from one of the smallest communities came to see them. He hesitated a moment, then said resolutely, "I want to talk about this water project."

"We discussed it with him," Mr. Caldwell continues, "and he said that he had talked to his congregation and they had finally decided to take a chance—that he thought this was a good thing and that the state was sincere. He wanted to know where to sign. It was only a small community, twenty-four families, but we were overjoyed. We finally had a project!"

The project was given "fanfare and wide publicity." Then the big day arrived. "It must be understood," Mr. Caldwell explains, "that in the areas where we were working, people did not understand that

you could drill a hole in the ground and get water. They had no idea
how a pump works, and a well-drilling rig was really something. You
can imagine the parades of people that thronged the highway leading into our little town when a well-drilling rig arrived, followed by
a truck with a 10,000 gallon storage tank on it, another truck loaded
with pipes and valves, plus the contractor and some of his men."

As a spectacle, the trucks and equipment were exciting, but when
the rig started punching a hole in the ground the reaction ranged
from superstitious terror to derisive mockery. "Old-timers were betting
we'd never get water," Mr. Caldwell remembers with a wry smile.
"They were sure the whole thing would fail and told us that it was
in no way sensible. Everything we were doing was contrary to their
custom and belief, and they were angered that some of their own
people were helping with such a ridiculous project." Some tried to
pull the workers away; others laughed and poked fun at them, and
some even threatened them. "But the minister and his group stayed
right with us," Mr. Caldwell says, "and we developed an excellent
well, installed the pump, set up the tank, and in short order twenty-
four families were running around smiling because they no longer
had to drink the dirty ditch water."

But now the people had a problem: what to call this miracle that
brought water up out of the ground. A new word must be coined.
Then suddenly from the lips of a child it came—"El Pumpo!"

With clean water the attitude of the people in the village changed
completely. Children's faces were scrubbed, the men wore clean shirts
and the women fresh dresses. Soon other villages were clamoring for
"El Pumpo," and the department was able to carry out seven additional projects. The legislators were delighted and increased the water
appropriation. "There is never any question about the 'Little Water
Projects' bill any more," Mr. Caldwell says. "It is passed unanimously
at every session on a bi-partisan basis."

Most of these communities today have a water distribution system,
with practically every home supplied, but the department long ago
stopped trying to explain bacteria except to a few; in most cases safe
water is installed so the people won't have to haul muddy water from
the ditch any longer.

Not only has the attitude of the people changed but their life
pattern has been altered. Many have bathrooms with hot and cold
water and most of them have washing machines. Children can play

instead of feeding fires and hauling ditch water. Their parents too have leisure for other activities, and have learned the value of organized community life.

The next project will be sewer systems and the same plan will be followed. Once a community has been assisted in financing a water project it carries on from there, paying the maintenance costs, but additional help will be given when the sewer system is constructed. This arrangement encourages community initiative and responsibility, and encourages also the establishment of sinking funds and sound planning.

Pollution Research

Providing money for research is another way in which citizens can help in the conservation of natural resources. No other investment pays such high dividends. Research might develop a less costly method to control water pollution by sewage and industrial wastes. Dr. Ruth Patrick, Curator of the Department of Limnology at the Academy of Natural Sciences in Philadelphia, Pennsylvania, is seeking the answer in nature by studying how a stream purifies itself. This is known to be accomplished by living organisms, both plant and animal. The secret apparently lies in the maintenance of a proper balance among organism populations—a system whereby the numbers are kept in check by feeding upon one another. When a substance, entering the stream, upsets this balance, the stream loses some of its ability to recover. Dr. Patrick is trying to determine how much waste the organisms in a given stream will tolerate without damaging its natural power to recover. If waste disposal can be kept within the limits of the stream's power to cleanse itself, the cost of treatment might be reduced considerably. In connection with this research, the academy has developed a device which indicates how "sick" a stream or river is, much as a fever thermometer measures illness in a person.

Our soil, forests, minerals, and wildlife *could* be depleted to the point of disaster without most of us realizing what was happening until too late, because we are not affected directly or immediately by their loss. This is not true of water. The slightest shortage in our community is felt at once, and no one has to tell us how serious a water famine would be. Every day we are becoming more fully aware that we must conserve water, use it wisely and without waste.

CHAPTER VIII

SCIENTIFIC SOIL
CONSERVATION

Soil conservation begins in your backyard. But just what *is* your backyard? The Department of Agriculture says: "Your backyard consists of that little plot of ground that lies in back of the house where you live. It is here that you nurse a lawn, grow a few tomatoes, raise petunias, or build a rock garden. Your backyard is the farmland that surrounds your community, the land a thousand miles around that provides you with the necessary food, clothing and shelter. Your backyard is the forest land, the rivers, the marshes, the mountains and the plains where live your 180 million or more fellow Americans. *Your backyard is the good old U.S.A.*"

Every homeowner with even a postage stamp of a backyard knows the value of topsoil, but most people are not aware that our big backyard—the U.S.A.—has been robbed of millions of tons of topsoil by erosion, over a third of our original heritage. Wind and water scour the fertility from some 400,000 acres of food-growing land each year. When the Pilgrims sat down to their first Thanksgiving feast, the average depth of our topsoil was about nine inches. The average depth today is estimated to be between five and six inches. As we know, we *live* from this thin layer of irreplaceable soil that blankets the earth. It is the source of our food, the chief support of life. Our survival depends upon it.

Soil scientists say that well over 282 million acres of crop and grazing land in this country have been seriously damaged or ruined by soil erosion. This is about equal to the combined areas of Illinois, Iowa, Missouri, Kansas, Nebraska, and Wyoming. Another 775 million acres of land are moderately eroded, and 700 million more are slightly eroded. Most of our land is, in fact, subject to erosion if not protected, since the greater part of it is more or less sloping. This applies to much of our 478 million acres of productive cropland, including 69 million acres of rotating pasture. Thus, combating soil erosion becomes one of our most critical conservation problems.

Like every other natural action, erosion has an essential function, playing an important role in the formation of soil. But it takes from 300 to 500 years to create *one* inch of topsoil. When soil scientists speak of erosion as a destructive force, they are not referring to "natural" or "geologic" erosion, which has been going on for millions of years. They are referring to an accelerated type of soil erosion, caused by man's interference with natural processes. As we have explained, the roots of tough grasses, shrubs, and trees anchor soil to the ground, protecting it from wind and water which would otherwise carry it away. Some soil is lost even when the surface is protected, but under natural conditions the amount lost is more or less balanced by the creation of new soil. This is possible because the action of wind and water is slowed by protective covering, giving nature time to work. However, if this covering is removed and the land left unprotected, erosion may be speeded up a thousand times. That is what man has unwittingly done. The erosion he has induced deprives us in a few years of soil that took nature countless centuries to build.

Soil erosion has been called an enemy of civilization, a digger of graveyards, the conqueror of empires. It has damaged or ruined for practical use hundreds of millions of acres of once-productive land all over the world. Authorities say that for those who know how to read the story, the rise and fall of civilizations is written on the lands they have occupied as clearly as words in a book. In his dynamic booklet "Conquest of the Land Through 7,000 Years," Dr. W. C. Lowdermilk, former Assistant Chief of the Soil Conservation Service, U.S. Department of Agriculture, shows how civilization after civilization has risen to power on the strength of abundant resources, only to crumble and fall as the land became exhausted and unable to support the people. At the request of a congressional committee, Dr. Lowdermilk was sent on an eighteen-month tour of western Europe, North Africa, and the Middle East in 1938-39 to gain information which would help solve soil erosion problems in this country. Before that he had spent several years in China studying soil erosion and land use. The desolation he found in areas where civilizations had once flourished burned into Dr. Lowdermilk's consciousness "the full and fateful significance of soil erosion." "My experience with famine in China," he writes, "taught me that in the last reckoning all things are purchased with food. If we in this country are to be safe in the security of our land," he continues, "we must conserve the physical integrity of the soil, for if the soil is destroyed, then our liberty of choice and action is gone."

To the colonists, coming from over-crowded countries where the land could no longer support the population, the New World must indeed have appeared "a land flowing with milk and honey." Before them lay a vast wilderness, with seemingly inexhaustible resources. The soil had never felt the touch of a plow, the streams were clear and teeming with fish, wildlife was plentiful, the earth an unopened chest of priceless minerals, and great primeval forests stretched over the land. Some of these people may not have known much about land care but most of them did. Among the English colonists were men who had owned small farms and been noted for their industry and independence of spirit. They knew how to care for the soil for, through necessity, they had husbanded it with painstaking care in their homeland. And in spite of the abundance of fertile soil all around them, many continued to do so here.

But there were others who went on a land-spending spree. They farmed their land until it was no longer productive, then abandoned it and moved on to fresh fields. Indeed, the practice of pulling up stakes and moving on when the soil lost its fertility became all too common and continued throughout the development of this country until there were no more new lands to "conquer." Loss of fertility was not the only reason for abandoning a farm, however. Sometimes land was abandoned because it turned out to be unsuitable for agriculture: it was land that should never have been plowed. Such land accounts for much of the "land nobody wants" in our country today. Usually such land is heavily eroded since it was left without any protection from wind and rain. From the beginning, far-sighted men protested this practice, among them Washington, Jefferson, and Patrick Henry. Surely it is more than a coincidence that the same men who envisioned liberty as the foundation of the land also recognized the land as the foundation of liberty.

For the most part, the people who settled the United States came from the British Isles and northern Europe, and naturally they used the farming methods familiar to them. But the long straight furrows that were the Old World farmer's pride turned out to be ruinous on the sloping land of North America. For almost 300 years we did not realize what was happening. That is why soil erosion is so dangerous— the damage is usually done before we even suspect trouble. It was not until the tragic dust storms of the thirties that erosion was finally recognized as a critical national problem.

There are a number of reasons why erosion got such a stranglehold on our soil before anything was done about it. First, there was so much land compared to the population that no one thought of being careful about it. Second, the country was developed at such a headlong pace that there was no time for soil problems. Third, land was cheap and, like most things that are both cheap and plentiful, it did not command the respect accorded it in densely populated countries. Japan too is subject to severe erosion, due to steep slopes, erodable soil, and heavy rains. But the Japanese have had an active erosion control program since 1885, and have developed systems of soil conservation in mountainous and hill lands that authorities say are perhaps unexcelled anywhere in the world. The Dutch too have a deep feeling for the land, having wrested most of it from the sea. And those who know the Riviera have seen the soil husbandry of the thrifty French. It might also be said that anyone who has seen the deeply eroded hillsides of North Africa and the poverty of the people there can never dismiss erosion with an indifferent shrug.

There is little doubt that squandering, indifference, and greed were contributing factors in the injury done our soil through erosion. However, such motives do not provide the whole answer, or even a major part of it. There are always those who have no regard for anything, in every age and country. But that could not be said for most of the pioneer men and women who trudged across this land of ours to establish homes and towns. These people would not knowingly have maimed the land or undermined the security of future generations. A logical explanation might be that they were not familiar with the type of erosion we have in this country, and would not have known what to do about if they had. They knew other land care, it is true. But our type of erosion is something they probably had had little or no experience with in their homelands.

The climate of the British Isles and northern Europe is generally mild, with gentle winds and rains. Under such conditions, erosion is gentle too, especially on a rolling landscape like England's. Dr. Lowdermilk found that the English had comparatively little trouble with erosion. On the other hand, our climate is varied, with strong winds and torrential rains that develop suddenly. Broad areas are subject to prolonged drought. By contrast, England has abundant rainfall, coming in mists, while a state like Utah has a desert-type climate similar to that of Iran. On sloping land such as we have, long straight furrows invite accelerated erosion. Gusty winds and heavy rains sweep down them unhampered, carrying the topsoil with them. If a drought comes, the soil may become parched and powdery, so that a strong wind can sweep tons of it into the air in great choking clouds within a short time, while the land aches for rain. People from the arid and semiarid regions of the Old World might have foreseen what could happen, but those from a moist maritime climate, who had never heard of a dust storm, could hardly have been expected to understand.

We must consider too that when the homesteaders migrated westward there were people of almost every type driving those covered wagons. Not all were skilled farmers, knowing the needs of the soil, but most of them managed rather well as long as the fresh fertility of the soil lasted. But by the time that was gone and erosion had set in, they were in no economic position to correct matters even if they had known how. This was also true in the South, said to be one of the most heavily eroded sections of the country. After the Civil War, many plantation owners were forced to sell their land at auction for whatever they could get. Others, burdened by debt, resorted to share cropping. Even landowners who were able to keep their holdings were in no financial position to practice erosion control.

It is easy to condemn our forefathers for what happened to the land, but lack of knowledge and economic necessity probably had more to do with those millions of eroded acres than anything else.

The point is, will future generations condemn *us* for not having done our part to rebuild the land when we have the knowledge and the resources to do it?

How the Soil Conservation Service Works

A Brief History of the Service

Someone has said that necessity is the mother of conservation. Certainly that is true in the United States. The Soil Conservation Service, our first line of defense today in the battle against erosion, was born of emergency work undertaken in the depression years of the thirties. Some projects in erosion prevention and control were undertaken in 1933 primarily to provide jobs for unemployed men. Then, on May 11, 1934, we had our first giant dust storm in what has since become known as the "Dust Bowl." This brought to acute focus the need for erosion control on a national scale. Clouds of dust, lifted from the Great Plains, blew across two-thirds of the nation. The sky grew so dark as far away as Washington that lights burned in the Capitol at high noon. Strong winds carried the dust into New York City where it drifted into skyscrapers and covered office desks with a gray film. The people of the United States were shocked when they learned that this was *soil* blowing away—topsoil from fields that had been seas of ripening wheat. The rest of the world was shocked too, especially those who remembered that these same wheatfields had meant bread to so many hungry people in war-torn Europe a few years before.

But the greatest shock came to the people in the panhandles of Oklahoma and Texas, the heart of the dust-stricken area. They stood by helplessly while the wind brought them desolation and ruin, making their fields look like a desert in a sandstorm. Huge banks of dust piled against fences, barns, and houses like drifts of dirty snow. In the fields, expensive farm equipment lay buried in the dust. Almost overnight self-respecting farmers became paupers, and thousands of families had to leave their land and become migrant workers, welcome nowhere.

From its inception, the Soil Conservation Service has had inspired leadership and is characterized today by dedicated personnel of top-flight ability. Its first chief was Dr. Hugh H. Bennett, known affectionately to his men as "Big Hugh," with Dr. Lowdermilk as assistant chief. There were many problems facing the fledgling SCS, which started as one-man desk space in the Department of the Interior and later became an important branch of the Department of Agriculture. First, scientific soil methods had to be worked out both for the prevention and control of erosion and for the best and most productive use of all types of land. This meant research. Second, if the program— of necessity a long-range one—was to succeed, public and congressional support must be maintained long after the dramatic impact of the dust storm was forgotten. Third, that rugged individualism so dear to the American heart must be respected. New methods, however necessary or sound, could not be forced on anyone. Farmers, ranchers, and other landowners must be educated to their use—sold, not told. And of course there was the matter of finding trained men. This was a large order, but the stature of the men in the SCS was equal to the size of the job. Within a few years our genius for know-how had worked out scientific soil methods that today are unsurpassed anywhere, and they are still being improved.

When this country was founded, a bold new pattern of life was cut for the New World, based on liberty and equality. Unfortunately, there was no new pattern for the new land. Instead, an age-old pattern was used, one that had destroyed countless civilizations and brought famine from time immemorial. But now the land also was to have a bold new pattern, based upon its rolling contours.

As the SCS explains it, "we had put a square pattern on round land." Our farms were a patchwork of square fields set down every which way, without much thought for the character of the land. All too often the land had not been treated according to its needs or used according to its capability. For example, some land in the Dust Bowl was not suited to continuous cultivation and should never have been plowed. It belonged in grass which would have held the soil in place and helped to retain moisture. In other cases grasslands had grown so thin from overgrazing that the soil had no protection from the hot sun and drying wind. When strong, steady winds swept over these acres after recurrent droughts, millions of tons of topsoil went along with them.

The first step then was to use the land according to its capability, the second to treat it according to its needs. For the first, the SCS worked out land classifications to help farmers determine the proper use of their land. (The same farm may have land that falls into several classifications, in which case each piece is used accordingly: in cultivation, meadow, woodland, pond, and so on.) For the second, after years of neglect, new designs were created for the land, as individual as a couturier's pattern. Instead of straight furrows on slopes, the land was to be plowed on the contour, following the lay of the land instead of running counter to it. There is a definite reason for this: curved furrows catch rainfall and allow the water to soak into the ground, thus saving both water and soil. On soils that erode easily, or on steep slopes, strips of close-growing plants such as grass and clover were to be set between alternate strips of row crops such as corn and potatoes. This is especially helpful in controlling erosion during heavy rains. The same principle was to be followed on level stretches of the western plains where rainfall is scant and winds blow with great force. However, in this case the strips were to be straight rather than curved, running *across* the path of the wind and helping to break its force.

These are only a few of the methods that were worked out to save our topsoil, but the broad waving lines of this new design can be seen from an airplane, streamlined like a fine automobile. Other simple techniques were found that worked minor miracles in the battle against erosion. Every southerner knows what porch-vine is. It has been used for years to screen front porches. Soil conservationists tested it on small gullies to see if it would hold the soil in place. It did. Then they discovered that cows like it. Today the porch-vine is famous as kudzu, a plant that is protecting thousands of acres from erosion while providing valuable food for livestock.

Scattered water holes and salt blocks on rangeland are another aid. Three-fourths of the land in the western half of the United States is used for livestock, producing more than half of our cattle and most of our sheep. But before we learned sound range management, ranchers often put too many animals on the range, more than the land could support. As a result many of our rangelands are seriously overgrazed, and in such poor condition that soil experts say it may take a hundred years to get them back to their original vigor. Restoring them calls for careful planning, skill, and time. Ranchers must make a living, livestock must eat, we must have meat and wool, and the range must be restored to good condition, all at the same time.

Here again simple techniques have helped. When the range is in poor condition, more land is needed to support a given number of animals. Therefore, using the whole range is important. But this is dry country, and the water-hole is just as important to the animals as grass. They have a tendency while grazing to stay near their water supply, and this is true also of the salt blocks which are so necessary to them. As a result the grass near the water is likely to be cropped so closely that the soil is bared and erosion begins. Range conservationists found that by scattering water-holes and salt blocks throughout the range, the animals would wander from one to another, thus cropping the grass more evenly over the whole range.

In its early days the SCS concerned itself mainly with research and experimentation, of which Dr. Lowdermilk's tour was a part. Then the educational program was undertaken, with hundreds of demonstration projects carried out in all parts of the country to show farmers and ranchers how scientific land use and care would benefit them. Later, soil conservation districts were established, making technical advice and help available to all who wished it. This proved so successful that the work is now carried out entirely through these districts. SCS men fought hard for their program and are still fighting for it. As Dr. Bennett said: "If a foreign nation should invade this country, every man, woman, and child would immediately rise to the defense of our land. We would throw the enemy out regardless of cost. *Now we have gone to war against erosion.*"

Today there are 2,800 conservation districts, established in all fifty states, as well as in Puerto Rico and the Virgin Islands. Scientific practices are being followed on millions of acres, for which the SCS most assuredly deserves the highest honors. However, the fight against erosion has really just begun. True, we have the knowledge, but human nature being what it is, many people are not receptive to new ideas and different ways of doing things. This applies to farmers and ranchers as to other people. We have in the SCS and Forest Service what many consider to be the best scientific knowledge in their respective fields of any in the world. Such knowledge avails us nothing if it is not used. In the case of the Forest Service, the national forests have provided a dramatic demonstration of good forestry practice, proving to private owners what can be done. But with the SCS, the road has been rougher—almost farm to farm and ranch to ranch. Time too has been against them since results are often not apparent for several years. "We have enough good land in this nation to keep us prosperous and well fed if we conserve and improve it," these men say. "We know we can do this, and we know how to do it. We can make most of our land produce more and more, year after year. But—will we do it in time?"

Brackettville's Soil Conservation District

The manner in which people tackle the job is as American as cowboy and Indian movies—each community handling it in its own way. The farmers and ranchers in and around Brackettville, Texas, are all using scientific land practices today although most of them opposed the formation of a conservation district a few years ago. Credit for the changed attitude goes to the New World Study Club, a member of the General Federation of Women's Clubs. The members of this club are the first women to be responsible for the formation of a district. Indirectly, they were also responsible for others, established as a result of the success of this one.

There are some farms in what is now the West Nueces–Las Moras Soil Conservation District, but this is mostly ranch country, rich in frontier history as part of the "Old West." The area is in the southwestern part of Texas, below the Big Bend of the Rio Grande. To the east is San Antonio, site of the Alamo and a lusty, roaring "cow town" in the trail-driving days after the Civil War. To the southeast is the fabulous King Ranch, reminiscent of the days of the open range, when cowboys drove the longhorns over the trails to the Kansas railheads, or on up to Montana. To the west is Mexico. Through the Brackettville section flows the Nueces River which Mexico once claimed as the boundary between the two countries rather than the Rio Grande. This dispute triggered the Mexican War.

Texans are no longer fighting Indians and rustlers, with a man's life depending upon a fast draw. They are fighting erosion, an enemy insidious and ruthless, and a way of life depends upon how fast it is conquered. The Brackettville area pivots on livestock and through the years the land has become badly overgrazed. As a result, floods and prolonged droughts have been very damaging. In many places the thick native grasses have been replaced by invading plants that are worthless and even poisonous to livestock. Ranchers have suffered livestock loss from all three causes and since this is beef, wool, and mohair country we have all been affected indirectly. In addition to high-bred cattle, sheep, and goats, the area produces Quarter horses that are known the world over.

Some ranchers felt that the answer to their common problem lay in the organization of a soil conservation district. Others strongly opposed the idea. In this case the opposition did not stem from antipathy to modern techniques, for most ranchers realized the urgent need for scientific ranching. Apparently it sprang from a deep-rooted reluctance to "tie up" with the government in any way, for fear of relinquishing their right to do as they pleased with their land, and putting themselves into a position where they could be "pushed around" by the government. Texas fought a revolutionary war of its own before becoming a part of the United States. It had its own army of independence under General Sam Houston and won its freedom from Mexico in 1836. Living in the theater where the drama was enacted, the past is still too vividly real for a Texan to take his freedom lightly. When the rumor spread that, by becoming a member of a soil conservation district, a rancher would be putting his land under government control, most Texans stopped listening right there and voted the project down. When the issue came up a second time they voted it down again.

Meanwhile droughts persisted and poisonous weeds became a greater menace, with livestock losses increasing steadily. The women decided to take charge. There is in Texan women much of the courageousness that marked our pioneer days. The important thing, members of the New World Study Club decided, was to get the true facts about conservation districts and present them to the men. Mrs. O. R. Davis, then conservation chairman, arranged a joint meeting of the civic and service clubs, open to all farmers and ranchers in the area. Then she invited SCS men to address the meeting and explain how a district operates. The soil men gave demonstrated talks on what they were doing, why they were doing it, and how they went about it in language the people understood. They made it clear that no individual liberties would be surrendered if a district was formed, that the SCS was rendering technical assistance in scientific farming and ranching as a public service. The people were free to refuse it or take advantage of it. When the Texans realized that they would set up and run their own district, under Texas laws, their attitude changed.

The club arranged similar meetings in other localities, making sure that everyone had an opportunity to get the facts firsthand, and that any lingering misapprehensions were dispelled. Then they went from ranch to ranch, distributing SCS literature and getting out the vote. This time the district was voted "in" almost unanimously. Farms and ranches in the area are now work-plotted and long-range programs are under way for the restoration of the land. Drought is still the major problem, but conservation measures, employed expertly, make the best use of every drop of rain.

The Role of Women in Soil Conservation Districts

Women everywhere are taking an active part in these districts. The Women's Auxiliary of the National Association of Soil Conservation Districts, with headquarters in League City, Texas, has assumed much of the responsibility for the educational activities of the districts. This program includes strong support of Soil Stewardship Week each year, distributing brochures, giving information; serving as guides at district pilot and demonstration projects, working with youth groups, and bringing conservation into the programs of women's organizations. They also provide libraries with books and other material about natural resources and work closely with school authorities to make conservation instruction a part of the school curriculum. At home they teach their children good land use and the effect scientific soil practices have on nutrition.

"Soil conservation used to be considered strictly male territory," George Peterson wrote editorially in the *Minneapolis Star-Journal* a few years ago. "Now the women want in. Not only *want* in . . . they *are* in. And the men are encouraging it."

Plowing Contests with a New Twist

Soil conservation districts enable communities to tackle, cooperatively, land problems affecting large areas which may include several farms or ranches—problems that landowners cannot solve individually. In this way a farmer or rancher who uses conservation measures on his own land is assured that his efforts will not be offset by the negligence of his neighbor. But getting everyone in an area to cooperate is often a ticklish problem since people can be "pretty set in their ways." Lack of cooperation makes effective management difficult for more progressive landowners if the particular soil problem affects a whole area. The SCS has overcome such opposition by various means. One way has been to tie up with plowing contests, a tradition in many rural communities. A typical example is provided by an account of the National Plowing Matches at Wabash, Indiana, in 1955.

For generations farmers have held plowing contests at county and state fairs to see who could plow the straightest furrow. These straight furrows, as we have seen, are suitable on flat, or nearly flat, land but disastrous on land that slopes. The problem was how to get this point across without attacking a time-honored tradition and possibily arousing greater antagonism toward scientific soil use. The SCS solved it by having two contests: one for straight furrows and one for contour plowing, both with generous prizes.

The Wabash affair was a big four-day "World's Fair of Agriculture," combining the State and National Plowing Contests, National Conservation Days, and the city's Diamond Jubilee of Electric Light. Thousands of people came from all over Hoosierland to visit the 2,000-acre site chosen for the event. Among the host of attractions was a Queen Contest, the winner to reign over festivities at the Plowman's Banquet as "Furrow Queen." There were also special features for women, classified euphoniously as "Charm on the Farm." But the two major events were the Plowing Matches and the Wagon Tours. Visitors were taken on a five-mile, hour-and-a-half wagon tour, with sixteen stops at ten farms, and shown the new pattern of the land. Before them were practical demonstrations of the scientific agricultural practices the SCS has worked out for saving soil and increasing the productivity of the land. They saw strip cropping, terracing, pond construction, diversions, woods improvement, grass plots, and contour cultivation demonstrated and clearly explained. Later there were demonstrations of aerial seeding.

After the tour came the plowing matches. The traditional straight furrow contest was billed as a "Level Land Plowing Contest," while the new method for sloping land was designated as a "Contour Plowing Contest." One competition of each type was scheduled on alternate days as the main feature. The men signed up for the type they wanted to enter, or they could enter both. Contour plowing was not too popular at first, but the men were urged to "try to get the hang of it." Since no one was expert everyone had a fair chance at the prizes, with "mom" and the children on the sidelines to cheer. Some of the younger men, sleeves rolled to the elbow, were the first to try. Then one by one the others, skilled at straight furrows, stepped up to try. It was not long before they were vying with each other in good-natured rivalry, each determined to be the first to master this new way of plowing. By the time the contest got under way competition was even keener than it had been on the straight furrow matches. The second contour plowing contest was held on the third day of the fair. By then no persuasion was needed to secure entrants. Everyone had a good time and the SCS had put its point across in the largest event of its kind ever held.

Indiana is a part of our vital corn belt, its fertile farmlands yielding richly in grains, particularly corn and winter wheat. In some sections of the country scientific soil methods are important as a means of *restoring* abused land. But in this case, as with most of the agricultural land in the Midwest, they are essential to keep good farmland productive and even increase its fertility.

Teamwork in Tupelo

People who live in small towns or cities sometimes forget how dependent we are upon the farmer, failing to recognize that his welfare is related to our own, and that the land is the foundation of our way of life. The SCS sums it up in a succinct statement: *good soil, good living—poor soil, poor living.* This fact, it emphasizes, applies to the community and the country, just as it does to the farmer. Civic-minded leaders in Tupelo, Mississippi, actively aware of this, have developed a cooperative program for farmers and townspeople that not only has inspired similar programs in other communities and states, but attracted the attention of other countries.

Mississippi has all the charm of the Deep South, with its traditions of hospitality, its old plantations and antebellum mansions, its oleanders, magnolias, and magnificent live oaks—its "Ol' Man River" atmosphere. But there is also the tragedy of deeply eroded soil, drained of productivity when cotton was king. Tupelo, in the northeastern corner of the state, is a town of about 11,000 with a trading area that includes five counties and 175,000 people, mostly rural. There is good farmland in the valleys, but this is largely hill country, where people have struggled for generations with impoverished soil. The farms are small. A little more than half of the people own their own land; the rest are tenant farmers. Three times this area has been struck down by a major disaster, but each time it has pulled itself up by the boot-straps, stronger than ever. It is proud of its achievement and should be. There is a close relationship between the town and country. The leaders of the town think in terms of the farmer's welfare and, in turn, the farmer thinks of himself as citizen of a Tupelo without city limits. Consequently both have prospered.

The Tupelo story begins with the closing battles of the Civil War when the town was burned to the ground by Union troops—its first disaster. Out of the hopelessness and desolation of the years follow-ing the war grew the kinship and cooperative spirit so characteristic of the community today. "Tupelo grew slowly," the people will tell you, "but it grew together." There are many illustrations of this unity of spirit during those years, but for brevity's sake we skip to 1916, the year of the second disaster. Cotton was all these people knew at that time. When the boll weevil, sweeping through Mississippi like a virus, wiped out the cotton fields, the whole area was prostrated, farmers and merchants alike. To the farmers it was a sledge-hammer blow. At best, many had been able to wrest only a meager living from the unproductive, eroding hill lands, some of which could hardly be called land any more. Now with even that little gone, they did not know which way to turn. The merchants too were at the breaking point, having stretched credit as far as they dared. As for the banks, they were holding notes no one could pay—too many such notes.

The person who put Tupelo on the road to recovery was S. J. High, then president of the People's Bank and Trust Company. He realized that the answer to their mutual problem lay in the restoration of the land, but that took time as well as money. And, like money, time was running out. Once land has become exhausted it takes years for it to recover, even with today's advanced soil practices. The prob-lem was even more nettling then. On a large farm a skillful farmer can rotate his crops, rest part of his land, and still maintain sufficient production to make a comfortable living. But these were very small farms. The farmers were uneducated and for the most part not highly

skilled; scientific soil knowledge was not then available for the asking
as it is today. Furthermore, even though it was like whipping a tired
horse, the land must be made to yield its utmost every year or many
already undernourished people would go hungry. If the soil did not
grow cotton, it must produce something equally lucrative. Mr. High
found the answer in livestock.

Poultry, pigs, and dairy products! A factory on every farm! This was
his idea. His purpose was not necessarily to replace cotton growing,
but to supplement it. Farmers would not be wholly dependent upon
the cotton crop. Diversification would help them financially and
at the same time relieve the punishing burden cotton and tobacco
place on the soil. If the land could rest and proper restorative measures be applied, Mr. High pointed out, it would eventually produce
larger yields on less acreage, at less cost to the soil. The additional
products would give the farmer the necessary income for fertilizer and
other land needs. At the same time the slack in employment for hired
workers would be relieved, as cotton provides less than half a year's
work. Where the land was not suitable for cotton, or too exhausted to
make the crop practical, the new products could take its place entirely.
Meanwhile, they would tide the community over this cropless period.

The bankers in the area were accustomed to giving advertising
calendars at Christmas time at a cost of about $5,000. Mr. High per-
suaded fellow bankers to use the money to underwrite his program,
hire a livestock expert and help the farmers get started. The county
board of supervisors agreed and employed a county agricultural agent.
Mr. High then sought an outlet for the milk. The Carnation Milk
Company was so impressed with the earnest efforts of this community
to help itself, that it established a huge plant at Tupelo, its first
in the South. Thus a new era was born.

The bankers bought a second-hand projector, and the county agent,
Sam Durham, along with V. S. Whitesides, a bank employee who later
became president of the People's Bank and Trust Company, toured
the countryside, teaching the people dairying and soil conservation
practices. They did everything possible to put the idea across, from
sowing experimental plots of pasture grasses for farmers who would
let them, to distributing agricultural handbills, and setting up a
chicken-house in the Court House Square. When hybrid corn was
introduced, they promoted it through 4-H Club boys and girls, reach-

ing the parents through the children. Meanwhile the other banks were doing their part, one having hired a poultry expert, another a top dairy man. Practical help was offered anyone who would accept it and would help himself, Negroes as well as white. Slowly, but surely too, the community began to recover.

Then in 1936 the third disaster struck. A tornado ripped through Tupelo, killing 203 people, injuring hundreds more, and destroying almost half the town. But again, this small community, which never had been one to waste time feeling sorry for itself, pulled itself together and continued on its way. The business section was rebuilt in modern style, a symbol in its way of Tupelo's progressiveness and unconquerable spirit. During this period a young newspaper owner and editor, George McLean, was developing as a civic leader, championing the cause of the underprivileged and giving generously to community development programs.

When Mr. McLean left the Navy after World War II, he had soil experts make a study of the land around Tupelo and work out a plan for its best use. The land was found suitable for three types of farming: (1) a combination of dairying and cotton raising, (2) the raising of poultry, fruits, and vegetables, and (3) part-time farming and industrial occupation. Mr. McLean's next step was the organization of a Community Development Council, composed of twenty-three business men and farmers. The Council mapped a Rural Community Development Program based on these findings. It is this program which has aroused so much interest throughout the South and in other sections with similar problems, as well as the Philippines, Egypt, and Pakistan.

The Council organizes farmers by communities, defining a community as a number of rural families centering around a common meeting place, such as a school or church, and usually having a few services available such as stores and filling stations. Each community, in turn, has its own council and officers, with a civic group in Tupelo acting as its sponsor. Prizes are offered for *community* achievement rather than for individual effort. Awards are based on organization, adult and youth leadership, farm and home improvement, community improvement, and the use of scientific farm and soil practices. The prizes are provided by business men and civic groups. The contest, the Council stresses, is based on the conviction that "there is no limit to what an organized community can do—*if it wants to do it.*" And it puts power into its slogan by raising $43,000 every year to finance the program.

Many interesting promotional ideas have been used. One was to have the farmers draw lots. Then everyone, businessman and farmer alike, was invited to help to do a face-lifting job on the winner's farm. The house was repaired and attractively remodeled, given a new roof and a coat of paint. The barn and out-buildings also were repaired and painted, and a fence built around the pasture. Conservation measures were carried out on the land, including the seeding of the pasture to permanent winter grazing, the cleaning of ditches, and the filling in and planting of gullies. This aroused the people's interest, showed them what could be done and how to do it, and instilled a spirit of teamwork. But it went beyond that. It brought home-spun neighborliness to the community level. Community work days, on which the farmers gather to help a sick neighbor, to rebuild a house that has burned, or to turn an old homestead into a community model farm have become a feature of Tupelo's community development program. This promotional idea also proved sound from an educational point of view. Every community now has a demonstration farm where the recommendations of the Soil Conservation Service, working with local agencies, are put into practice. All able-bodied persons in the community contribute two or three days of work during the year to the development of this model farm and home.

The work of the Council, however, covers more than farm management. Its field embraces health, education, religion, recreation, beautification, and practically every phase of community life. On all counts the Tupelo area has made amazing progress, the Council reaching into remote and backward sections that usually take little or no interest in finding a better way of life.

This thriving union of town and country has raised the living standard of the whole area. It has encouraged and developed home-grown businesses and brought in outside industry to provide an outlet for its products and a market for surplus labor. Most important, it is nursing sick land back to health, strengthening the foundation of its own prosperity and ours. Once again the banks are giving calendars at Christmas time, but instead of decorative landscapes they use photographs taken in the Tupelo area which show good farming practices.

Pride and Its By-Products

The American Farm Bureau Federation states that there are about 1,500,000 farms in the United States supporting families on incomes of less than $1,000 a year. Moreover there are a thousand counties in which more than half of the farmers live on poor income farms, too small to benefit from mechanization or government price legislation. These people cannot be permanently helped unless the land is restored to productivity and used according to its capabilities, but they are the least likely of all to seek the advice of soil experts or to initiate a soil conservation program. How to reach them is a problem.

The Asheville Agricultural Council of North Carolina, patterned on the Tupelo model, has an original way of interesting small farmers in scientific land practices. Like Tupelo, Asheville is surrounded by small farms, many with worn-out, deeply eroded soil. The Council's objective was to heal the land and encourage good farm management, with well planned diversification rather than dependence on a single crop. But, instead of starting with the soil, it began with a mail-box painting contest. Why? Council members feel the key to their astonishing success lies in the answer to that question.

Before you can talk to these people about soil conservation, the Council believes, you must first make them want to improve their economic situation, to create the desire for something better. "The man who won't change his way of farming to save his land," says Morris L. McGough, executive vice-president of the Council, "will frequently do a right-about face when it comes to a church organ, a community prize, or when a neighbor is able to build a new barn because modern soil practices have raised his income. People who were satisfied with oil lamps, outdoor toilets, and wells become interested in electric lights, bathrooms, and running water when the house gets a new foundation, an extra room, or an attractive coat of paint. If interest is aroused in improving the home and community, interest in better land use follows as a means of producing the income needed for better facilities."

There were many reasons for the mail-box painting contest. Painting a mail box is a quick, easy, tangible accomplishment that permits a contest of short duration without complicated directions. It is a contest teenagers can enter, and that is often like a foot in the door when it comes to breaking down adult apathy. A mail box gets *noticed.* A freshly painted mail box in front of a run-down house makes the house look even shabbier and points up the need to do something about that too. Such a contest can be repeated whenever and as often as desired, paving the way for more ambitious contests.

Church remodeling and cemetery cleanup programs are among the first community undertakings the Council promotes. It was found that when all other appeals fail, a sense of pride in the home and community can usually be aroused when people work together to build, remodel, or beautify a church. The whole program hinges on this spirit of working together. What happened in Cane Creek, one of some 107 communities now participating in the program, illustrates this spirit. One year the Baptists helped build a Methodist parsonage, and the next year the Methodists helped build a home for the Baptist minister. Applied to soil stewardship, it was found that a farmer working alone on a long-range program often gets discouraged before benefits appear; but as part of a community that is tackling the soil problem he is likely to see the job through.

"Competition has played an important part in this program," Mr. McGough says, "not so much from the standpoint of the prizes, but mainly because of the recognition, interest, and backing of business and civic leaders." A civic group may sponsor one or several communities, but the members do not go out to the farms and give advice, nor do they lead the rural community. This is a partnership of progress based on fellowship, with leadership developed from within the community. Recognizing that their welfare and problems are interlocked, farmers and business men plan and work together for their mutual benefit. "Through extensive promotion and publicity," Mr. McGough points out, "outstanding community accomplishments are made known to people all over the area."

The cardinal feature of the program today is the Rural Community Development Contest which runs for a full year, with cash prizes donated by agricultural organizations, civic groups, and business firms in Asheville. It covers community organization and improvements, improvements in the appearance, convenience and comfort of homes, and increase in family income. The civic group which does the best sponsoring job wins a plaque. To sustain interest, the Council encourages community social activities and the organization of Boy and Girl Scout Troops, 4-H Clubs, and similar groups. One-half of the total community score is based on the improvements made by individual families. For this phase, the Council distributes printed forms describing the contest, which the farmer is asked to fill out from a daily record he is to keep. This record not only shows the farmer and his family the progress that is being made, but serves to remind him of things yet to be done. It inculcates in their minds the good land practices that have made a higher living standard possible. Often childish handwriting reveals that some boy or girl is carefully keeping the family tally on restoration of soil that almost perished because nobody cared about it.

The program, now in its eighth year, was inaugurated by a group of Asheville businessmen who, hearing of the Tupelo project, sent a representative to see how effective it was. They were so impressed that they immediately had an inventory made of their own area and presented the findings to a mass meeting of rural and urban dwellers.

The Asheville project has paid high dividends, bringing conveniences most people take for granted—gas and electric lights, inside water, attractive homes, library books, vitality and good health through an adequate diet—to people who never had them before.

The Cherokee Indian Reservation is about fifty miles from Asheville. A young Cherokee farmer, excited about what was happening in drab neighborhoods and on worn-out farms, decided to see what could be done in the Indian colony. He invited Mr. McGough to address a meeting of fellow Indians and show them how to organize a community. Only eight attended the meeting, but they formed a council and elected officers. Others soon became interested. What the Indians wanted most was electric lights. This meant cutting a right-of-way through wooded mountains, but today the reservation has electric lights and other conveniences too. This is also true of the Negroes in the Asheville area, many of whom are participating in the program.

Businessmen have profited through increased buying power, higher bank deposits, and a more stable prosperity. With eggs and poultry as a sideline, farm women now have "pin money," which is reflected in increased sales of clothing and home furnishings. But most important of all is the fact that barren land is turning green again.

Educational Programs in Land Conservation

Demonstration in a Train Car

An interesting example of American ingenuity is the Agricultural Improvement Car of Utah, a modern version of the old traveling medicine show. But instead of cure-alls, this air-conditioned-motion-picture-theatre-on-wheels educates people in the wise use of land and water. It is drawing record crowds in rural areas of Utah and Nevada.

Both states are large, with sparse populations scattered over the broad distances between towns. Both have serious erosion problems. The annual tours, begun in 1948, are sponsored by the Union Pacific Railroad, the Utah State Agricultural College, and The Utah Associated Garden Clubs. Accompanying the specially designed, bright yellow railroad car are soil, forestry, and range experts who are taking information about scientific land practices to people in remote sections. Instruction is given in informal talks and discussions, by motion pictures and slides, models, and exhibits. Question and answer periods are an important part of the program. The car is equipped with tiered seats for good visibility, and microphones so that all may hear during the question and answer sessions. Since this is mostly cattle and sheep country, with farming dependent upon irrigation, the programs deal mainly with problems relating to better soil and water practices, but home improvement is featured too. Landscape and horticulture specialists travel with the car, and one year the entire program was devoted to the improvement of home grounds and backyard beauty, with models of well planned farm and ranch landscaping. In its first seven years the "Ag" car visited 673 communities and counted an attendance of 110,772 people. Every year it becomes more popular.

Successful Farm Management for Future Farmers

Henry Robinson, a progressive vocational agriculture teacher at the Flathead County High School in Kalispell, Montana, believes that farming is a business and should be run as such. He turns out graduates who are businessmen, as well as skilled farmers. So successful are his training methods that his students have won the highest award of the Future Farmers of America, the Gold Emblem, for thirteen consecutive years, in competition with 8,900 high school chapters throughout the country.

By the time these young men finish their four year "vo-ag" course they not only are qualified as farmers, but most of them are farming and have good-sized investments in machinery, land, and livestock. They may graduate in debt (which most of them do), owing for a tractor, a Holstein cow, purebred hogs or sheep, but they graduate as scientifically trained farmers with firsthand experience in management of a type their fathers could glean only by years of experience. Robinson's high school students own approximately $80,000 worth of cattle, sheep, hogs, poultry, and grain, as well as $12,000 worth of farm machinery. What is more, they have been getting 3 per cent interest on their investment, and consistently gross about $4,500 a year from the demonstration farm. Since initial investments in farming are so large today, Robinson teaches his students to regard indebtedness as a necessary step toward professional independence. They learn the value of bank loans and sound credit. Through his help, many borrow the money to start their own farming programs while still undergraduates. This, however, is all done on a business basis, the boys submitting to the bank a detailed analysis of their plans, with costs figured down to the last hidden cent. The banks find these earnest, level-headed, thoroughly trained boys, with their business-like and scientific approach to farming, a good risk.

Profits from the demonstration farm are put into a pool of high quality livestock, which helps boys get started on their own through what Robinson calls "revolving projects." This is a program whereby purebred animals are placed with the boys as foundation stock, the young breeders repaying the pool in equivalent stock as their herds grow. Then these animals are in turn passed on to other boys. In each case the transaction is covered by a written contract between the boy and the Flathead Chapter of the Future Farmers of America. "After all," Robinson explains, "this is a business proposition. The chapter is not giving the member livestock worth so much money—it is merely affording the member a chance to get started for himself, after which another member receives the same opportunity." Hundreds of young farmers have made their start in this way. There is no fixed contract. Each is written to fit the individual case, often by the boy himself, then reviewed and approved by a chapter committee. "The chapter has never suffered a loss from default on any of its contracts," Robinson says proudly. This speaks well for the motto of the Future

Farmers of America: "Learning to Do, Doing to Learn, Earning to Live, and Living to Serve."

Robinson's program grew out of his faith in "plain dirt of almost any kind," and his belief that "schools should lead and not follow in a community." But the demonstration farm—the nucleus of the program and the pride of the whole area today—was once ridiculed as "the Future Farmer's Folly."

The Flathead Valley is in the northeastern part of Montana, near Glacier National Park. In 1949 the farmers operating small wheat farms in the area were caught in a price-cost squeeze and wheat growing became increasingly unprofitable. Most of them felt that their land was too poor for other crops, but Robinson, who had taken his master's degree at Michigan State College of Agriculture, was convinced that the farmers did not need to be at the mercy of poor soil. He wanted to show them how to restore their land through scientific soil practices and make it pay by growing high-profit specialty crops. To do this, he and his students scouted for the sorriest piece of land they could find, which he planned to turn into a demonstration farm. The sorriest, they discovered, was the county poor farm, a ninety-three-acre tract of badly eroded land that had not paid its way for years. Most farmers would have considered it hopeless, but it was exactly what Robinson was looking for. When he approached the Future Farmers Advisory Committee (a group of business men and farmers) with his plan to lease the land as a demonstration farm in connection with the chapter, none of them would have anything to do with such a "foolhardy" venture.

For the first time, Robinson decided to go against his committee's advice, so convinced was he that his idea was sound. The boys had already run soil tests. With the help of the Soil Conservation Service, along with college, county, and state agricultural experts, a master plan for the farm was developed. To finance the project, the Flathead Chapter of the Future Farmers of America incorporated and sold itself $2,100 worth of memberships at $10 each, with some boys buying several. Armed with the master plan and their notebooks, showing in detail how it was to be carried out, they asked the bank for a $5,000 loan to buy fertilizer and machinery. It was granted. The boys then formed labor crews and went to work.

The next two years were hard for Robinson and the boys. The

words "Future Farmer's Folly" rang often in their ears. But all that is forgotten now. By the third year these young farmers were getting 140 bushels of oats and barley to an acre from soil that had previously yielded less than ten. By the fourth year their farm had become one of the major producers of certified seed in the nation, some of it seed in which national shortages existed. About this same time the Montana State College of Agriculture, impressed by the skill of these hard-working lads, had them conduct fertilizer tests. The Montana Seed Growers Association, equally impressed, asked them to help propagate an important new orchard grass. Agriculturalists from other states and from Canada began visiting the farm. Throughout the area, farmers who had been held back by the heavy weight of tradition watched the program intently, listening thoughtfully when Robinson suggested switching from wheat to speciality crops, dairy farming, poultry, or swine.

There is more than pride behind the farm today, for it has pointed the way to a more prosperous agriculture and a higher living standard for the whole area. In 1956 farmers in Flathead County grossed a million dollars more income than in 1955. Today the valley is a land of well kept homes, lush pastures, fat livestock, and abundant crops, attracting families from hundreds of miles away who want their sons to attend Kalispell's fine vocational-agriculture school. To show their faith in these young farmers and their belief in Robinson, the people have floated a bond issue giving them one of the best-equipped "vo-ag" buildings in the West.

Robinson does not confine his training to farming. He has the ability to bring out the best in his boys, and in so doing is developing rural leadership. Among his graduates are thirteen known masters of local Granges, two Pomona masters, and one state master, as well as over a hundred 4-H Club leaders and assistant leaders and a state legislator.

A Unique School for Girls

The Pennsylvania School of Horticulture for Women in Ambler, Pennsylvania, is something of a counterpart of the Kalispell school. Modeled after the famous European colleges of gardening for women, it offers a two-year course in horticulture, ornamental horticulture, landscape design, and agriculture. The grounds cover 150 acres—120 devoted to a demonstration farm and twenty to a forest, with emphasis placed on conservation practices. A number of demonstration livestock units are maintained, including sheep, hogs, horses, cattle, and poultry. There are orchards, gardens, greenhouses, extensive plantings of ornamental shrubs, and a dairy, all doubling as outdoor laboratories. As at the Kalispell school, the students learn by down-to-earth practice as well as by classroom study, with those majoring in agriculture expected to take part in all farm operations. Blue jeans are the order of the day for classroom and laboratory.

The Ambler school was founded in 1911 by Jane Bowne Haines, a graduate of Bryn Mawr College, after she had visited similar schools in England, France, Germany, and Switzerland. The first year it had only three students, but in recent years thirty-five states and eight foreign countries have been represented in the student body. Among its graduates are many successful professional women such as authors, editors, and assistant editors of magazines relating to horticulture and landscape design, garden center directors, seed analysts, flower shop owners, and assistants in botanic gardens. But even more are farm women, wives of men upon whom we are dependent for the care of the land.

Replacing Vanished Plants

To people remote from forests and grasslands, a forest fire or a dust storm—if it is large enough to make the headlines—may be disturbing for a day or two, but as it ceases to be news it is quickly forgotten. To people living near such areas it is a different matter. They *know* what a forest fire means in terms of water shortages and erosion, what has happened when the topsoil swirls into the air in clouds of dust.

The garden clubs in Colorado have for a number of years carried on a project which is among the most worth-while undertaken by any garden club. Working with the U.S. Forest and Soil Conservation Services, these clubs honor retiring officers, individuals who have done outstanding club work, or the club itself, through the government's reforesting and reseeding programs. They contribute money for trees and grass seed to restore burned and overgrazed areas and protect them from erosion. Some clubs have subscribed again and again, and most of them have participated in the program. In years when there is sufficient rain, they concentrate on reforestation, in drought years upon re-seeding, according to the government's program.

Youngsters, too, participate in this program. Through the Johnny Grass Seed movement, which originated in Mesa County, Colorado, school children and members of youth groups plant grass seed wherever they go—on grazing lands and pastures, in gullies, at fence corners, on road cuts, stream banks, bare hillsides, and other wastelands. Certified seed, approved by the Colorado Game and Fish Department, the Forest Service, and the SCS, is packed by the Izaak Walton League and distributed to children through the cooperation of sporting goods stores.

The project, started in 1949, soon became a state-wide activity with a Johnny Grass Seed Week proclaimed by the Governor. It has now spread to other states, with garden club members, hunters, fishermen, picnickers, and the general public participating. In one week, in Colorado alone, 250,000 packages of seed were distributed. The project has now been expanded to include legumes and shrubs.

Community Composts

Maplewood's Fallen Leaves an Asset

Many think of soil conservation as applying only to farm and forest land. But erosion also steals from cities, suburban areas, and small towns. Control of soil erosion is one of the most costly and time-consuming maintenance problems of Central Park, in New York City. The tragic carelessness with which the public treats protective ground cover—grass, shrubs, and trees—underscores the need for people everywhere to know more about conservation, what is being done and why.

Take the matter of fallen leaves. If someone in our neighborhood heaped dollar bills into a pile and set fire to them, we would be horrified. Yet we burn money when we burn our autumn leaves. The annual leaf crop is one of the main sources of organic matter for the creation and maintenance of topsoil. "One average mature shade tree yields approximately one bushel of leaf mold a year," says Richard Walter, superintendent of Parks and Shade trees in Maplewood, New Jersey. "In a community with 25,000 shade trees this amounts to an estimated 1,000 tons of the finest soil-building material devised by nature. At $15 a ton the estimated yearly loss in that community would amount to $15,000."

But the monetary loss is negligible compared to the loss to soil health and plant vigor. In the forest, fallen leaves and decayed grass add to the organic matter which makes the soil rich, dark, and crumbly. Leaf burning deprives the soil of its rightful share of organic matter. Beautiful residential areas often degenerate over a span of years because the soil has been allowed to deteriorate in this way. This is also true of new home developments, intended to become more attractive over a period of years, as young plants and trees mature. "The pattern is familiar," Mr. Walter says. "In the new development the soil is fresh, the plants young, and the gardening enthusiasm of the home owner runs high. For ten or fifteen years all is fine, then the first trouble signs appear. The maturing trees compete with the grass and shrubs for the last ounce of nutrients and water in the soil. As the yearly leaf crop is burned or moved to the city dump, the last traces of organic matter in the soil are moved along this one way street, and trees, shrubs, turf, and flowers show the increasing effect of soil devitalization." Beautiful parks frequently deteriorate in the same way. "Exempt from this downward trend," Mr. Walter adds, "are landscaped areas where leaf mold, compost or manure are applied as needed." Summing up, he says: "No amount of commercial fertilizer will prevent a decrease in productivity of the topsoil, since the best soil, depleted of organic matter, must revert to what is commonly called subsoil."

Through example, literature, lectures, and demonstration the Department of Parks in Maplewood has, with emphatic success, encouraged the people to make compost instead of burning their leaves. Nearly every home now has its compost heap, and composting is a main topic of over-the-fence conversation. The compost pile is usually tucked away in a spot where it is not visible, but the results of its use are evident in the lush lawns, lovely gardens, and rich loamy soil. The department utilizes all excess leaves on public grounds. "We now produce yearly about 300 tons of leaf mold and fifty tons of wood mulch, obtained from woodchips, a waste product of our tree pruning operations," Mr. Walter states. "This is all utilized in the maintenance of parks, playgrounds, and shade trees, for soil improvement, top dressing for turf, for transplanting shrubs and trees, and as mulch for conifers, broadleaved shrubs and herbaceous plants in the greenhouse and nursery."

The Garden Club of America has had leaflets printed, telling how Maplewood uses its leaves. These have been distributed to all affiliated clubs.

A Community Compost in Chestnut Hill

The townsfolk in Chestnut Hill, Massachusetts, also count nature's annual leaf fall among the community's assets. Composting is a regular practice among homeowners, and excess leaves are utilized in a community compost.

Formerly, tons of leaves were thrown on the town dump every year. The idea for a community compost originated with the conservation committee of the Chestnut Hill Garden Club, which carries it out in cooperation with the Town of Brookline. The town supplies the leaves, cleaned up from the streets and parks, and the club supplies the manure, phosphate rock, lime, and loam. The town mixes, chops, screens, and bags the material and provides storage. The club pays the town a flat fee, plus the cost of making the compost, which is sold at a small profit. This money is used for park and other community improvements, sending boys and girls to Audubon camps, and for conservation education purposes. The Chestnut Hill project has inspired a number of other garden clubs to sponsor community composts.

Individual Effort

A Conservation Crusade Along a Mail Route

George Bennett has been a rural mail carrier in Connecticut for thirty years, but he carries more than mail to the country houses along his thirty-five mile route in the Woodbury–Southbury valley. Wherever he goes he puts in a word for conservation as he makes his deliveries. In his quiet, friendly way he tells people about bad places he has noticed on their land. Always his comments are followed with a neighborly offer to help. He has some extra multiflora rose roots from the Soil Conservation Service that would be just the thing for that eroding slope. For the bare patches in that field he has some flowering crab seedlings he grafted onto an apple that is well adapted to the stony Connecticut soil. As for that wooded area needing attention, he has more red pine seedlings than he can ever use himself. Weeping willows would be fine along that brook. If the property owner will drop by his place over the week-end and pick them up he will have all these things ready. "The nice thing about plantings of this sort," he explains, "is that they combat erosion and at the same time retain water, provide food and cover for wildlife, help prevent floods, and beautify the landscape." Because they cannot let him down, people *do* pick up the plants and trees Bennett offers them, and they *do* plant them on the danger spots. Thus, a country mailman carries on his conservation crusade over some 51,000 acres that border his route.

CHAPTER IX

ORGANIZED ACTION

The peace-time problems facing our nation, however crucial, usually break down into many smaller problems, with a share of the responsibility for everyone. The conservation of our natural resources, surely one of the most crucial, is no exception. It was, I believe, the historian Green who said: "The world is moved not only by the mighty shoves of the heroes, but also by the aggregate of the tiny pushes of each honest worker."

The United States has never been a nation of followers, nor has its strength or greatness ever depended upon one man. It has always been a nation of individuals, of many leaders, with leadership springing up when needed. Perhaps that is the essence of what we mean by "our way of life." We may call it "grass roots" leadership, "operation bootstrap," or any of a dozen names, but it is still an outcropping of the pioneer spirit so deeply rooted in our character. To express it in another way, one of our cherished heritages is the privilege of individual responsibility. This may be why public-spirited groups have been so amazingly successful in this country, their accomplishments often astounding people from other lands.

There are thousands of such groups in the United States, with a total membership in the millions. Their combined efforts constitute a staggering potential for keeping America beautiful and bountiful. It is mostly a matter of each group taking care of its own corner and shouldering a part of the national responsibility for protecting our natural resources. During a war we often say: "If only people would use the same creative energy for good that they use for destruction!" There has never been a greater opportunity, or a greater need, to do just that—than *now*.

Conservation Education

A Radio Series

Probably ever since man first began to till the soil, a few farsighted men have tried to influence others in its wise use. Vergil wrote about soil erosion, and the Romans had several good manuals for farmers. In our own country there have been many such men, beginning with colonial days. "Since the achievement of our independence," Patrick Henry wrote, "he is the greatest patriot who stops the most gullies."

Influential as many of these men were in their day, they could reach only a limited number of people. With new media of communication this is no longer the case, and the United States is becoming conservation minded at last, through the efforts of dedicated individuals and groups. The educational program is being carried out in many ways. A method of unusual interest is the "Today and Tomorrow" project of the Conservation Foundation, a non-profit organization in New York City devoted primarily to research and education.

The project is a thirteen-week radio series in conjunction with the National Broadcasting Company. First presented in 1956, the series was so successful that it has been broadcast over many independent stations and the demand for it continues to grow. The programs are narrated by actor-farmer-ranchowner James Cagney, an ardent conservationist and a trustee of the Foundation. Another contributor is Bernard Baruch, who says in the introduction to each program: "Since our wealth is drawn from the earth, in always limited quantities, as minerals, food, water, wood, and wildlife, destruction of the earth's surface and waste of its products, have a cogent meaning that touches the life, today and tomorrow, of every human being."

Among the programs in the series is a story about the "black gold" of east Texas in the oil booming days of the thirties; a story of tree farming in Louisiana, showing how the lumber industry is encouraging people to grow trees as a crop; a story of the Florida Everglades showing the reclamation of wasted land for truck farming and cattle raising; and a dramatization of the water pollution problem in Kalamazoo, Michigan. Since "Today and Tomorrow" was launched, the foundation has prepared a number of other radio and television programs in connection with its extensive conservation program.

Montana's Conservation Caravan

Because of its great size and sparse population, alerting its citizens to conservation needs posed a problem in Montana, but these resourceful people have met the challenge in a manner as American as this frontier country itself.

Montana, our third largest state, covers about 146,997 square miles. It is larger than either Italy or Japan, but its population is 1 per cent that of Italy and a little more than ½ per cent that of Japan.

The massive Northern Rockies dominate the western part of Montana, occupying about 40 per cent of its total area. Within and on the edge of this mountainous region are the extensive mineral deposits of copper, silver, gold, zinc, lead, manganese, sapphires, and other minerals for which the state is famous, including the fabulous copper mountain at Butte. There are about 20 million acres of forest land, most of it in the west, with Douglas fir, ponderosa pine, lodgepole pine and Engelman spruce among the principal species. Much of this acreage has been set aside in national forests, including nearly two million acres of forested treasure designated as wilderness areas. In the northwest is Glacier National Park, joining with Canada's Waterton Lakes National Park to form the Waterton-Glacier International Peace Park. In the western valleys are cherry and apple orchards and, to the east in the rolling tablelands, millions of acres of wheat. In the southern counties, where rainfall is scant, are vast cattle and sheep ranches. Thus, one can readily understand why a state-wide educational program sponsored by a small group of conservationists would be a remarkable undertaking.

The Montana Conservation Council was created in 1948 to provide a means of coordinating the activities of all similar groups in the state. Among its members are representatives of civic and farm groups, educational institutions; business, industrial, and labor organizations, and public and government conservation agencies. Membership, however, is not dependent upon affiliation with a group. Any person over fourteen years of age may join. Indeed a goal of the Council is to have every Montana family represented. On its Board of Directors are

two members of the Montana University faculty, the state super-
intendent of public instruction, a member of the Soil Conservation
Service, the Montana Wildlife Federation, the U.S. Forest Service,
and the Montana Grange. Representatives of the Montana Power
Company and of several soil conservation districts also belong. The
Council was incorporated in 1954, with headquarters at Billings.

The program of the Council is primarily educational. One of its
objectives is to provide a public forum for the study and discussion
of specific Montana needs and problems. This is done at an annual
conference, attended by people from all over the state. "Many public
agencies, private organizations and individuals are engaged in worth-
while conservation activities," Mrs. Robert Hamilton, former president of the Montana Federation of Garden Clubs and a member of
the Council, explains, "but each is apt to be most interested in some
particular phase, seeing only a segment of the picture. Bringing these
people together is not only advantageous to Montana conservation-
wise, but enables Council members to keep informed about needs and
accomplishments throughout the state and the rest of the country."

Many progressive measures have resulted from this unitized ap-
proach—the establishment of soil conservation districts in all counties,
the creation of college and university conservation workshops to train
teachers, conservation instruction in the schools, more general use
of scientific forestry practices on private land, and laws to control
water pollution. Montana's resources have not been exploited as
ruthlessly as those of many states and the Council wants to make sure
they never are. Many of its measures are preventative. Several hundred
people attend these two-day annual conferences which climax "Conservation Week," and a monthly newsletter helps sustain interest
during the rest of the year.

A unique feature of Montana's educational program is the "Conservation Caravan." Like Utah's "Ag" car, but making use of a
chartered bus, the caravan makes a five-day tour of the state. The
purpose is to study the resource problems and the methods being
used to meet them rather than to teach or demonstrate the solution
of the land problems of individuals. The 1954 caravan traveled through
the northwestern section of the state, covering the Missoula area, the
Flathead section, and Glacier National Park. In the Missoula area
are some of the most rugged and inaccessible wilderness areas in the

United States. Here the group saw the modern way of combating forest fires in remote areas. Once, a fire in such a forest could be reached only by foot, and fire fighters often struggled for days to get to it—across deep canyons and up high mountain divides—with their equipment strapped on their backs. Today this work is done by smoke jumpers, trained men who plunge like paratroopers from planes and helicopters, sometimes in squads of a hundred or more. Packages containing fire-fighting equipment, radios, rations, and drinking water are hurtled down after them. By this method, a fire that might otherwise rage out of control for days can often be smothered within an hour or two. We can more fully appreciate modern fire-fighting methods such as these when we consider that one fire in Peshtigo, Wisconsin, in 1871, burned over 1,280,000 acres of pine, destroying entire towns and causing 1,500 deaths, five times the loss in life of the Chicago fire which began on the same day. Even so, the Forest Service estimates that over 83,000 fires burn and scar about 3,500,000 acres of trees *every year*.

The 1954 caravan also studied watershed management at Goat Creek, water development at Hungry Horse Dam, game management at Wolf Creek, and spruce beetle control in the Holland Lake area. They saw demonstrations of modern timber-cutting methods, selective logging, timber utilization, Christmas tree management, forest recreation, aluminum production, and mineral management.

Due to prolonged droughts, small-scale farming has not proved too practical on Montana's plains where high grasses once fed countless herds of buffalo. In the Flathead section, however, it has been more profitable, in some cases with the aid of irrigation. The group studied the problems of farm management peculiar to this area, learning how they are worked out through scientific soil practices. The agricultural school at Kalispell also was included in the tour.

The caravan was by no means all work and no play. The tour was highlighted by a trip through Glacier National Park, which covers 984,000 acres. Winding through the mountains along famed Going-to-the-Sun Highway, so-named by the Indians, the caravan viewed lofty snow-capped peaks, plunging waterfalls, colorful canyons, forested valleys, zenith-blue lakes.

Each year the Council makes a caravan trip to some specified area,

studying thoroughly what is being done, or needs to be done, to conserve Montana's rich natural resources.

A Tour of Maryland and Pennsylvania Farms

The tour idea is becoming increasingly popular as a means of
stimulating interest in conservation and developing leadership. When
the General Federation of Women's Clubs held its 1953 convention
in Washington, D.C., the program included a two-day tour of farms
in the surrounding area. It was conducted by the Soil Conservation
Service, Forest Service, and the Maryland Extension Service.

The group, representing fifteen states, traveled through the uplands
of central Maryland, crossed into Pennsylvania at Gettysburg, and
went as far as York, then returned through Manchester, Westminster,
and Cooksville, Maryland. The first stop was at the Thrasher Farm
near Frederick, selected because, in 1947, it had been rebuilt in a
day. Of particular interest was a "sky" pond—a farm pond that depends entirely upon rain and snow. A soil conservationist explained
the benefits of ponds for irrigation, stock watering, fish production,
fire protection, and to provide water for many agricultural uses. He
also told how they help maintain the water table.

Maryland has many thriving dairy farms in this section, among
them the 1,100-acre Lawson King and Sons farm, famous for Holsteins.
The King farm is in the heart of the Montgomery County Soil Conservation District. Here a Maryland extension conservationist explained how a soil conservation district operates. The drive through
York County, Pennsylvania, was particularly interesting, since this
is one of the most notable areas in the country for water, soil, wildlife, and forest conservation, and for the control of water pollution.
A SCS work-unit conservationist showed the group the new pattern
that had been worked out for the land, and pointed out the significance
of multiflora rose hedges, strip cropping and diversion terraces.

Among the stops the next day was the Municipal Water Works, in
Hanover, Pennsylvania, a 1,514 acre tract on which white, scotch,
and red pines are being planted in a large reforestation program.
There are only two private farms in this area but it was evident that
soil was being washed from them into the reservoirs, while on the
forested portions no silting occurred.

Community Outdoor Natural Resource Laboratories

In July 1959 the U.S. Junior Chamber of Commerce launched a "fundamental conservation education effort at the community level across America." This has great potentialities. The Jaycees plan to promote the establishment of Outdoor Natural Resource Laboratories where simple examples of good soil, water, forest, wildlife, and recreational management will be shown, together with exhibits explaining how such practices operate and their value to the community. A basic kit of material has been prepared by experts to guide Jaycee conservation chairmen in the planning and development of these laboratories.

Leadership from Sportsmen

Ohio's Unified Department of Natural Resources

Every major war burns up resource reserves like a gargantuan furnace. This affects the entire country but creates especially acute problems in the areas from which the resources are drawn.

In World War II, Ohio's rich mineral resources were in great demand. When Ohioans took stock after the war, they found that many of their land and water problems had been seriously aggravated in meeting these needs. A commission was formed to analyze the situation and suggest methods to improve it. The commission recommended establishing a Unified Department of Natural Resources. The recommendation was presented to the Ohio legislature for consideration in a Senate bill but the bill was tabled at adjournment.

Conservation-minded people throughout the state were sharply disappointed, and in many cases incensed, at the failure of the legislature to pass the bill. Angered to the point of "doing something about it," Miami Valley Outdoors, a sportsmen's club, decided to try organized action. It invited conservation-minded groups from all parts of the state to send representatives to a meeting in Dayton in August, 1947, where "much needed improvements in conservation affairs in Ohio" would be discussed. At this meeting a round table discussion was held, with everyone present invited to express his opinion. A copy of the minutes was then mailed to every sportsmen's club and conservation group in Ohio, along with a request for suggestions, opinions, and criticisms. These groups were asked if they would send representation to a state-wide mass meeting to discuss Ohio's need for a unified department of resources and other matters relating to conservation. "Please understand," wrote Miami Valley Outdoors, "that we do not feel this meeting should simply be a one-time gripe session at which a number of hastily conceived resolutions will be passed, then put aside and forgotten." The meeting was being arranged, the club emphasized, because there was a definite need for a state-wide federation of conservation-minded organizations which could work together in the interest of Ohio's natural resources.

More than a hundred groups agreed to send representatives. Out of this and subsequent meetings came "The Ohio Conservation Congress," formed in June 1948 and composed of two representatives from each group. A year later, at its first annual convention, the Congress represented 65,000 sportsmen as well as other groups featuring conservation in their programs. The following year it represented 100,000 and it is still growing.

These people had sound reasons for wanting a *unified* department of natural resources, and for their feeling about conservation. We usually think of Ohio as an agricultural state, which it is. There are 22 million acres of farm and ranch land, of which over 11 million acres are in crops. But Ohio is also a leading industrial state. Although it ranks thirty-fourth in area among the states, it is fifth in population, with many large cities. Therefore Ohio has most of the problems common to our more densely populated states—a vanishing countryside, the threat of water shortages and floods. There are other conservation problems, some of which are common to this general area, although not especially to the country as a whole.

Ohio is rich in coal, clay, salt, gas, and oil. Bituminous coal is mined from easily accessible seams in the eastern and southeastern sectors, which are part of the great Appalachian coal field. It produces large amounts of sandstone, limestone, sand and gravel, and silica. Rock salt is worked in the northeastern section, valuable natural gas deposits are located in many areas, and there are petroleum fields in the northwestern and southeastern sections. Its position as an industrial state is based largely upon this wealth of natural resources, in addition to good transportation facilities and proximity to markets. Iron ore is brought across the Great Lakes from Lake Superior mines for the manufacture of iron and steel products, Ohio's leading industry. An estimated 80 per cent of its workers are employed by industry and about 90 per cent of the state's income is from commerce and manufacture.

This emphasis on heavy industry, however, has its price. Many square miles of virgin forest once blanketed the plains south of Lake Erie. Only vestiges remain today. Once the countryside was beautifully carpeted with green. Today much of it bears ugly mining scars. Where streams ran clear and teemed with fish, water pollution is a major problem. Perhaps more than any other industrial toll Ohioans resented the scars left by strip-mining operations. There are four kinds of coal mines, three of which are underground. In open cut or surface mining, commonly called "stripping," all operations are above ground. The earth and rock over the coal seam is drilled and blasted into small fragments to make their removal easy. Then giant power shovels remove this debris and put it aside. The coal is then taken out and loaded on big motor trucks or railroad cars. While this has its advantages for the miner, who works in the open, and the mine owner, who must consider costs, the unsightly blemishes created are heartbreaking to those who love the countryside.

Some mine owners, conscious of the public's unfavorable reaction to these scars, made sincere attempts to revegetate the spoil banks after mining operations ceased. But up to 1947 no laws required the restoration of such land and the general practice was to abandon it. Thus thousands of acres were turned into "land nobody wants," adding little to the tax rolls, but much to Ohio's already serious water problems, especially pollution. The public finally became so aroused by the practice that a law was passed requiring mining operators to restore the land.

Although the Ohio Conservation Congress was organized primarily to secure a unified department of natural resources, its purposes and objectives went far beyond that. It was just as important, members thought, to follow through on legislation and see that laws were properly enforced and, if not, that enough teeth were put in them to make them serve their purpose. Also it wanted to support the department once it was established. In other words, Miami Valley Outdoors wanted a long-range program on a state-wide basis. It planned to work for further legislation, to keep affiliated groups informed of pending bills, and to initiate projects which would help restore depleted resources and protect those that remained. These projects included the restoration of eroded areas to fertility, reforestation of denuded land, and the restoration of wildlife and wildlife habitats. Also high on the list of activities was an educational program in conservation, both for the general public and for school children.

Due largely to the concentrated efforts of the Congress, Ohio got its unified department of natural resources. The Congress was instrumental also in passage of the Debbens Bill, setting up a Water Pollution Control Board under the supervision of the Ohio Department of Health. It has played a major role in the passage of other legislation designed to improve Ohio's conservation picture—the strengthening of the strip-mining restoration law, providing sufficient funds to enable the Department of Natural Resources to function effectively, and a law making it mandatory that conservation be taught in Ohio schools. Through its scholarship program it is training teachers and students in this field, and through its "Citations of Merit" it is stimulating interest in conservation among business houses and industrial organizations. This collective action is showing results in many ways. In 1952 the Chairman of Forestry reported that, by the efforts of individuals and many cooperating groups, over 17 million trees had been planted that year.

Voluntary Reclamation

As in most states, erosion is a problem in Ohio. Consequently, the loss of additional land through mining operations was doubly disturbing since stripping is done in the areas that are most susceptible to erosion. It was necessary to strengthen the reclamation law twice for a number of reasons. First, too little was known when the law was passed about ways to restore such land to use. Second, although the law required the posting of a bond before land could be stripped, some operators simply forfeited the bond rather than go to the trouble and expense of restoring the land.

On the other hand there were companies who not only found it advantageous to restore the land, but believed it was their responsibility to do it. In all fairness, the projects of these companies have a place here.

A number of years ago, members of the League of Ohio Sportsmen became so disturbed about what was happening to the land around them that they approached several of the large mining companies directly to see if anything could be done about stripped areas. The result was the formation of the "Ohio Reclamation Association" in 1945, an organization created voluntarily by mining companies for this purpose. The Association has done extensive research in the best use of stripped land, working with local, state, and federal soil and forestry experts, and with conservation groups. Among the purposes to which such land has been put are grazing, orchards, growing Christmas trees, recreation, housing developments, commercial buildings, and airports. However the major portion has gone into forests. In many cases dams have been constructed across the final cuts in the operations, forming lagoons, ponds, and lakes which are stocked with fish.

A Stripped Area in Mingo Junction Reclaimed

An illustration of what one group has done with such land is the project of the Mingo Sportsman Club in Mingo Junction. In 1950 this group of 200 anglers purchased 950 acres of old mining land from the Powhattan Mining Company for a nominal sum, payable in annual installments over a period of years. The men believed the area could be made into an ideal sport and recreation preserve, since it was only partly stripped, the company having carried on an anti-erosion tree planting program through parts of the area since 1937. There were many wooded areas and small ponds, providing cover for wildlife. When negotiations were completed the men divided into teams and went to work, the mining company furnishing heavy equipment for levelling and for building dams and roads. The group united several ponds to produce an eight-acre lake, planted hundreds of shrubs and trees, and later built a club house. The streams and lakes were stocked with fish. Today the area provides recreation for the men, their families, and local children. The club entertains hundreds of children there every year, taking orphans for outings, providing activities for Boy Scouts and other youth groups, and nature study for school children. The Mingo Sportsman Club also sponsors three other projects—"Adopt a Stream," "Adopt a Lake," and "A Fishin' Hole for Every Kid."

Good Fishing at Sportsmen's Park

"Sportsmen's Park" near Stuebenville is a similar project carried out by the Jefferson County Sportsmen and Farmers Association. The development was started in the depression years when lack of money to travel in search of good fishing and recreational facilities made it necessary to work out something near home. In this case the stripped area was a desolate waste of "raw yellow earth" and "gaping holes and ditches." Its only redeeming feature was a four-acre lake which had been used as a reservoir for the water in the steam shovels. Somehow the lake had escaped pollution and abounded in giant-sized bluegills and largemouth black bass. The club leased the land from the coal company for a dollar a year. Then, like the Mingo Club, the men rolled up their sleeves and went to work. There was little money for materials, but this coal company also helped by lending heavy equipment. Through the years these men have worked on their park, often laying aside their fishing rods to pick up a hammer, saw, or trowel while the "bass were leaping and begging to be caught"— and they are still working to improve it. Where there was once an ugly earth scar, there is now a beautiful 550-acre park, with lovely lakes and lagoons, shrubs and trees of all kinds, a picnic area, playgrounds, a $40,000 lodge, and one of the best trap ranges anywhere around.

Better Farms, Better Homes, Better Business

Rotarian Leadership in Tennessee

Everywhere fine projects are waiting to be sponsored. The first need to activate them appears to be an individual or group able to trigger action. Once a project takes hold, accomplishments often far outstrip the highest hopes of those who started it. What the Rotarians did in Tennessee is a good illustration.

About three-fourths of Tennessee is in farms and two-thirds of the population is rural. Erosion is widespread with much of the state affected by sheet and gully erosion. At a meeting in 1944, members of the Rotary Club in Knoxville concluded that business too often forgets that "Main Street's prosperity originates where Main Street ends." In an effort to learn how business men and farmers could work together, a group of them talked with agricultural extension specialists at the University of Tennessee. Extension Service people had learned from experience that every neighborhood has farmers whose talents for leadership often go to waste and that these men are an almost unlimited reservoir of local leadership. "Why don't you help the communities organize so they can solve their own problems?" they asked.

The Rotarians liked the idea. They set up a fund for prize money, with communities competing in farm and home improvement, then stepped into the background and let the University Extension Service take over. Agricultural agents in county seats all over the mountains of eastern Tennessee were promptly informed of the plan. The idea caught on and the result has been a transformation in rural sections throughout the state. In a spirit of neighborly friendliness, people in more than 700 communities are gathering in churches, homes, and schools to work out cures for deeply entrenched community ills. A more general use of fertilizer and other scientific soil practices have brought about an increase in farm income and a higher standard of living that has benefited the entire state. Conveniences such as electric lights, running water, telephones, and bathrooms are accepted today as a matter of course in many rural areas where they were uncommon before. Beautification of homes and communities has become a source of pride in sections where there was once little or no interest in such matters. The movement has gained such momentum through the years that the university has set up a special department to help rural communities plan their work and train their leaders.

Block Projects in Chicago

Sometimes it is a section of a city that urgently needs help. Residents in the Hyde Park–Kenwood section of Chicago, Illinois—once known for its fine old homes—faced the problem of neighborhood deterioration following World War II. Of the two areas Kenwood was luckier, remaining essentially a community of private homes, with a high percentage of professional people, professors from the nearby University of Chicago, and civic and business leaders. But large apartment houses surrounded it and the slums were not far away. Neighboring Hyde Park, also very exclusive at one time, was less fortunate. In the twenties, spacious apartments were built, and later small apartments and hotels. In the thirties many of the gracious old homes were divided into tiny flats or converted into rooming houses.

During World War II, war workers poured into Chicago, cramming into all available housing. Along with the rest of the city, Hyde Park–Kenwood felt the impact of the sudden influx of people and of the housing shortage that followed the war. Many homes which otherwise might have remained one-family dwellings were turned into rooming and apartment houses. Due to overcrowding, marginal and aging buildings became dilapidated, often slum-like. The number of well-kept homes, owned by the families living in them, began to decline and the number of badly kept rooming and apartment houses increased. A less desirable type of person began to move in. By the late forties, wealthy families were moving to the suburbs, real estate values were on the down-grade, and the whole section was wavering under the insistent pressure of the bulging slum sections around it. Sociologists predicted that in two years it too would be a slum.

The outlook for people with established homes was gloomy. Should they "get out while the getting was good?" If they did, it meant selling at a heavy loss, buying in the suburbs at a time when houses were scarce and prices high, and commuting to the university or city after years of living close by. If they stayed, it meant raising their children in a decaying community and probably being forced out eventually anyway. Neither prospect was cheerful.

Some people moved, but the majority watched, waited, and worried while the rumors flew. One day in 1949 a group of residents, refusing to believe the situation hopeless, met and discussed the possibilities of doing something about their situation. The formation of the Hyde Park–Kenwood Community Conference was the result.

The Conference faced an overwhelming task. There were 72,000 people of different races in the area and their income range was wide. Any program undertaken must have the support of everyone in the two communities, otherwise it was doomed from the outset. In the war and housing emergency, zoning restrictions had been violated, making it difficult to enforce zoning and building codes now. Because of many uncertainties, homeowners were reluctant to make repairs and improvements. Rumors of this or that "element" taking over were having a telling effect, causing wave after wave of panic selling and deepening the atmosphere of apprehension that hung over the area. The city became remiss in its services, children were careless about littering, and juvenile delinquency was on the rise. There was no precedent to follow, no example of a community having reversed a downward trend through its own efforts.

Working with the university and church groups, the Conference held a series of discussion meetings in an effort to define community problems and determine whether resuscitation of the neighborhood was more than a daydream. Later, a citizens' meeting was called, to which representatives from all sections of the two communities were invited. At this meeting a working plan was developed and special committees were appointed to deal with specific problems such as the redevelopment of slum pockets, sponsoring cleanup and home maintenance drives, providing new recreational areas, gaining the cooperation of city officials, and enforcing the zoning and building laws. Because of the many professional men and women in the area, naming the committees was easy, but it takes more than a small group of courageous individuals to put such a project across and everyone knew it. The nucleus of the program was to be block by block organization of the two communities. The central office of the Conference would supply help and advice and coordinate the efforts of the block groups when programs to be undertaken involved the entire community. Each block group, however, was to work out its own program.

As members of the first group began to realize that they could do something constructive about their common problems, their fears yielded gradually to enthusiasm. None wanted to move, but as individuals they had felt they had no other choice. A policy was adopted of trying to enlist the cooperation of everyone in the block in improving the neighborhood. It was a modest start, but it set the pattern for other block groups.

Only when the anxieties of residents were quieted would they willingly invest in neighborhood improvements, it was felt. Therefore, two top priority projects were tracking down groundless rumors and halting illegal conversions. Throughout that year Conference officers went from meeting to meeting, explaining their objectives and mustering community support.

The idea took hold more quickly than might have been expected, possibly because of the thoroughness of the groundwork and the concrete problems that were tackled. People soon learned the advantages of working together. For instance, by hiring a contractor to do all of the major repairs and improvements at one time, reduced rates were obtained, and special prices were given when several people in a neighborhood had similar jobs done at the same time.

Although work in the beginning was all done on a voluntary basis, the Conference developed finally into an established organization with paid officers, supported by membership dues and grants. The project became so successful that it has inspired a number of similar ones. It has also been the subject of study by such organizations as the Metropolitan Housing and Planning Council, and a demonstration area for the Community Conservation Board. The Chicago Land Clearance Commission chose it for the first urban renewal project in Chicago—a program now under way.

Puerto Rico's "Operation Bootstrap"

Puerto Rico has been burdened for generations with one of the highest population densities in the world, and long suffered from the inflexibility of a one-crop (sugar) economy. Under the leadership of Governor Luis Muñoz Marin, an economic and social development program "based on faith born of desperation" was launched in 1948. The project has attracted thousands of visitors and observers from almost a hundred countries. This program, called "Operation Bootstrap," is strengthening the island's economy and raising its living standard through the use of improved soil practices, diversification of crops, reforestation, and industrialization. But the feature that is creating the most interest is a unique low-cost housing project, part of a long-range program.

The Social Programs Administration of the Commonwealth Department of Agriculture is the motivating force, but the project is still a typically American grass-roots affair. One of the many challenging goals of Operation Bootstrap was the elimination of slums and the provision of adequate homes for even the poorest farm families. At that time the typical dwelling of poor families was a flimsy, one- or two-room wooden shack with a roof of rusty, corrugated steel sheet. This was perhaps sufficient shelter in Puerto Rico's warm climate, but such homes are an easy prey of hurricanes and wood-boring insects and are almost completely lacking in privacy. Through the "Aided, Self-Help Housing Program," low-cost, hurricane-proof, concrete houses are now being built for as little as $300. The government contributes up to $150 for materials and the occupants pay $15 down and the balance in small monthly payments.

What makes the low cost possible is the manner in which the project is being carried out. A small group of fifteen to thirty families, wanting better homes, forms a building cooperative. They pledge themselves to help each other and decide by drawing lots, or a similar method, whose house will go up first. The Social Programs Administration then sends a small team of technicians to meet with the adult members of the "co-op" to explain the program, go over the plans, demonstrate construction techniques, and get the first house started. A series of evening and weekend building parties follows and in a matter of months every member family is living in a sturdy, vermin-proof, hurricane-proof house with at least two bedrooms, a living room, kitchen, and bathroom. While the basic construction is identical, each homeowner chooses his own interior and exterior decorations.

In the past three years, build-it-yourself homes have been going up in rural areas at the rate of 2,000 a year and the pace is increasing. The plan has been extended to urban areas, although the city houses will be more expensive—from $1,200 to $1,500.

Community Clinics in Arkansas

As a number of the preceding projects show, a community renaissance is occurring in the South. Basically most of the programs are similar, one inspiring others, but each is individual in some way. The program in Arkansas pivots on the community clinic.

A state of great natural beauty, Arkansas is heavily wooded, with more than 20 million acres of forest land. Lying within the drainage basin of the Mississippi River, it has a wealth of streams, rivers, and lakes. There are hundreds of mineral springs, the curative properties of which were known to the Indians long before Spanish exploration. Consequently the state attracts vacationists, sportsmen, and health seekers from all over the section. Lumbering and the manufacture of wood products are important, Arkansas ranking second among the southern states in hardwood timber stands. It yields, among other mineral resources, more than 90 per cent of the nation's bauxite, source of aluminum, and enjoys the distinction of possessing our only known diamond mine. Predominately though, Arkansas is an agricultural state with more than half its total area in farm and range land. It produces a variety of crops, but cotton is the major cash crop, the state ranking third in national production.

Indeed, it was the cotton boom of 1818 that brought the first large wave of settlers to Arkansas, and the southern plantation system was set up in the alluvial plains in the southern and eastern parts of the state. After the Civil War this system was replaced by share cropping and farm tenancy, a practice responsible for the poor condition of the soil in many areas. The tendency is to take as much from the land as it will yield and to give back as little as possible—in most cases an economic necessity. The poorer the land becomes the more distressing become the living conditions of those dependent upon it. Because of this strong reliance upon the whims of the cotton market, the depression of the thirties struck Arkansas hard and many people were forced to leave the state. Then the war boomed new industries, notably aluminum production, and increased purchasing power. This temporary boom awakened business leaders to the potentials of a higher living standard state-wide and the possibility of achieving it through a diversified economy. As an experiment, a business group called in community planning experts from other states to survey various communities and make recommendations. The planning experts did a competent job, but it soon became clear that any improvement program, to be successful, had to come from the community itself. People did not like outsiders telling them what was wrong with their town, although they accepted willingly criticisms and suggestions from "one of their own." Through trial and error, civic leaders developed the community clinic. It is working wonders among Arkansas communities, and attracting investigators from other states and countries.

At a community clinic a diagnosis is made of chronic ailments and a formula is worked out for their cure. As Arkansas does it, a state expert in such matters, accompanied by soil, planning, and other specialists, visits a community and goes over its problems with the townspeople in a series of discussions. This may require several days or more, as only small groups are taken at a time. There is no "lecture." The expert, usually born and raised on an Arkansas farm himself, discusses community problems in a down-to-earth way. Toward the end of the meeting he passes out cards and asks each person to fill one out, stating what he thinks is the most urgent need of the community and whether he would be willing to work on a committee to do something about it. The cards are taken to Little Rock, the state capital, where they are tabulated and analyzed. Then they are sent back to the town authorities, or whoever sponsored the program, with comments and recommendations. The services of the University of Arkansas, state conservation and planning agencies, and industrial specialists are all available to any community wanting to improve itself.

As with most community improvement programs, a contest is used to stimulate interest and action. In this case the contest is sponsored on a state-wide basis by the City Planning Department of the University of Arkansas, the Arkansas Industrial Development Commission, the Chamber of Commerce, and a number of utility companies. Communities are classified according to population and each competes with others in its population range for a cash prize. Awards are made for the greatest improvement during the contest year. The basis of the contest is five-fold: industrial development, better business, improved living, better environment, and better planning. High on the list of considerations for an award is an active city planning commission, citizen and civic support and understanding of planning, and evidences that the plan is being carried out. As in similar programs, the use of scientific soil practices, the raising of highbred cattle, and more diversified land use according to its capability become an integral part of the plan as a means to achieve better business, better homes, and better communities. Begun in 1948, the project becomes more far-reaching each year, with more and more clinics functioning as the list of contesting communities grows longer. Among those that have won awards are Decatur, DeQueen, Prairie Grove, and Paragould.

Kentucky's Reawakening

When a disaster strikes a community, people forget their differences and work for the common good. But it is often difficult to get them to cooperate when there is no emergency and the larger the area is, the more difficult it becomes.

In the 1800's Kentucky was considered a progressive state economically, well advanced in social welfare, education, and public health. Toward the close of the century it declined and by the 1940's it was considered backward in fields where it had once assumed leadership. The Committee for Kentucky, representing 450,000 members of agricultural, business, educational, labor, professional, and social organizations, was formed in 1943 to try to correct the situation. Its objective was to stimulate communities to organize for action by developing "a moral climate for progress."

The committee had made a thorough study of conditions in the state, digging into the darkest corners for facts—a procedure likely to bring out shocking revelations almost anywhere. It learned that Kentucky's per capita income was well below the average for the rest of the country, that it ranked 47th among the states in literacy, and 41st in expenditures for education. At one time it had led the South in industrial payrolls: now it ranked next to the lowest. Agriculturally, conditions were especially sad, though Kentucky is predominately a rural state with 70 per cent of its economy based on farming. A large percentage of farmers were in the "below $1,000 yearly" income class; 75 per cent of the farms did not have central station electric service; 84 per cent had no telephones; and 97 per cent had no inside toilet facilities. About 40 per cent of the farms needed major building repairs. Many farmers were hauling water for stock four or more miles, and 42 per cent of the farms were not reached by improved roads. Population was declining, with one native Kentuckian in every four leaving the state.

Committee members were aware that every state has its shortcomings and that in many ways Kentucky was no worse off than others; nor were they overlooking any of its good features. This, however, was not the point. Many things were tragically wrong and could be corrected only by united action.

The committee decided to take a bold course. It would spread the facts throughout the state without any cushioning. This would be a gamble, it knew, for Kentucky is a proud state—proud of its world famous horses, its beautiful women, its traditions, and hospitality. The people would not like their shortcomings made public, but that was a chance that had to be taken. A publicity drive was launched with the slogan, "Wake up, Kentucky!"

The publicity program was as thorough as the search for facts had been. Reports were sent to the eighty-seven member organizations of the committee for use as program material and a roster of speakers was made available to them. The statistics were also incorporated in the curriculum of high schools, colleges, and universities and were used in social science classes, and distributed to libraries throughout the state. For more than a year, radio station WHAS, powerful enough to reach almost every hamlet, conducted as a public service a weekly fifteen-minute dramatized program called "Wake up, Kentucky!" Seventeen other stations rebroadcast the program without charge. The program won a National Peabody Award in 1946. The Kentucky Press Association, a member of the committee, cooperated with complete news coverage, editorials, and a weekly syndicated column by Ewing Galloway, a New York photographer and Kentucky farmer. Thousands of brochures were distributed, essay contests were conducted in the schools, and editorial contests among the newspapers. Special exhibits were arranged for the state fair and other gatherings. The plan was to encourage the citizens in every community to study their local problems and take action. For this purpose the state was divided into nine areas. A caravan—a thirty-three-foot trailer with a public address system and facilities for showing slides and films—spent a month in each section, setting up community workshops. As part of the "moral climate" it was trying to create, the committee emphasized that corrective measures would cost money, and that the taxpayers must be willing to pay for them.

Some protested the publicity and condemned the work of the committee, but the majority were in sympathy with its objectives and many communities cooperated. In May 1946 the first farm housing conference of its kind in the United States was held at the University of Kentucky under the auspices of the committee. Its results were published in a pamphlet and distributed throughout the nation by the National Committee for Housing. Under the auspices of the Kentucky Medical Association, a medical scholarship fund of $200,000 was established to train doctors for rural areas. Many of the bills the committee recommended in the fields of education, welfare, and agriculture became state laws. A state Agricultural and Industrial Development Board was established, the salaries of rural teachers were increased, the state university received an increase in funds for research and experiment. Public Welfare appropriations were increased, and the physical condition of a number of institutions was improved. New hospitals were built in strategic areas, new roads and highways constructed. But more important perhaps than any of these achievements, citizens' groups all over Kentucky are now working together to meet their present problems and to plan for the future.

One of their primary concerns is to reach into the rural areas to help the small farmer, the "forty-acre man and his mule."

"We need this man," C. V. Bryan, extension agent of the University of Kentucky says, "and we should make sure he isn't pushed out of the American picture. His rugged independence, his rugged individualism on our rural frontier is the very bulwark of democracy, the clue to a strong America."

The Committee for Kentucky aimed to pave the way for progress rather than undertake specific projects. Once it had attained its goal, it went out of existence (1950). The Kentucky Chamber of Commerce, established upon its recommendation, and the Agricultural and Industrial Development Board took over where it had left off. They are now carrying forward an active community improvement program. The Committee for Kentucky has received inquiries about its work from nearly every state and from many foreign countries. A number of similar committees have been patterned after it.

International Contest for Better Communities

The General Federation of Women's Clubs is the world's largest organization of women. It was formed in March 1890 when representatives of about sixty clubs in eighteen states attended a meeting in New York City at the invitation of the Sorosis Club. The objective was closer association. Today nearly 16,000 clubs in the United States are members and the world membership is approximately 11 million women, representing fifty-eight countries. Members of foreign affiliates are sometimes American women living abroad but usually their membership is cosmopolitan. The *Club International de Mujeres* in Mexico City, Mexico, represents fifteen nationalities, while the Woman's Club of Rio de Janeiro, Brazil, represents twenty-four. Headquarters of the Federation is in Washington, D.C.

The early women's clubs were chiefly cultural and social, but when women entered public life, club programs went right along with them. The General Federation has many worthwhile civic achievements to its credit—the establishment of libraries, pioneer work for kindergartens, influence in securing pure food laws, the eight-hour day, and child labor laws. It contributes effectively in the conservation field and has a very active conservation and natural resources department. Like the garden clubs, these groups give hundreds of conservation scholarships every year to young people, teachers, and club members; promote conservation education programs and the teaching of conservation in the schools; contribute books on the subject to libraries; sponsor tree planting programs (3,401,936 trees were planted in twenty-nine states in 1956); support state and national legislation in behalf of our natural resources, and carry out conservation programs and projects in the individual clubs.

A number of years ago the Federation launched an annual "Community Achievement" contest that has since become one of the most outstanding of its kind in the world. Up to 1955 the contest was limited to clubs in the United States, but today it is international in scope. It is conducted under the joint sponsorship of the Federation and the Sears-Roebuck Foundation, with $65,000 in cash prizes. Projects, to be eligible for a prize, must represent *community* achievement as contrasted to *club* achievement, with community participation. The projects must benefit the entire community—improve its appearance, supply added conveniences, advance its civic spirit, or enlarge the opportunities of its people. Suggested projects cover conservation and beautification, education and culture, health, youth, citizenship, government, and safety. In order to provide a greater opportunity for carrying out long-range projects, the duration of the contest was increased recently from one to two years. It is possible for a club to win as much as $10,000 for a conservation or community project. In all cases, the prize money must be used for the benefit of the community.

The projects undertaken in this contest are remarkable in their scope. Most of them are not big and few are spectacular, but that is not the purpose. In each case the project fills a *need* in the community and that is the basis upon which entries are judged. Clubs fall into either of two categories, depending upon the size of their membership—those with seventy-five or more members and those with less. Small clubs whose resources may be limited do not compete with clubs in large communities that have unlimited resources, nor do clubs in this country compete with those abroad.

Representative Contest Entries

A number of entries in these contests have already been described in this book, such as the Abbeville Planning Commission and several recreation and swimming pool projects. In selecting projects as illustrations, it is always a little unfair to those who have carried out projects equally fine, or possibly even more outstanding in some ways, but that cannot be helped. Those included were not necessarily chosen because they were considered the best, nor were they all prize winners. They were selected to show the variety of the projects undertaken and the ingenuity used in carrying them out. The following are a few examples.

Women's organizations in Lafayette, Indiana, banded together and established a Girl Scout camp on a 120-acre tract as their entry, and used the prize money for buildings and expansion. The Woman's Club of Laramie, Wyoming, campaigned to put a woman on the school board in order to establish a public kindergarten that was opposed by the all-male board. They were successful in getting it. In Glenrock, Wyoming—twenty-five miles from the nearest physician— the club secured a doctor for the community. Water pollution was the concern of club members in Belfair, Washington; their entry was a successful program to "Keep Hood Canal Waters Clean." In Lamoille, Nevada, there was no place for community gatherings so the seventeen members of the Woman's Club decided to correct matters. They enlisted the interest of the townspeople and residents of the surrounding area. As a result, part of an air base hospital unit was moved 300 miles from Tonopah to Lamoille and remodeled into a community hall. Club women in Lexington, Nebraska, undertook a variety of projects in one of the contests. These included a summer theater, improvement and beautification of the city park, the coordination of health facilities and projects, and the formation of a community council representing thirty-five civic organizations.

Boulder City's Hospital

In Boulder City, Nevada, the only hospital was operated by the government and it was running at such a heavy loss that it was scheduled to be closed. Everyone felt that the hospital was essential but, as closing time approached, no one had done anything about it. A large sum was needed for running expenses until arrangements could be made for its maintenance and no one was willing to assume the responsibility. Taking the money accumulated for its own building fund, the club assumed the running expenses of the hospital for a month to keep it open. Then the members raised more to keep it functioning until it could be turned over to the community.

A Children's Playground in Forest Grove

In Forest Grove, Oregon, the need was for a children's playground. The City Recreation Council had bought a tract of land for a picnic area, but after a swimming pool had been built with funds raised by public subscription, no money was left to equip a play area for small children. The Woman's Club undertook this project, then found that the older children had no play equipment either. The members successfully carried out both projects, with children and businessmen actively helping.

Safety and Sanitation in Seward

Seward is a small Alaskan community about 400 miles from the Arctic Circle. It had a new post office, a new hospital, a new high school, a supermarket, and housing areas. Construction was going on everywhere, but it still had many characteristics of the frontier town. Wind, dust, and black smoke drifted over the town from an open city dump, in contrast to the clean clear air from the snowcapped mountain peaks that rimmed Seward.

The Woman's Club called upon all civic groups to join them in a "Safety and Sanitation for Seward" campaign. Mass meetings were held to arouse interest; city officials were bombarded with letters and phone calls, and regular marches were made on the City Hall, demanding action. In a comparatively short time Seward had voted a street-paving bond issue, the dump was on its way out, and other improvements were sufficiently advanced to warrant the club's project being chosen as a prize winner.

Spunky Women in Mississippi

A "small" project sometimes takes more determined effort than a big one. In Iuka, a little town in Mississippi, there was a garbage dump behind the stores on Front Street. In spite of repeated efforts to get rid of this eyesore, it remained year after year until most of the people accepted it as an unavoidable nuisance. But members of the Woman's Club felt differently about it. When their patience was completely exhausted, they set a date and appeared at the dump *en masse*.

Wielding rakes and shovels, they started loading the garbage and debris into the city truck. In a matter of minutes they had an audience—a big one. A group of men watched them, open-mouthed. Convinced that they really meant business and were not going to give up until the last shovelful was gone, one old fellow exclaimed admiringly: "You girls got more spunk than anybody in Iuka," and invited them all across the street for soft drinks. Needless to say, the dump has been removed permanently.

Prize-Winning Community Councils

The first prize of $10,000 in the 1956-58 contest was won by the Woman's Club, the Zenith Club, and the Junior Woman's Club of St. Helens, Oregon, a town of 5,000. The clubs organized a community council which planned and carried out an extensive community improvement program. Among the accomplishments of the council were a bond issue campaign for a new $872,000 high school, the establishment of a sewage treatment plant; the creation of a community center; a cleanup and fix-up drive for homes and business houses; a new court house; neighborhood playgrounds, and the beautification and equipment of a park.

A $5,000 prize was awarded the Woman's Club of Wild Rose, Wisconsin, a village of about 600. This group also worked through a community council, composed of representatives of civic groups, working with government officials. The program included a successful effort to bring new industry to the community and new job opportunities for young people, a soil conservation program, a recreational program, a nursery summer school, a village and highway beautification program to make theirs a "village of roses," a new well stocked library, fire protection, a Civil Defense program, and the annual planting of 1,250,000 trees on submarginal land.

Affiliates Active in Community Improvement

Foreign affiliates and territorial clubs, like those in this country, also play active roles in community improvement. The Cristobal Woman's Club was founded when the Panama Canal was being built and survived when the others disbanded. Today it has a membership of 170 Americans, Panamanians, French, English, and Chinese. Scores of families in Colón are receiving food, clothing, and medical aid weekly through this club. Among its other accomplishments are the establishment of the first library on the Atlantic side of the canal, organization of the first Red Cross committee, and the establishment of a free clinic in Colón.

Throughout the world these little groups are doing what they can to build better communities. The American Women's Club in Sydney, Australia, maintains an iron lung fund. A group of 170 Austrian women in Vienna runs a home for elderly women. In Brussels, Belgium, the American Women's Club awards an annual scholarship of approximately $1,500 to a Belgian girl for a year's study in the United States. The Jamaica Federation of Women in the British West Indies operates play centers for children of pre-school age and provides lunches and clothing for school children. The Constantinople College Alumnae Association in Athens pioneered in establishing playgrounds in Greece. In Lima, Peru, the American Women's Literary Club was responsible for starting the Scouting movement and is sponsor for the Girl Scouts in Lima. The American Women's Club of Bombay, India, raises $15,000 annually for its work in settlement houses, schools for the blind, rescue homes, and hospitals.

Two women's clubs in Japan, both started by American naval personnel, belong to the General Federation—one in Tokyo and one in Yokosuka. Over 21,000 Japanese women belong to the Shinsei Yokosuka Society today. Among other projects, these women have charge of garbage and trash collection (they own twenty trucks, three barges, and employ 160 people), run a widows' home and a day nursery, operate a blood bank, collect for the Community Chest, are responsible for paroled juvenile delinquents, and conduct an active get-out-the-vote program. The Cairo, Egypt, Woman's Club, founded by fifteen American and British women, established the first village nursery in Egypt, the pattern for many others.

A Day Nursery in British Honduras

The projects in the preceding paragraphs are a few of the regular activities of foreign affiliates. Contest entries are equally remarkable. The projects are too varied to permit the selection of a typical example, but the entry of the Woman's Club in Belize, British Honduras, will give some idea of the fine work inspired by this contest.

Distressed by the deplorable housing conditions in Belize, this club decided to provide the community with a nursery so that working mothers would have a safe and healthy place to leave their children. A survey of the slum areas had shown over 30,000 people living in fewer than 4,000 houses, many just tumbledown shacks. The club-women secured a site, then set out to raise the money they needed. They had $422.23 in their treasury and this was to be the basis of the fund. It paid for sinking shafts and laying a concrete foundation. The women then collected foundation stones for the groundwork. Now they needed 800 concrete blocks. They raised the money for these through a "block drive," in which people were asked to buy a concrete block for fifty cents. This crisis met, they set out to get a roof, doors, and windows by staging a huge Mayan Mestizada (harvest festival) for the entire community. The Mestizada netted $1,500 and created enthusiasm for the nursery throughout Belize. After that, raising money for the actual building was comparatively easy, and today the town has its nursery.

An International Organization of Rural Women

The Associated Country Women of the World is an association of nearly six million women, with consultative status with the United Nations. It actively supports the UN program, working closely on a volunteer basis with the Food and Agriculture Organization, the World Health Organization, and the United Nations Educational, Scientific and Cultural Organization. In its position as a bridge uniting the country women of the world, it plays an important role in agricultural and nutritional programs in less developed countries. Mrs. Raymond Sayre of the United States, while serving as president, explained its contribution in this way: "Women are the creators of attitudes in the home and in the family in every country, no matter how subordinate their position in the life of the community. If changes in traditions and habits are to be made, women must first see their value."

Many instances confirm Mrs. Sayre's statements. In Greece, after World War II, the people were nearly prostrate from hunger and malnutrition and in 1947 the Greek Government asked FAO for help. Soil experts recommended improved agricultural practices, and a nutrition specialist suggested changing the food imports from high to low cost food staples like salted roe and soya flour. If these women had not been taught proper nutritional habits and encouraged their families to eat and like the new diet, the program probably would have failed. Again, in rural Japan disastrous floods were ruining farmland largely because farmers were cutting so many trees for fuel. The Japanese Department of Agriculture, as part of its conservation program, introduced the use of charcoal burners. This of course meant a complete reorganization of cooking methods and the women met the challenge. India too is changing age-old habits and traditions as women take their place in public life. The A.C.W.W. is strongly represented there and has also reached into Pakistan, Egypt, Zululand, and many other places where women are advancing toward brighter horizons

The history of this immense sisterhood dates to the latter part of the nineteenth century, when women in widely separated parts of the world began to form clubs to overcome their isolation and loneliness. It might even be said to go farther back than that, as the first recorded founding date for such a club was 1797 (Finland).

A home tragedy led to the organization of Canadian country women. The baby son of Mrs. Adelaide Hoodless of Ontario died after drinking impure milk. Knowing that if she had had more knowledge her child would not have died, Mrs. Hoodless determined that the necessary instruction should be brought within reach of country women. She campaigned for education in homemaking and the first Women's Institute in Canada was established. Lady Aberdeen, wife of the Governor General, devoted much of her energy in its behalf. Several years later, Lady Aberdeen and Mrs. Alfred Watt, who had been associated with the institute, met in England. From this meeting the Associated Country Women of the World came into being. Triennial conferences are now held in leading cities of the world. The home office is in London, England.

The original goal was "to promote and maintain friendly and helpful relations between country women's and homemakers' organizations of all nations and to give any help possible to their development in the economic, social, and cultural sphere." In the fulfillment of this purpose, the sphere was broadened until such subjects as conservation became an important part of the program. In trying to maintain "friendly and helpful" relations during a depression, a war, and a post-war period, it encountered the matter of well-being, and that brought it to the problem of malnutrition, and malnutrition led to the land, "the basic raw material of all activities." When it studied the land, the problem devolved into the matter of worn-out soil and the urgency of doing something to rebuild it.

The country women worked out a "Memorandum of Reconstruction," dealing with the practical issues of food, housing, health, and education on an international scale, with suggestions and plans for action. The section dealing with food was quoted at the International Nutritional Conference held in 1943 at Hot Springs, Virginia, from which the Food and Agriculture Organization emerged. In 1950 six lessons in conservation, "You Owe the Land a Living," were prepared by United States members of the A.C.W.W. and distributed widely.

Conservation today is a basic part of the program and all organizations belonging to the A.C.C.W. carry out projects in accordance with the needs of their area or country. Mrs. J. F. Van Beekhoff Van Selms of The Netherlands is president at this writing.

Influence of Women's Institutes in Ceylon

The objectives of the A.C.C.W. are well illustrated by work of the *Lanka Mahila Samiti* (Association of Women's Institutes in Ceylon). The Mahila Samiti were introduced into Ceylon in 1930 shortly after women were given the right to vote. The purpose was to raise the living standards of rural people, comprising about 85 per cent of the total population. This association was the pioneer group in this field in Ceylon and is cited in all United Nations literature dealing with rural development as an outstanding example of co-operation between governmental and non-governmental agencies. There are Mahila Samiti in more than 1,300 villages today and the membership is about 100,000 women.

The backbone of the movement is a band of trained workers, which are of two kinds: the paid worker (*grama sevika*), and the voluntary worker (*sweccha sevika*). The paid worker is something of a traveling supervisor. She goes wherever she is sent, sets up the Samati, and runs it for three months, until the voluntary worker, a local village girl, can take over and continue the work for the village, many of which are in remote areas of the island. These women are trained in health measures, nutrition, home crafts, conservation, gardening, child care, and many similar subjects. The impact of their new knowledge is being felt today throughout the island.

Neighborly Help from America to England

The spirit of international neighborliness which motivates the association has been evidenced in many instances. In the spring of 1947 thousands of English farms were inundated after a disastrously cold winter. There was a fund for farmers, and gift parcels poured into England from country women all over the world. One of the services most appreciated, however, was the helpful advice offered by women of the Mississippi River area of the United States, who had themselves often experienced the damaging effects of flood water. They told the harassed English women how to remove stains from carpets and furnishings, how best to dry and restore furniture and mattresses, and how to cope with the many other household problems created by floods.

The Community Development Program of the United Nations

It is estimated that between one-half and two-thirds of the world's people are undernourished. A tragically large percentage live on the edge of starvation with the threat of famine always lurking in the shadows. Close to two-thirds are illiterate; nearly half the world's children do not go to school, and many of those who do receive inadequate training. In the past most of these people had no hope for a better way of life, but fortunately this is no longer true. Throughout the world people are awakening to the realization that poverty, ignorance, famine, and disease do not have to be. The British historian, Toynbee, believes that future generations may see as the greatest achievement of the twentieth century—not its scientific discoveries, but its realization, for the first time in human history, that man's knowledge can be shared with peoples all over the world for the common good.

The United Nations represents over two and a third billion people of differing nationalities, beliefs, habits, languages, and loyalties. It has many programs to improve conditions among the less fortunate. One of those holding the most hope is the Community Development Program of self-aided help inaugurated in 1950. In this project the UN provides technical assistance, with the governments of the countries wishing help providing the money for the program and the people themselves doing most of the work. The UN stands ready to provide assistance in this field, but the request must come from the country desiring aid. After such a request is received, the UN sends a technical expert, or group of experts, to help and advise the requesting government, using and training local leadership. In some instances a pilot project is set up, then similar projects are established in other communities. Salaries of the technicians are paid by the UN but the cost of the program is borne by the participating country. The technicians are highly qualified men and women from many countries. They must be people who can teach their skills to others so that the work can be continued when they are gone. The program pivots on local leadership and its success depends upon community cooperation.

Since most communities asking help are rural, the core of the program is wise land use to improve crop yields; irrigation to make use of arid land; the prevention of soil erosion, the protection of water supplies, farm diversification, and reforestation.

One of the most important contributions of the United States to the UN program is in the field of higher education. A large percentage of the technicians and potential leaders comes here to be trained. Among countries having advanced programs are Ghana, India, Pakistan, Viet-Nam, Indonesia, and Ceylon.

International Union for Conservation

It is not possible in a book such as this to include the work of all groups and agencies dealing with conservation, nor is this necessary. The accomplishments of most are well known. However, mainly because they are new, there are some which may not be familiar to the public, but whose aims and purposes should be known. Among them is the International Union for Conservation of Nature and Natural Resources. This is an international body composed of governments, international organizations, and organizations within various nations that are concerned with the preservation of man's natural environment and the conservation of renewable natural resources. It was founded in 1948 at the international conference sponsored jointly by UNESCO and the French Government at Fontainebleau, France, with thirty-one nations participating.

The objectives of the Union include the conservative use of renewable natural resources in all parts of the world, and the preservation, through appropriate legislation, of outstanding areas and flora and fauna having scientific, historic, or esthetic significance. It is supported entirely by membership dues and special grants made by individuals, organizations, foundations, or agencies for specific projects. The secretariat is located in Brussels, Belgium, the seat of the Union and the center of its activities.

CHAPTER X

FOR TOMORROW'S SAKE

Whatever its faults, the American way of life has brought us the greatest productivity and the highest standard of living of any people in the world. But let us not forget that neither would have been possible without our wealth of natural resources. With "progress" nibbling away at the good earth from every angle and our population increasing steadily, there is little doubt that conservation will become more and more important as the years go by. Consequently we cannot start too early to train our children to cope with the resource problems they will have to face.

Creating Conservationists Among the Nation's Youth

Young "Citizens of Nature"

Most experts agree that instruction should begin in the lower elementary grades, and that the best way to proceed is to make the children "citizens of nature." How this can be done effectively is well illustrated by the educational project of the seven garden clubs in Greenwich, Connecticut.

Three of the Greenwich garden clubs belong to the Garden Club of America, a national organization of some 165 clubs, and the other four are affiliated with the National Council of State Garden Clubs, Inc. Formerly each club had its completely separate conservation interests and endeavors. Then, in 1950, the Garden Club of America brought out a natural resources educational packet for distribution to schools and youth groups. This so interested garden club members that the conservation committees of all seven clubs decided to work together on the project.

"The World Around You" packet contains a number of pamphlets and booklets about our national parks, our wildlife heritage, soil, water, and other natural resources, keyed to various age levels. It includes a guide for teachers and youth leaders, with suggested topics for study and discussion, recommended books and films, and radio recordings, suggestions for field trips, conservation exhibits that children can make, and projects they can carry out. Included for older students and teachers is a copy of Dr. Lowdermilk's fine booklet, "Conquest of the Land Through 7,000 Years."

The packet was excellent, the clubs agreed. The question was how to make the best use of it. Little purpose would be served by distributing the packets through the schools if the material was simply to be read once, then put aside and forgotten. After consultation with school authorities, it was recommended that the project be carried out through Audubon Junior Clubs.

Since 1910 nearly ten million boys and girls have become "citizens of nature" by means of these clubs, which are formed mainly in elementary schools and youth organizations such as the Boy and Girl Scouts. There are Audubon Junior Clubs in all of our states and territories, in every province of Canada, and in a number of other areas, including Mexico, South and Central America, South Africa, and Australia. Since the National Audubon Society is the largest organization for the conservation of renewable resources in the world, the committee felt that the junior wing was uniquely qualified to instill in children a love and appreciation of nature and to impress upon them their obligation to protect their heritage.

The projects, games, and activities of the Audubon Junior Clubs are all highly instructive and entertaining. At the same time they have a very practical purpose, such as the protection of our birds by encouraging children to build bird houses and maintain feeding stations at their schools, camps, and homes.

Activities of the clubs, however, cover far more than birds. Among their many fine projects is the "Adopt a Tree" program. Each child selects a tree he can see every day either at home or on his way to school. He records its name, facts about its leaves, its height, the reach of its branches, what plants live under it, what birds and animals use it, whether it has moss or lichens growing on the bark, what its wood

is like, and its range in the United States. Soon he is discovering why
the leaves change color in the autumn and drop to the ground, the
significance of tree rings, the many uses of wood, and its importance
in his daily life. He becomes interested in the forest, the forest floor
and the plants that grow there, and the wildlife that it supports. He
begins to understand the interdependence of plants, animals (in
cluding himself), soil, water, and climate. By now he is ready for a
simplified explanation of watersheds, the water table, good and bad
forestry practices, and the importance of using our forests and other
resources wisely. Thus he is led naturally and easily into the world of
conservation, which will be just as fascinating to him as his other
interests. By such instruction small citizens learn early that one of
their most important responsibilities as citizens of the United States
is good stewardship of the land and its resources.

When the committee made its recommendation to the garden
clubs, there were only five Junior Audubon Clubs in the twenty-one
schools of the Greenwich area. Their total membership was 151
children. Working closely with the Audubon Center nearby, each
committee member made herself responsible for contacting three
schools, calling upon the principals and teachers. A year later there
were forty-five clubs with a total membership of 1,105 children. The
membership has been increasing steadily every year. So successful has
this pilot project been that many other garden clubs have adopted it
as a program for their junior departments.

It is the conviction of the National Audubon Society that the combined thinking of the millions of people who have been members of
its junior clubs "has a profound effect on governmental policies affecting conservation of natural resources."

Opening Nature's Doors to City Children

The wonderful door to nature can be opened to city children too.
In Worcester, Massachusetts, the Natural History Society has an extensive program. It has prepared loan boxes for distribution to schools,
and any item in the museum that will help in nature studies is available as a loan. The Society conducts a four-week Nature Training
School every summer for city boys and girls in the second-to-eighth
grade group. Two sessions are held every year at the museum's forty-
acre wildlife sanctuary. For children unable to attend this school there

is a two-month summer program at its Children's Museum. From October to May a nursery school for smaller children is conducted in which they are taught the wonders of the world we live in and the fundamentals of conservation. A branch of the Children's Museum has been established in a particularly congested area of the city in order to reach still other children. This center operates as a separate unit. It has its own field trips and an outdoor summer session in a nearby wooded area.

For high school students, the Society conducts an eight-week school of forestry and conservation every summer on a 1,200-acre tract owned by the museum. Instruction here is of the highest caliber. The Harvard School of Forestry, the University of Massachusetts, and the Massachusetts Department of Natural Resources cooperate by supplying teachers and equipment. There is also a collegiate division open to students in the first two years of college. Other educational projects include adult conservation instruction, a once-a-week radio program called "Nature in New England;" a center of information for the community about natural science, horticulture, and conservation, and a voluntary body of women working for conservation on a community, state, and national basis. The program of the Society is made possible by generous gifts, family and contributing memberships, and volunteer workers.

Virginia's Nature Camp

The Virginia Federation of Garden Clubs operates a Nature Camp which members call their "stake in the future." It is located on Big Mary's Creek in the George Washington National Forest, near Vesuvius, where it is tucked between two mountains in a beautiful little valley that is rich in its variety of native plants, shrubs, and trees. The usual activities of a summer camp are included in its program and the boys and girls who go there have the time of their lives, but its primary purpose is to promote conservation.

The federation makes no attempt to provide for large groups, but seeks outstanding boys and girls with qualities of leadership. Its aim is to give them an opportunity to learn more about their natural heritage and "to develop in them a sense of responsibility for the future of this country." Courses offered are designed to create strong interest in our natural resources, and the purpose is to encourage these young people to select forestry or other conservation work as a career. A progressive course of instruction is offered those who return year after year. The personnel, exceptionally fine, includes instructors from the Virginia Forest Service, the Commission of Game and Inland Fisheries, and other departments of the state. The camp is open to boys and girls from the fifth grade through senior high school.

The camp is a state-wide project, all member clubs contributing toward expenses. The idea originated with Mrs. Fred Shilling as state conservation chairman in 1941 and she is still executive director of the camp. The clubs raised $6,500 to start their camp, which was opened in 1942 in leased government buildings. It was moved to its present site ten years later. The federation financed a large swimming pool and erected a number of buildings, the newest being a building to house a library, workroom, museum, and two additional staff bunk rooms. While a fee is charged, it is not the purpose of the clubs to make a profit, nor do they require the camp to pay its own way. It is supported by gifts from the clubs and hundreds of life memberships, and relies heavily upon voluntary workers. It is incorporated as a non-profit organization under the sponsorship of the federation. The Virginia clubs raise money for their camp by staging flower shows, conducting garden tours, and by giving luncheons.

Boy Scout Magic

Magic is a part of the Boy Scout program these days and thousands of members are working for merit badges in this field. They are not awarded magic for pulling rabbits out of hats, which is "kid stuff," but for "conservation magic," helping to restore idle and abused land to usefulness.

The merit badge in soil and water conservation, a requirement for the rank of Eagle Scout, is one of the hardest to earn—especially for city boys—and one of the most coveted. The Scouts in the two Kansas Citys, however, found a way to fill the requirements. They are lending a hand in the Blackwater Pilot Watershed program in Johnson County, Missouri. Nearly a thousand Scouts have earned their conservation badges by working on the watershed, to the mutual benefit of themselves, the farmers, city people, and their country.

When the Blackwater Pilot Watershed program was undertaken in 1953, Paul Hallam's 375-acre farm became a part of it. A conservation plan was prepared for his farm with a flood prevention phase that included an earth dam to impound a ten-acre permanent lake, with additional acreage for temporary water storage. This body of water appeared to be a good possibility for wildlife development. The Missouri Conservation Commission already was cooperating formally with the Johnson County district and had planting stock available. Hallam was anxious to cooperate on the wildlife phase as on the rest of the program. It was agreed to enclose the lake and two grass waterways leading into it with a multiflora hedge to protect the area from farm animals and to provide food and cover for wildlife. This meant planting about 15,000 rose bushes and 500 scotch and loblolly pines as a windbreak.

Many Scouts of the area were familiar with the Hallam farm because Paul Hallam is a counselor for the Kansas City Scout Council, and many outings had been held there. When the opportunity came to do something in return, the Scouts responded enthusiastically. At 9:30 one November morning in 1954, two troops—160 boys—arrived at the farm with about thirty fathers in tow to fix "chow." A Scout ceremony was held, then the boys were shown how the planting was to be done. The area was divided into 400-foot stations, with a Scout patrol—six to twelve boys—headed by a Powder Horn Scout and an adult, to each section. By noon the job was finished and, in addition, the boys had planted a 600-foot windbreak and a quarter-of-a-mile rose hedge on a nearby farm.

The project was so successful that all 10,000 Scouts in the greater Kansas City area wanted to earn their soil and water conservation badges in the same way. Consequently the boys have been going to the farms in groups, sometimes of several hundred. The watershed program is progressing, with everyone benefiting, especially the city boys who are able to earn their conservation badges. Soil Conservation Service men say the quality of the boys' work is on a par with that of professionals.

Erosion Control in Hawaii

A project similar to the Missouri watershed plantings is being carried out in our new state, Hawaii. Scouts of Troop 83 in Lihue on Kauai Island had never earned a conservation badge up to 1953, when the East Kauai Soil Conservation District was organized. The program for the district seemed to Scoutmaster Tonaichi Fuji to offer a good opportunity for the boys in his troop to learn about the classifi-

cation of land according to its capabilities, terracing, and other conservation practices. He also hoped a way could be found for the boys
to earn their badges.

Soil and forestry men, glad to cooperate, suggested that the troop
take as a project the planting of an eroded hillside on Kalepa Ridge, a
few miles from Lihue. The Board of Agriculture and Forestry furnished the necessary ironwood seedlings and on the day selected the
Scouts moved in with their picks and shovels. Four hundred seedlings
were planted that day. When news of the tree planting reached other
Scout troops, they became interested too. Today the project on Kalepa
Ridge is progressing nicely, one Scout troop succeeding another so that
as many boys as possible will have a chance to earn conservation
badges. The Kalepa Ridge project has also led to other plantings
in Hawaii.

Oregon's Young Forest Builders

Millions of trees have been planted by the Scouts, Camp Fire Girls,
4-H Clubs, Future Farmers of America, and other groups of young
people. America's youth is making a tremendous contribution to the
nation through countless "trees for tomorrow" projects. In Oregon,
Portland school children have set out more than 350,000 seedlings to
help restore the 267,000 acres of black stumps left by the disastrous
Tillamook forest fire of 1933. The annual tree planting expedition of
the children to the Tillamook Burn has become a tradition. This ugly,
sprawling fire scar is about thirty-five miles from Portland. The children go out by bus, form into platoons, and set out bundles of
Douglas fir and other seedlings under the supervision of foresters. The
job is a big one, and its completion will take years. Foresters say that
the full benefit of the children's work will not be realized for eighty
to one hundred years, but thousands of Oregon's children will have
participated in the planting and learned first hand the value of
our forests.

Conservation Training

Teaching Conservation in the Schools

Although opinion differs as to method, the majority of conservation-
minded people agree that conservation fundamentals should be taught

in the public schools. Today a growing number of states require such instruction. Wisconsin law requires it not only in elementary and high schools, but in all teachers' colleges. Montana has similar legislation. Among other states insisting upon such instruction are Tennessee, Florida, North Dakota, and Ohio. Indiana recently established conservation studies as a requirement for teachers of science, social science, and agriculture, and for all elementary teachers. To meet the Indiana requirements, Purdue University now offers a Master of Science degree in conservation, as well as a four-year undergraduate course with a major in this subject.

Many other states also have strong programs in conservation education, providing instruction in the public schools, though this is not required by law. A few have full-time state directors, supervisors, or consultants in the department of education. Some have the part-time service of general consultants or supervisors, and a number have special directors of conservation education in the state departments of conservation, or in the game and fish agencies. In most states having active programs, a state committee has been organized by the department of education, or with its cooperation, such as the curriculum Committee on Conservation and Education in Michigan. Indeed Michigan has a very effective program, with a fine School of Natural Resources at the University of Michigan. Many states have prepared texts for students and curriculum guides for teachers, have provided excellent conservation slides and films to schools and colleges, and have broad programs of teacher training. Even so, such programs represent just a beginning in conservation education, and there is much that public-spirited groups can do to help bring this vital subject more strongly into the school curriculum through legislation or persuasion.

Conservation Education in Marion County, West Virginia

One of the most successful attempts by a group to have the study of conservation included in the public school curriculum is the project of the Green Hills Garden Club in Fairmont, West Virginia. This group of thirty women sponsors the Marion County Conservation Plan, which won the Ritter cup, a state community achievement award, and also a conservation award from the National Council of State Garden Clubs, Inc.

The project was conceived in 1953 when Walter C. Gumbel, conservation consultant for the Monongahela Power Company and a member of the board of directors of Friends of the Land, addressed the club. He strongly underscored the need for conservation instruction in the schools, emphasizing that the subject should be presented in a dynamic manner. Inspired by Mr. Gumbel's talk, Mrs. C. Howard Hardesty, who was president of the club, and Mrs. Clay D. Amos, its conservation chairman, called on J. J. Straight, superintendent of the Marion County public schools, and asked his advice as to how this could be done. "Only through a realistic and far-reaching program," he replied, explaining the difficulties of introducing new material into an already crowded curriculum. However, he was interested, and the two women arranged another meeting to discuss the matter further, with Mr. Gumbel attending to help present the case for conservation. As a result of the second meeting, it was decided to outline a conservation course suitable for young people in the junior and senior high school group.

Five science teachers were invited to join in the next meeting. Once more Mr. Gumbel presented the case for conservation, then Mr. Straight explained to the teachers what he had in mind, with Mrs. Hardesty pledging the full support of the Green Hills club in carrying out the program. The next step was a review of available source material and the preparation of a teaching manual. Mr. Straight, a committee of science teachers, and Mr. Gumbel collaborated on this and after months of hard work developed "An Outline for Teaching Conservation and the Wise Use of the Renewable Natural Resources," which is now being used in the Marion County schools. This outline, which includes source material, suggested projects, and basic facts, was approved by the state superintendent of schools and many requests for copies have come from schools in other states. "Most encouraging of all," Mrs. Hardesty says, "the program has been excellently received by the students from the very beginning."

As its part in getting the project started, the club purchased source material for the school libraries, and has continued to do this. To date the members have contributed nearly 300 books, countless booklets, pamphlets, charts, maps, and films. They raise money for this material by importing bulbs from Holland and selling them at a "Gardener's Corner" during flower shows. The club also features outstanding conservation exhibits of Marion County students at its shows and gives radio and TV programs on the subject.

When the teaching of conservation in the junior and senior high schools of the county had become established, the club arranged a panel discussion on "Our Next Step in Conservation Education," with Mr. Gumbel as moderator. Mr. Straight, most of the science teachers in the county, and Dr. John W. Pence, president of Fairmont, an accredited state college for teachers, were among those attending. This meeting led to the introduction of conservation activities into the elementary schools of Marion County. The college, which had cooperated, added day and evening courses on resource use and arranged conservation workshops for teachers.

The project has spread to other counties and there is now a teachers' handbook entitled "Living, Learning, and Loving West Virginia." More than 30,000 copies have been printed for distribution to teachers throughout the state.

The State federation of garden clubs in West Virginia was so impressed with the Marion County conservation education plan and the work of the Green Hills club that it has made conservation instruction in all West Virginia schools a state project. Other state federations too are taking a thoughtful interest in the Green Hills project, and so is the National Council of State Garden Clubs, Inc.

Mrs. Hardesty believes that the unusual success of this project was largely due to teamwork between club members and school authorities. Groups seeking to have conservation taught in the schools sometimes fail, school officials say, because their members unintentionally give teachers the impression that they are trying to tell them how to teach. "Civic groups," Mr. Gumbel says, "can best implement the efforts of teachers and educators by providing basic information, encouragement, and other helps in the form of books, awards, scholarships to camps, and recognition of teachers. The teacher, by virtue of her training, has the technical skill to adapt and use the materials provided by promotional, professional, and technical resource leaders. This is an important concept and must be thoroughly understood by everyone concerned with conservation education in the public schools."

Conservation Workshops and Clinics

In an article titled "America's 'Amazing Women,' " which appeared in the *Reader's Digest*, Clarence W. Hall quotes a European sociologist as saying: "Americans seem unaware of what makes their nation the most compassionate and socially competent on earth today—the strength of their woman power."

The United States, perhaps more than any other country, has availed itself of the talents of women. This is particularly true of women in the community where they carry a heavy share of civic responsibility. The millions of women who contribute to community welfare throughout the country, most of whom have families and do their own housework, "make up a volunteer army five times the size of all our armed forces," Mr. Hall states. "If paid for, at the minimum wage scale, their services would cost two and a quarter billion dollars a year." And the amazing American woman does all this, he points out, "without missing a trick as wife and mother."

Garden club members are among the most active of such women in the field of community betterment. But perhaps their most significant contribution is in the field of conservation. They have fought consistently against the exploitation of our natural resources by selfish interests and have as consistently endeavored to make the general public conscious of the need to use such resources wisely. However, they realized long ago that making people "aware" is not enough—that conservation is an attitude toward natural wealth and must become a way of life. They also realized that it would never become a way of life as long as the old notion of "inexhaustible" resources prevailed. Working in conjunction with educational institutions, conservation agencies, and departments of the government dealing with natural resources, they are sponsoring and supporting workshops all over the country which are designed to train people in conservation and develop leadership in this field.

A typical workshop is the Iowa Teachers Conservation Camp, held each summer in Springbrook Park near the State Teachers College at Ames. The camp operates for three sessions of three weeks each and college credits are given. Mrs. Toni R. Wendelburg, former conservation chairman of the Federated Garden Clubs of Iowa, says: "These teachers visit nearby farms and see how farmers locate their crops according to the nature of the soil; they see modern farming methods and machinery, the use of fertilizers, crop rotation, contour plowing, and multiflora rose hedges. They study plants and see how they establish themselves in colonies, prosper, and give way to other societies. They learn what a water table is and why it fluctuates; see how trees and wildlife in bottomlands differ from those in the uplands." But this is only part of the program. They also visit marshes, parks, flood control projects, water survey stations, sewage disposal plants, sawmills, farm woodlots, fish hatcheries, forest nurseries, and research areas.

The camp is staffed by instructors from Iowa State Teachers College, a representative of the State Conservation Commission, and resource specialists from various conservation agencies and groups.

Teachers return to the classroom with a new appreciation of the urgency and importance of resource conservation and a sober realization of their responsibilities in teaching conservation.

Washington's Workshops

The state of Washington has a number of natural resource workshops, all strongly supported by garden clubs. The first state-wide workshop was held in 1953 at Rustic Inn near Easton. The purpose of its ten-day program for teachers was to "teach those things out-of-doors that can best be learned out-of-doors," and to explore materials and techniques in conservation suited to instruction at various grade levels. The instructors were members of the staffs of Washington's four teachers colleges and resource specialists from federal, state, and private agencies. Consultants from schools already teaching conservation demonstrated methods of instruction.

This pioneer venture was so successful that three more state-wide workshops were established the following year, and a number of others are being conducted on a local basis. As a result, Washington has become known as one of the more progressive states in outdoor natural resource education. Schools from other states and from Canada send representatives to these workshops to study Washington's conservation education plan.

Workshops for Others Besides Teachers

Conservation workshops are not solely for teachers. Club members and other interested individuals attend, such as leaders of youth groups, librarians, writers, and college students. The federation of garden clubs in South Carolina co-sponsors a summer conservation clinic with Clemson College of Agriculture. Each club in the state is asked to send a teacher through a scholarship, as well as a club member or some person in the community who will pass the information along to others. In the fall the federation holds a symposium in conjunction with the University of South Carolina and in the spring sponsors a youth conservation camp for girls, providing fifty scholarships. The Federated Garden Clubs of Michigan has a state-wide scholarship program in which all clubs are asked to send two or more teachers to the conservation training school at Higgins Lake for a week during the summer. In the fall there is a session for club members.

In many cases the garden clubs have been responsible for the establishment of these workshops and, in all cases, they give generously to support them. The workshop at Storrs, Connecticut, one of the oldest, was initiated by The Federated Garden Clubs of Connecticut, Inc. From 50 to 80 per cent of those who attend its two sessions each summer receive scholarships from garden clubs.

The garden clubs are among the staunchest advocates of conservation education in the schools and have perhaps done more to further this cause than any other civic group. However they are fully aware that the wise use of our natural resources is a problem that must be met by today's citizens while those of tomorrow are being prepared to take over. One of the fundamental purposes of the workshops is to train conservation chairmen as community leaders. The Florida Federation of Garden Clubs has a most effective method for training and developing its chairmen. In cooperation with the Florida State University in Tallahassee, it established a conservation workshop in 1955 which club chairmen as well as teachers attend. The state conservation chairman, Mrs. Robert L. Fairing, went a step further. Taking a tip from business, she holds a series of district conferences each fall for club conservation chairmen, much as a sales manager conducts pep meetings. In this way the chairmen not only get a broad view of the resource problems of their state and country, but have an opportunity to discuss local problems with specialists and receive help and advice.

Participation in Conservation Through Scholarships

Public-spirited groups in cities sometimes feel that there is not much they can do about conservation other than being "aware" of problems affecting the land and supporting needed legislation. They can, however, also provide scholarships to train college students and others in conservation and related fields. The Woman's National Farm and Garden Association, a constituent society of the Associated Country Women of the World, has an outstanding scholarship program. Its city branches contribute heavily to this program, and through the years many of its scholarship winners have distinguished themselves in the conservation field.

Film Strips and Plays

A Conservation Film Strip Done by School Children

A number of civic groups have found film strips an unusually effective way of presenting conservation to children, especially when the children have had a part in creating them. The Riverside Garden Club in Connecticut works closely with the Greenwich schools and is one of the seven clubs that participated in the Audubon Junior program. As an extension of this program, the club wanted a good movie that would bring the conservation story to the children on their own level and "in their own backyard." Unable to find what they wanted, they enlisted the help of the high school photography club. None of the members had ever done any photography of this sort before but, as one said afterwards: "You'd be surprised what you can do if you just do it." The result is a delightful strip called "Conservation in Our Town." It was so successful that it was followed by another called "Our Water Supply," and the program has become a continuing project of the school. The strips are done in color, the garden club paying for the film. Charts and cartoons, used to illustrate certain points, are made by art students. Each film takes almost a full term to prepare in its entirety because the pictures usually cover the four seasons. They are used in connection with classroom study.

"Conservation in Our Town" presents basic facts about the soil illustrated with pictures taken in and around Greenwich. To these children erosion is not something that happens elsewhere. It is the rain washing mud down the street and into the drain right in their town. It is topsoil being swept from the hillsides of a Connecticut farm because furrows are straight instead of contoured. It is something that is happening on the beach where they go swimming. They know how water runs off bare soil while grass absorbs it because they demonstrated it for the film and then took pictures to prove the point. They understand the relationship between fertile soil and their own healthy bodies because they made charts and drawings of scientific soil practices, then scoured the countryside taking pictures of good and bad land use. They have a mental picture of what happens when they turn on a faucet because this was part of "Our Water Supply," and they know how water is purified in their town because they did that story too. And they are aware of the abuses that result in contamination. Finally they realize the importance of voting "for people who will make laws to save our land and keep our waters pure" and of writing to their congressmen "urging them to support special bills dealing with conservation" because that too is part of their film.

A *Children's Play About Water, Grass, and Trees*

Children are enchanted by make-believe and love to do a play. At first thought, conservation would seem a difficult subject to dramatize but a number of children's plays have been very effective.

One of the best known is "The Big Three," published and widely circulated by the Forest Service. The original version of this play, which was later shortened and made into a playlet for children, was written by two members of the Shippan Point Garden Club in Stamford, Connecticut. The leading characters are the three subjects the club had taken up in its monthly conservation round tables that year: water, grass, and trees. The dramatization was so well received that it was repeated at the annual state-wide conservation meeting of The Federated Garden Clubs of Connecticut, Inc. The federation liked it so well that copies were made and distributed to member clubs and it eventually came to the attention of the Forest Service. The playlet is easy to produce, adaptable to various age levels, calls for simple costumes and few props. It can be presented as a classroom or group program. Copies can be obtained from the U.S. Forest Service in Washington, D.C.

A *Conservation Play Written by School Children*

"Are You a Litterbug?" is another conservation play for children, written and originally produced as a class project by seventh grade students of Cleveland Hill High School, Cheektowaga, New York. The play was done in connection with the "Our Woodlot" project described in Chapter VI, under the guidance of Miss Grace Heacock, general science teacher. Keep America Beautiful, Inc. sent mimeographed copies to Parent-Teacher Associations throughout the United States and the Conservation Forum of New York State awarded it a prize.

A Play in the Form of a Trial

One of the most imaginative projects is a one act drama called "Conservation Play." The action takes place in a court of law with Mr. Farmer, Mr. Lumberman, and Mr. Hunter on trial for maltreatment of our natural resources. The time is the present, the place almost anywhere in the United States, and the attorney for the prosecution is old Mother Nature. It is the type of thing that children love to do, and it offers a refreshingly different program for school and youth group activities, as well as garden club and other adult group programs. The play was originally produced in Dulce, New Mexico. It was written by Henry W. Benedict, fifth grade teacher, at the Jicarilla Apache Boarding and Day School, in collaboration with Leland D. Chase and Julian N. Franklin, Branch of Soil Conservation, U.S. Indian Service.

CHAPTER XI

METHOD OF PROCEDURE

As the reader has surely noted, the projects described in this book more or less follow a pattern in spite of their diversity. Indeed, most successful projects of this nature seem to follow the same general pattern, whether they are neighborhood efforts or nation-wide programs. These are the steps:

(1) A *public-spirited individual or group recognizes a need and determines to do something about it.* That need may be a recreational area, the elimination of water pollution, or the restoration of a sick watershed. It might be a beautification program, anti-litter drive, a community forest, a soil conservation district, a town planning commission, or workshops to train conservation leaders. Whatever it is—the most successful projects are those which fill a basic need in the community or nation.

(2) *An analysis is made of the problem—with the advice of experts sought where necessary.* There are many instances where a civic-minded group has plunged headlong into a community project on a sink-or-swim basis and been highly successful, and there are others where a fine project never got off the ground because there was too much discussion and too little action. On the whole, the most successful groups have been those which made a careful analysis of the problem before they tackled it, drawing upon the advice and experience of experts. When this is done, the difficulties likely to arise are anticipated and plans can be made to meet them. Mrs. Slifer expected many people to oppose the saving of Bergen Swamp (Chapter I)

because of the widespread notion that swamps serve no useful purpose and should be filled in. Her first step was a consultation with authorities in various fields, who established the *value* of the swamp to the community as a means of helping to maintain the water table, a place to study plants and wildlife, and as a potential for scientific discoveries. Thus she gained, in addition to the support of nature lovers, the support of those people who must have a *practical* reason for saving natural areas.

(3) *Teamwork is important.* Teamwork is the common denominator of every project, whether it involves forty families working for a rural recreational area, or conservation-minded groups all over the country joining in a fight to protect our national parks, or to keep the new highway system free of billboards. Small groups are limited in what they can accomplish alone, however public-spirited they may be. When the strength of all such groups in the community is combined, each taking a share of the responsibility, the possibilities for accomplishment are limitless. This is because, together, they represent a cross-section of community life and thinking.

(4) *A plan of action is worked out.* In judging the entries in its highly successful Community Achievement Contest, the General Federation of Women's Clubs puts strong emphasis upon the manner in which the project is carried out. And it is significant that the top winners in the last two contests have both been responsible for the creation of centralized planning organizations. (Chapter V, How Abbeville Got Its Planning Commission, and Chapter IX, A Community Council in Oregon.) In both instances there were many things the community needed, and in both instances the townspeople in general were apathetic about the situation. The contesting clubs might have tackled some one problem and, in doing so, would have made a worthwhile contribution to their communities, but they went a step further. They created a *permanent* means of achieving improvement, thereby changing the whole atmosphere and way of life in their towns. And yet, in each case, the membership of the group or groups initiating the program represented only a small segment of the population. What made the difference was their *plan of action.*

(5) *A program of public education is undertaken.* There is little purpose in talking about the restoration of a sick watershed to people who do not know what a watershed is or how its condition affects

them. A farmer is likely to be indifferent or even hostile toward a soil conservation district until he understands how it operates and what it will mean to him and his family. A sewage treatment plant, however badly needed, may well be voted down unless the people are made to see its importance to their welfare. All too often voters go to the polls and vote against an issue simply because they know nothing about it, and their general inclination is to vote against anything that will increase taxes. One of the essential ingredients, and in some ways the most essential, in almost any successful project is a well organized program of community education.

(6) *The project is made the responsibility of the whole community.* In its own way, each community is a little America, representing what this nation stands for and its democratic processes. The most worth-while project, regardless of size, is one in which the community is led, or inspired, to help itself rather than have something done *for* it. Community participation should include young people and the older people because both have much to contribute and like to feel they "belong."

(7) *Finances are not always a major problem.* Where and how to raise the necessary money is a primary consideration in undertaking almost any project. When large sums are needed, as in the acquisition of the California redwood forests, big fund-raising drives must be planned and executed. In local projects more and more people today are cutting costs by contributing man-hours, applying the do-it-yourself idea to the community. Where money must be raised, they make it fun by having a dance, a bazaar, auction, or similar event. Indeed the successful group is usually one that has made the financing of its project a challenge rather than a problem, an opportunity for members to prove their ingenuity.

(8) *Successful groups work in harmony with public officials.* There are some public officials who conveniently forget their obligation to those who elected them when it is in their interests to do so, but the majority are honest, hard-working individuals with the best interests of the community and nation at heart. Many groups have been frustrated in their efforts to carry out very worth-while projects simply because they overlooked the fact that these officials are often in the best position of anyone to help them. An excellent example of how public officials and voluntary groups can work together is the

"Blue Star" project of the National Council of State Garden Clubs, Inc. (Chapter II, "Blue Star" Highways).

(9) *Many groups use contests as a means of creating interest in their projects.* Competition apparently has a strong appeal to most people. A spirited contest, properly conducted, is useful in carrying out most projects, especially where the support of young people is sought. Contests have been used very effectively in the anti-litter drive and have contributed tellingly to its success. (Chapter II, Campaigns Against Roadside Littering.) They have also proved valuable in promoting scientific soil practices. (Chapter VIII, Plowing Contests with a New Twist, Teamwork in Tupelo.)

(10) *Interest is sustained by publicity and progress reports.* Starting a project is one thing: following it through to successful completion is another. As we have pointed out, many projects in this book are of a size and nature beyond what could be reasonably expected of the groups that undertook them. A number of them took years to complete. (Chapter III, Restoration of Patriot's Park by the Tarrytowns, Master Plan for an Entire Valley.) These groups were successful because they sustained interest by periodic encouragement. Publicity for publicity's sake is never desirable, but publicity to keep a long-range project going by means of achievement reports is sound business practice. In this connection the local newspaper editor is the best ally.

(11) *Provision is made for the maintenance and future security of the project.* It is sad that even the most public-spirited groups will sometimes spend a tremendous amount of time, money, and effort on a project, only to have it become forlorn and forgotten in later years because the members failed to provide for its maintenance, or its future security. This is often true of beautification projects and sanctuaries, or areas that have been set aside in their natural state for one purpose or another. These precautions should be considered a part of the project, an essential to its successful completion. In its roadside beautification program, the New Hampshire Roadside Improvement Associates give high priority to maintenance when awarding prizes, which undoubtedly accounts for the breathtaking beauty one finds along the roadsides of this state. Many examples have been given showing how to provide for the maintenance of projects. An unusually good way of ensuring the future of a project is told in Chapter I, The Salt Marsh of Conanicut.

(12) *The determining factor in the success of all community and conservation projects is enthusiasm.* One may ignore any or most of the rules for success in carrying out a project and still succeed, but enthusiasm is the lifeblood of all such projects. Without it the best of projects are doomed from the outset, for most of them entail a great deal of hard work, much of which is routine and unglamorous. A group may have every other ingredient for success, yet fail miserably for lack of enthusiasm. On the other hand, it may face seemingly insurmountable difficulties, with little *but* boundless enthusiasm—and do the job. There is ample proof of this fact in the pages of this book.

A FINAL WORD

There is drama in the devastation of a flood, a hurricane, or a forest fire. Such disasters strike swiftly, savagely, with powerful impact. Because we see these forces of nature in violent action, we know what they can do. Erosion, much more destructive, does not have the vivid personality of a hurricane or typhoon. Silent, unseen, relentless, it works its deadly destruction upon the fertile earth, stripping away the topsoil, making it unproductive.

There is drama in industrial progress—vast cities, smart shopping centers, super-highways, giant power dams, and factories. We can point to them with pride as examples of American achievement. But progress, like erosion, can also destroy. As we watch the relentless whittling away of the countryside, the tragic loss of productive land, the pollution of our streams and rivers, and try to stave off the threats to the natural beauty of this land of ours, many of us are wondering if the time has not come to decide just how high a price the people of the United States are willing to pay for "progress."

We have never had a consistent, clear-cut, long-term policy of resource conservation in the United States. Fortunately we have had a number of conservation-minded presidents, such as Theodore Roosevelt, who took steps to protect our natural resources. But for the most part the interest in this vital subject seems to have fluctuated with the interest of the president in conservation issues. Even so, a president must have the support of Congress, and Congress, in turn, must have the backing of the people. We must also bear in mind that congressmen are dependent upon the people of their own states, a fact which may well influence their attitude and thinking. Also, let us not forget that time is running out. We have recognized the need for a person of cabinet rank to further our progress in the field of science, to co-ordinate and unify all scientific efforts. Is it not plain common sense to have a cabinet member who could devote his entire attention to the wise use of our natural resources, and who would be in a position to see the picture as a whole, rather than from the viewpoint of any one section of the country, or one group of people? The time has come when conservation must become so much a part of our thinking as to be a part of the American way of life, and this attitude should be so strongly entrenched that, like our attitude toward liberty, it will remain unaffected by changes in representation or administration.

We cannot continue to leave the responsibility for the conservation of the United States' natural resources to a few dedicated individuals and groups. We must *all* share it, because far more is at stake than our standard of living. These resources are not only the source of our wealth, but the source of our strength as a nation. We are a valiant people, but many valiant peoples have been conquered because they did not have the resources to back up their bravery. We have a responsibility not only to those who will inherit this land from us, but to all people everywhere who value liberty and the dignity of the individual.

There is no better way to bring this book to an end than by quoting the "Eleventh Commandment" of a great conservationist. When he returned from his tour of the Middle East in 1939, Dr. Walter Lowdermilk wrote a brief paragraph which gives those who read it ample cause to ponder:

> Thou shalt inherit the Holy Earth as a faithful steward, conserving its resources and productivity from generation to generation. Thou shalt safeguard thy fields from soil erosion, thy living waters from drying up, thy forests from desolation, and protect thy hills from overgrazing by thy herds, that thy descendants may have abundance forever. If any shall fail in this stewardship of the land, thy fruitful fields shall become sterile stony ground and wasting gullies, and thy descendants shall decrease and live in poverty or perish from off the face of the earth.

INDEX

259